Claire Dale and **Patricia Peyton** are directors of Companies in Motion, offering Physical Intelligence coaching and training to industry leaders including one of the world's most recognised consumer brands, a global investment bank and a multi-national pharmaceutical organisation. A well-known British dancer and choreographer, Claire founded the Claire Russ Ensemble, a contemporary dance company that performed across Europe for fifteen years. She is also senior communications tutor at RADA Business, specialising in embodied leadership training. Patricia has spent over thirty years working with Fortune 100 and FTSE 1000 organisations to help individuals and teams improve their performance. She is also managing director of Sphere International, providing leadership and sales consulting, training and coaching across industries globally and sits on the board of trustees at Emerson College in the US.

PRAISE FOR *PHYSICAL INTELLIGENCE:*

'*Physical Intelligence* is essential reading for anyone with a body and a mind. It flows effortlessly from beginning to end, like a warm summer's breeze, infused with relatable stories, clearly described exercises, life hacks and insights from some of the most prominent and successful people in the arts, media and sport . . . I wish I'd read this book twenty years ago, but I'm delighted to have read it now. Dale and Peyton define the field of Physical Intelligence brilliantly and engagingly. A must-read.'

– Peter Lovatt, BSc, MSc, PhD in psychology and computational neuroscience, reader in the psychology of dance, University of Hertfordshire, and author

'This is a wise and generous book. I can't imagine anyone who wouldn't gain by dipping into it (better still, reading it from cover to cover) . . . In an age where we constantly ignore or abuse our body's intelligence and value the prizes of the education system over the benefits of learning, this book is an essential counterblast to a better, more integrated way of working and living.'

– Edward Kemp, director, Royal Academy of Dramatic Art (RADA)

'We have all heard a lot about the many benefits of being fit and healthy, but now imagine a world where you can actively influence and leverage your body to optimise your personal and professional well-being and success! Scientific research paired with practical experience and easy life hacks makes *Physical Intelligence* an inspiring read that will literally change the way you walk through life.'

– Dr Stefanie Teichmann, director, Google EMEA

'This book is totally brilliant; a super mix of the intelligent and the practical. Physical Intelligence is as important or more important than any other form of intelligence. That's hotly debated and not yet really respected and this needs to change.'

– Wayne McGregor CBE, resident choreographer, Royal Ballet

'Success in business requires a lot more than academic intelligence. We need to understand not only interpersonal relationships but also the physical processes that drive behaviours. This very readable and practical book is grounded in the evidence and speaks to us. I have seen these techniques transform individual performance and wellbeing.'

– John Trundle, CEO, Euroclear UK & Ireland

'An extraordinary, up-to-the-minute scientific blueprint for optimising your life, harnessing the natural intelligence of the body. Convincing, thorough, creative, pragmatic, well-organised: a brilliant resource book for professionals, practitioners, clients, families, those in good health, those in poor health. I can't imagine anybody – no matter how psychologically skilled or trained – who wouldn't learn a huge amount from this.'

– Roz Carroll, body psychotherapist and author

PHYSICAL INTELLIGENCE

Harness Your Body's Untapped
Intelligence to Achieve More, Stress
Less and Live More Happily

CLAIRE DALE AND PATRICIA PEYTON

**SIMON &
SCHUSTER**

London · New York · Sydney · Toronto · New Delhi

A CBS COMPANY

First published in Great Britain by Simon & Schuster UK Ltd, 2019
A CBS COMPANY

Copyright © Companies in Motion Ltd, 2019

The right of Companies in Motion Ltd to be identified as the author
of this work has been asserted in accordance with the
Copyright, Designs and Patents Act, 1988.

5 7 9 10 8 6 4

Simon & Schuster UK Ltd
1st Floor
222 Gray's Inn Road
London WC1X 8HB

www.simonandschuster.co.uk
www.simonandschuster.com.au
www.simonandschuster.co.in

Simon & Schuster Australia, Sydney
Simon & Schuster India, New Delhi

The authors and publishers have made all reasonable efforts
to contact copyright-holders for permission, and apologise
for any omissions or errors in the form of credits given.
Corrections may be made to future printings.

The authors are not health practitioners and do not purport
to give medical advice. If a reader is in any doubt as to whether
to adopt any recommendation made in this book on account of
an existing medical condition or health concern, they
should seek advice from a health practitioner.

A CIP catalogue record for this book
is available from the British Library

Trade Paperback ISBN: 978-1-4711-7090-4
eBook ISBN: 978-1-4711-7091-1

Interior illustrations by James Edgar
Typeset in Palatino by M Rules
Printed and bound by CPI Group (UK) Ltd, Croydon, CR0 4YY

MIX
Paper from
responsible sources
FSC® C020471

For Adam and Angus.

~

For my mother and John.

CONTENTS

PART 2: FLEXIBILITY

PART 3: RESILIENCE

PART 4: ENDURANCE

To enhance your experience as you
read this book, please visit:
www.companiesinmotion.com/physical intelligence

INTRODUCING PHYSICAL INTELLIGENCE

Our bodies are amazing examples of intelligent design and function, performing trillions of operations every second. Over 400 neurotransmitters and hormones influence how we think, feel, speak and behave. Physiology drives performance, and yet most of us *experience* physical reactions, emotions and thoughts without realising that we can *transform* them.

'Physical Intelligence' is the active management of our physiology – the ability to detect and strategically influence the balance of chemicals in our bodies and brains.

Through the practice of Physical Intelligence techniques, we can increase our *strength, flexibility, resilience* and *endurance*, enabling us to build our confidence, make better decisions, rise to more ambitious challenges and live more constructive, fulfilling and tolerant lives. Physical Intelligence may well be the most important intelligence for the twenty-first century.

The evolution of intelligence

The term Physical Intelligence was first used in *Frames of Mind: The Theory of Multiple Intelligences* by Howard Gardner in 1983. His work established our initial understanding of different intelligences and learning styles. Gardner proposed that 'bodily-kinaesthetic' intelligence (intelligence derived through physical, practical learning – demonstrated, for example, by those who excel in sport or dance) is equally valid alongside other types of intelligence.* Gardner also identified that 'intrapersonal' intelligence (understanding of self) and 'interpersonal' intelligence (understanding of others) are as important as the type of intelligence typically measured by IQ.

Then, in 1990, the concept of 'emotional intelligence' (EQ or EI) was formulated by two researchers, Peter Salovey and John Mayer, and in 1995 Daniel Goleman published his seminal book *Emotional Intelligence*. Emotional intelligence is the capacity to be aware of, control and express emotion, and to handle interpersonal relationships with good judgement and empathy in order to achieve personal and professional success for you and others.

Being emotionally intelligent requires a high degree of Physical Intelligence because we experience emotions largely in the body as physiological changes. Emotions are actually strands of neuropeptides – chemicals released into the bloodstream that arrive at receptor cells and activate circuits of response that lead to behaviour; sadness, elation, frustration and pride all have a different chemistry and a distinct *feeling* to them. For example, pride tends to move slowly outwards and upwards from the chest, while frustration often moves quickly inwards and down in a clenching action, forming isolated knots of tension.

Being physically intelligent is more than this, however. The internal state of the body motivates us to walk on the shady side of the street on a hot summer's day, to continue to read a book

---

* The eight 'multiple intelligences' Gardner identified were: linguistic ('word smart'); logical-mathematical ('number/reasoning smart'); spatial ('picture smart'); musical ('music smart'); interpersonal ('people smart'); intrapersonal ('self smart'); naturalist ('nature smart'); and bodily-kinaesthetic ('body smart').

we are enjoying, to reduce social activity when feeling unwell, to avoid contact with someone who isn't smiling, to go into business with someone we trust, and so on. The viscera (the organs in the body), limbs and digits (legs and arms, feet and hands, fingers and toes), senses (hearing, sight, taste, smell and touch) and musculoskeletal system (posture and orientation) are in continuous two-way communication with the insular cortex in the brain, a deep, central part of the brain that connects physiological experiences with thoughts and emotions and vice versa.

Two decades of neuroscientific research shows us, for example, that we are 45 per cent more likely to have a high-quality, innovative idea when we are walking as opposed to when seated; that an open and expansive body posture improves confidence and risk tolerance; and that paced breathing technique increases cognitive function by 62 per cent. Furthermore, there are over 100 studies that show that physical exercise improves intelligence, including IQ levels and task efficiency.

This evidence increasingly points to the fact that our Physical Intelligence not only sits alongside, but *underpins* our cognitive and emotional performance. Becoming more physically intelligent will help us create businesses and societies where people take responsibility for themselves, are more informed and thoughtful about how to use their capacity, and are equipped with techniques that foster harmony and help them and their organisations achieve and sustain peak performance.

Let's now explore physical intelligence in action.

Alex's story

Alex woke up one morning and took a deep breath. He had slept well and felt positive about the day ahead. He would be leading a client presentation he and his colleagues had been preparing for over a month. Everything was ready. Alex stood up, picked up his phone and opened a new email he had been sent.

It was bad news. The client could see them for only ten minutes of the thirty they had originally planned for. Alex frowned and cursed while his shoulders shifted subtly forwards and his stomach contracted. The back of his neck shortened, his chin jutted out in front of him, his spine sagged and his breathing became faster and more shallow.

Recognising the signs, Alex slowed his breathing down and did a quick internal scan of his body. He found his knees were locked, his jaw was clenched and his shoulders were tense. He felt like he had been punched and he momentarily considered pulling out of the opportunity. The news had really caught him off-guard.

Alex breathed again and sat up a bit taller, rolled his shoulders back and lengthened his spine. He relaxed the areas of tension and grounded himself. With this action came a subtle change of mood; whatever this news meant for his presentation, he felt able to handle it. All was not lost. He took another few breaths and loosened his neck and jaw, easing the tension, and placed his feet firmly on the ground beneath him.

He quickly updated his partner on the news and they hugged as he left the house. As Alex walked to the station, he concentrated on walking with ease, purposefully looking at the world around him to give him a break from worrying and to stimulate creativity. From experience, he knew that getting uptight about an unexpected change such as this, no matter how annoying, wouldn't help matters.

As he stepped onto the train, he focused on his breathing and suddenly had an idea about how it could work. The strongest presenter on the team could summarise the in-depth research in the presentation, which would save at least fifteen minutes. That left only five more to shave off. When he reached the office, he smiled as he walked in and asked the team to join him in the conference room. Without tension, he explained the situation, acknowledging that, although not ideal, he believed that with creative thinking and reorientation it would not be a disaster. He shared his idea and asked for others. Within twenty minutes, the team had a plan; within the hour, they had reworked the presentation, agreeing that Corrine, who had an engaging and flexible style as well as a strong physical presence, should summarise the research. The bid was successful and over the next ten years the partnership with that client flourished. It brought considerable growth to the company and their business eventually contributed to its being floated on the stock market.

In this everyday scenario of changing circumstances, Alex was using his Physical Intelligence, drawing on the physical data derived from changes in his body/brain chemistry, managing his emotions and transforming the outcome.

Our background

The Physical Intelligence techniques I have developed are drawn from thirty years of experience and a lifetime working with and researching the body – first as a dancer, choreographer and artistic director of a leading contemporary dance company, The Claire Russ Ensemble, then as founding director of Companies in Motion – all of which is supported by scientific research. The marriage between science and the arts has always fascinated me.

I help global leaders achieve their highest performance and head up 'The Leading Role', the flagship embodied leadership course at RADA (Royal Academy of Dramatic Arts) Business. My life's work now is enabling businessmen and women, sales teams, teachers, doctors, television presenters and professionals of all kinds to better understand and use their bodies to create positive outcomes in their work and their lives.

My co-author Pat also has a background in dance, as well as in voice work, and has been employed as a voiceover artist. However, she is best known for thirty-plus years working with Fortune 100 and FTSE 100 organisations, providing leadership, sales and communications consulting, training and coaching that helps clients improve their performance. In addition to being a founding partner of Sphere International (her own consultancy), Pat has served as chief design officer for Richardson (a leading sales training firm) and is a director of Companies in Motion. Her life's work is partnering with organisations to create environments that support the development of people and processes to provide personal fulfilment and commercial success.

Countless people we have coached have increased their levels of confidence and effectiveness, have been promoted to senior roles or have been inspired to pursue their dreams – all through the effective use of Physical Intelligence techniques. One client team in the pharmaceutical industry achieved a 12.5 per cent improvement in the quality of its commercial deals after just three months of practising Physical Intelligence techniques. With our help, a technology company achieved double-digit growth in the midst of the last recession. Physical Intelligence has been proven time and again to have a clear, measurably positive impact on the quality of our life and our work.

It makes you think, doesn't it? How many of our own failures could have been successes if we had managed our chemistry differently? And if we had learned from both our successes *and* our failures, how much more intelligent would we be now?

The four elements: Strength, Flexibility, Resilience and Endurance

At Companies in Motion, four elements – strength, flexibility, resilience and endurance – are the backbone of the Physical Intelligence training, as they are for many top performers in sport and the arts. We have devised and adapted techniques used by these same performers so that they can be used by anyone, anywhere. These four key elements are vital to life as a whole, and they also provide the structure at the heart of this book.

Strength is having a robust and stable foundation of the nervous and endocrine systems that enables us to take risks. It involves being focused; maintaining high cognitive function and good decision-making skills under pressure; being confident and positively assertive; establishing clear boundaries; and remaining committed.

Flexibility is being creative, innovative and collaborative; having high self-esteem and high respect for others; being great at adapting your style and influencing those around you; understanding others' agendas and being agile and quick-thinking in changing environments, ready to embrace and instigate change.

Resilience is bouncing back from adversity and conflict; being optimistic and constructive with failure; adopting a learning mindset; and developing a well-functioning immune system through emotional, mental and physical fitness.

Endurance is the capacity for staying power and determination; being able to focus on and achieve long-term goals and find intrinsic motivation to play the long game; to be strategic in order to plan, execute and maintain performance over the long term.

In this book you will discover over eighty Physical Intelligence techniques that you can integrate into your everyday life, forming new habits that enable you to actively manage your physiology and be at your best in this fast-paced, ever-changing and demanding world.

Learning and embedding Physical Intelligence

When we want to create new habits, it is easier to attach or 'stack' a new habit onto an existing one, something you *always* do that is already embedded into your long-term memory and therefore reliably part of your schedule. We call this 'habit stacking'. There are tips throughout the book on how to do this, using what we call 'triggers'. Woven through the chapters you will also find bite-sized 'life hacks', which provide immediate ideas for physically intelligent actions.

Think of this book as a manual that you will use to increase performance, 'habit stacking' in order to continually improve and deepen your Physical Intelligence for the rest of your life.

For example, if you want to get into the habit of stretching after going for a run, attach it to something you always do at that time – such as walking through the garden gate – and begin your series of stretches immediately after doing that. After only a few days, this new habit will become embedded and you'll start to enjoy the benefits, including breaking the cycle of self-recrimination that occurs when willpower inevitably fails.

New habits form small increments of substantial long-term

improvement. This is called 'incremental gain' – the theory that if you break down a process or challenge into its myriad constituent parts, whether that is taking a product to market or winning an Olympic gold medal, and make each part more efficient by just 1 per cent, the overall result will be improved markedly. Remember, there is always room for improvement.

THE PEOPLE YOU WILL MEET

In addition to our own life experiences and the work we have done, Pat and I caught up with friends, family and high performers in the arts and sport, as well as clients (renamed) we have coached and trained. They generously shared their personal experiences and applications of Physical Intelligence principles with us, and we have incorporated these insights and experiences throughout the book to give you additional inspiration. Specifically, you will hear from:

- **Jarrod Barnes**, learning and innovation specialist, former Ohio State (USA) football player (Safety) and coach and former member of the Detroit Lions (US NFL team);
- **Joan Beal**, vocal contractor, soloist and studio singer in Hollywood, former member of San Francisco Opera company and frequent guest artist;
- **Alessandra Ferri**, globally acclaimed and award-winning prima ballerina assoluta at the Royal Ballet, previously with American Ballet Theatre for twenty-two years and La Scala for fifteen years;
- **George Kruis**, professional rugby union player (second row, blindside flanker, No. 8) for England and Saracens in the Aviva Premiership, playing a role in England's Six Nations success;

- **Wayne McGregor** CBE, multi-award-winning choreographer and director, currently resident choreographer at the Royal Ballet, internationally renowned for trailblazing innovations in performance that have radically redefined dance in the modern era;
- **Megan Mitchell**, US morning news anchor, reporter and producer;
- **Camilla Ross**, accounting teacher and founding director of Emerson Theatre Collaborative, a theatre company that serves youth, community and artists with an emphasis on diversity;
- **Dawn Marie Flynn Sirrenberg**, classically trained singer, frequent soloist and vocal coach, Fulbright Scholar, performed leading roles with opera companies across Germany;
- **(Samantha) Claire Taylor** MBE, England cricketer and the mainstay of England's batting for ten years, leading run-scorer in the 2009 World Cup, recipient of Women's Cricketer of the Year Award;
- and **Karl Van Haute**, commercial airline pilot, former US Marine Corps captain and pilot.

For the Nutrition and Fitness chapters, we have collaborated with nutritionist Justine Evans ND, BSc (N.Med), and personal trainer and performance specialist Robert Devenport.

Explain, train, rehearse and perform

In the chapters that follow, we will learn more about the key chemicals in the body and brain that influence us, and then look at each of the four elements of Physical Intelligence (strength, flexibility, resilience and endurance), first explaining the science, physiology and the chemical story behind each element.

We will then train you in a set of techniques that will enable you to improve each element. Next, we will suggest you select a handful of the techniques and rehearse them for a week, exploring how you can make them work for you through practice and repetition. We'll then encourage you to make concrete decisions and perform these new techniques in the same order, using the same triggers, every day for the rest of the month. This will fully embed the new behaviours.

The same process will be repeated for each of the four elements, building your own Physical Intelligence programme over four months. You can start with strength and work through the elements in order or you can take our quiz: 'How Physically Intelligent Are You?' (www.companiesinmotion. com/HowPhysicallyIntelligentAreYou) and begin with the element that is a priority for you. After four months, you will have twenty techniques habit-stacked into your daily life (five per element), with sixty or more to go back to in time. As you gain experience, you can vary your approach, being creative with how you construct your physically intelligent lifestyle.

After just a few weeks using the techniques in this book, you are likely to notice greater mental focus and emotional stability. After a few months, you should be experiencing greater capacity, vitality and fulfilment. By applying Physical Intelligence techniques consistently throughout your life, you create the conditions for continued growth in cognitive capacity, wisdom, happiness and achievement; living the life you want, in the way you want. What feels extremely challenging today need not feel that way tomorrow.

We hope that you will write in this book, turn over the corners – visit and revisit pages for support and enrichment and share the book with others – inspiring those around you to build their Physical Intelligence along with you.

1

THE WINNING COCKTAIL

How to recognise the chemicals that drive our behaviour

Right at this moment, can you feel the pace of your heartbeat? Can you feel the movement of your breath entering and leaving your body? Can you feel the shape of your spine? Can you capture the feeling of your current mood and what is creating that mood today? Take a second or two to focus on each of these questions. As you do, you will likely become more aware, more actively present in your body.

There are eight key chemicals that work in combination to explain helpful and unhelpful, constructive and unconstructive, responses to situations at home, at work and at play. When the balance is right, we call it the 'Winning Cocktail'.

Ingredients in the cocktail

Acetylcholine

You've had a busy week, so you make it an early night and treat yourself to a long lie-in to start the weekend. On Saturday morning, as you go slowly about your day, you realise that you are breathing out in long sighs and having feelings of relief. This is your re-balancing and renewal system kicking in, driven by acetylcholine, the key chemical in the parasympathetic nervous system. Few people outside of the science or health fields know about acetylcholine, but it is responsible for hugely important areas like energy renewal, recovery from pressure, learning and memory. It brings the heart rate back to normal after intense activity and restores the balance of the organism as a whole in the process of homeostasis. This is true for all types of intense activity: emotional, mental, physical, or all three. The signature feeling of acetylcholine is balance.

LIFE HACK: To quickly relax and stimulate acetylcholine production after a hard day, take a hot bath with Epsom salts in it. Minerals such as magnesium and potassium (vital for renewal) will be absorbed through the skin and your energy will come flooding back – and you'll sleep better.

Adrenalin

We've all experienced it: on a fairground ride, skiing, going on a first date or even something somewhat negative such as accidentally hitting 'Reply All' on a sensitive email response. The primary functions of adrenalin are to 1) increase heart rate and blood flow in survival situations and 2) to release energy quickly from stored resources of carbohydrate and fat to provide the muscles and brain with a burst of energy and strength to facilitate immediate action.

Adrenalin creates excitement, activation and speed. It gives us the energy to meet new challenges, but it can speed us up or leave us feeling overly excited or nervous in presentations or negotiations, making it difficult to communicate succinctly or think clearly. Adrenalin is one of the two key operative chemicals of the sympathetic nervous system, the system that produces the fast action needed to respond to threats. The signature feelings of adrenalin are fear or excitement.

LIFE HACK: If you feel nerves building up, don't just sit there: move, shift position, walk, shake out your legs and arms to disperse adrenalin.

Cortisol

Do you ever worry or feel anxious about things? Do you sometimes react impatiently or angrily? Do you feel concerned about the future and whether you are up to it? Do you regularly believe that others are to blame for things? Or do you think things are always your fault?

These are all high cortisol speaking. Too many people are struggling to maintain their performance in today's fast-paced and demanding environments, and cortisol is part of the problem. It is a critically important chemical and the positive effects of it keep us alive. It numbs pain so that we can fight even if injured; it is the major player in our nervous system function that takes us into all challenging or competitive situations (arousal), improving short-term memory as we compete.

In a sustained period of working under pressure, with a lot of responsibility on our shoulders or in a sustained 'fight or flight' environment, cortisol builds, making us over-aroused and anxious so that we 'choke' and underperform; we make poor decisions. This happens either because we are in overdrive, pushing too much and taking unmitigated risks (hyperarousal) or because we have caved in (hypoarousal). We make attempts to think straight in complex situations but then often push our own agenda or decide on the path of least resistance, rather than what is right to do. The signature feeling of cortisol is anxiety.

DHEA

Dehydroepiandrosterone is *the* high-performance chemical. Synthetic DHEA is a banned substance for Olympic athletes, yet we can make it ourselves every day using a specific paced breathing technique. It supports vitality, longevity, stamina, cognitive function, immune system function, heart–brain function, long-term memory, responsiveness and many more functions of a healthy, high-performing organism.

DHEA and cortisol are, then, two sides of a balancing scale. DHEA is a biomarker of age and naturally drops beyond the age of thirty. For women and men, stress and high cortisol accelerate this drop in DHEA, which leads to premature ageing. Unless we manage pressure well, when DHEA levels drop too quickly, the overall stability of our nervous and endocrine systems are compromised. If we improve our capacity to perform under pressure without undue stress, we will age more slowly. The signature feeling of DHEA is vitality.

> **LIFE HACK:** Check your Fitbit, smart phone or Apple watch and find a breath-pacer app – then increase the amount of time per day you spend using a regular-paced breathing pattern. This boosts DHEA.

Dopamine

Have you ever felt disappointed on opening a birthday or Christmas present when it wasn't what you wanted? Or when you didn't get that promotion at work? Or when you finished a conversation feeling faintly put out by someone who took credit for something you played a big part in? These negative feelings are generated by a lack of expected reward, a lack of delivery of the pleasure chemical dopamine.

Dopamine is the great motivator. When we get it, we prioritise behaviour to make sure we keep getting it – for example, being annoyingly hooked on a rather poor but 'unputdownable' novel, or a box set where you just have to watch the next episode, or eating the entire bag of crisps. These are instances of the clever manipulation of our dopaminergic function – when our reward system is being played. It can feel so good yet be so bad for us.

Dopamine provides a powerful chemical drive for many things concerned with survival. It is no accident that we enjoy the taste of food, water alleviates thirst and sex feels good. Beyond that, what we are praised for when we are young sets up the mechanism for what we want to achieve and win later in life – at work or in a specialised area or skill, which is why it is so important to reinforce positive behaviours in children. Dopamine plays a huge part in goal orientation and engaging people in change. The signature feelings of dopamine are pleasure and need.

> **LIFE HACK:** STOP! Find something to enjoy and appreciate in this very moment. You just created a 'reward' and, in doing so, have given yourself a natural dopamine boost.

Oxytocin

Over a meal with family or friends, have you ever had that sense of feeling *right*? That you like being there, you feel safe and included, and believe that these people are looking out for your welfare? Hopefully, you regularly do. That's oxytocin being released. Oxytocin levels fluctuate in relation to our perception and processing of social information – whether we are in the 'in group' or 'out group', whether we feel safe or threatened. It is released when we trust someone; it enables us to feel responsibility to others and facilitates social bonding. Too much, and we may be overly dependent on relationships and lack the ability to make independent decisions; we may also want our group to be exclusive or elite. Too little, and we may feel isolated; we might not build professional relationships or know how to use our networks for support. We need to be able to boost our own levels of oxytocin, which we can do by empathising with others in order to create harmony or manage conflict.

Oxytocin is crucial to good teamwork because it is part of the emotions of liking, loving, pride and feeling included. It is a 'feel-good' chemical: with it, we feel stronger together, which also contributes to feelings of confidence – the confidence we derive from being part of a social group. The signature feeling of oxytocin is belonging.

> **LIFE HACK:** Send a text right now to someone who is in your thoughts and with whom you haven't spoken in a while. You may ask how they are doing, ask for their advice, or offer to help. You just boosted your oxytocin level. Notice how you feel happier – even better when they reply!

Serotonin

Serotonin influences levels of happiness, status and feelings of satisfaction and well-being. We believe that we are enough, have enough. We feel naturally balanced and empowered and can take responsibility for our role in society.

Serotonin is very important for the immune system and for deep-seated confidence. That killer chemical cortisol, if running too high, will drain serotonin levels until depression sets in. Smiling and laughing releases serotonin in ourselves and others when we smile at them. It is released when we eat bananas and good-quality dark chocolate. The signature feeling of serotonin is happiness.

> **LIFE HACK:** Use any form of meditation – mindfulness, a yoga breathing practice, Transcendental Meditation – or just sit quietly and focus on your breathing every day for ten minutes. Notice how you start to sail through the year without those annoying sniffles and flu viruses. Meditation boosts serotonin.

Testosterone

Testosterone (along with dopamine) drives your desire to achieve and compete. When you feel the confidence of a 'winner' or you have thoughts like *I did it!* your testosterone levels go up further, rising over a period of minutes.

Testosterone enables risk tolerance and confidence and is vital for feeling empowered. However, a warning about too much testosterone: if we are overly confident about a win, we may become arrogant and not prepare well enough (e.g. for that important job interview). Too much testosterone also impedes teamwork. If we have too little testosterone, however, we become risk-averse and avoid competitive situations. We can adjust levels of testosterone through the use of posture and through resistance-based physical exercise. The signature feelings of testosterone are power and control.

> **LIFE HACK:** To boost testosterone, the next time you achieve something good, put your arms in the air like a winner and say a big fat 'YES!' Don't suppress your elation. Feel it, and get used to being successful!

These are our 'Top 8' ingredients. Now we'll look at what happens when we start to put them together and influence their balance to create better outcomes.

Mixing the cocktail

Let's review Alex's success story from the Introduction through our chemical lens. Alex is well-rested when he wakes, indicating that cortisol (threat/stress/arousal) has been appropriately low during the night, allowing melatonin (sleep quality) to be appropriately high. Alex has used Physical Intelligence sleep techniques (more on these later) and knows how to achieve quality sleep, even before an important event.

Cortisol rises to wake Alex up in the morning, but as he reads the bad news on his phone he experiences a huge cortisol spike that manifests as tension in his shoulders and contraction in his stomach. He also experiences testosterone (confidence and risk tolerance) and dopamine (reward and goal orientation) levels dropping. He has been thwarted by circumstances and this manifests as a drop in motivation.

But then, recognising the signs, he uses posture to reboot testosterone levels, and shares the problem with his partner, boosting oxytocin (social bonding and trust). Oxytocin and testosterone both counteract high cortisol; he feels more balanced again.

Walking with expansive posture and stride further raises serotonin (happiness, status, self-esteem) and testosterone levels. Dopamine is released when we look at changing vistas, and this is associated with creative thinking. As he steps onto the train, the solution comes in a flash. Alex works on his breathing pattern on the train, balancing adrenalin (rising to the challenge) and acetylcholine (keeping a cool head) while boosting DHEA (increasing vitality/endurance).

As Alex walks into the office, he smiles at his team, which releases serotonin and oxytocin in himself and in the team members. He walks with expansion, pace, purpose, ease and confidence, which raises his and his team's testosterone and serotonin levels. As he shares his idea and asks for theirs, his voice is level and resonant, and he is purposely de-escalating his and their threat response, helping to keep their cortisol and adrenalin at optimal levels, preparing them to rise to the challenge and be productive and astute.

Alex knows exactly what he is doing. It is his knowledge of how the key chemicals impact his and others' behaviour that gives him the ability to achieve his own personal 'flow' state – influencing his internal cocktail. He is choosing behaviour that supports the combinations he needs.

We can instruct the body to achieve the balance we want by knowing more about our physiology, by practically creating new habits and by enacting the behaviour that shifts the levels of specific chemicals up or down.

Have you ever walked into an office and felt an air of tension, where people are charged with impatience, pushing or driving from a position of uncertainty, or where projects seem to regularly encounter problems and teams are often fire-fighting? Have you ever walked into a family environment where children and adults are self-assured, where creative ideas flow freely and people are able to question, discuss and collaborate without fear of conflict? Have you ever worked in a team and felt happy, making progress quickly in a dynamic, trusting and highly productive environment? Sports psychologists and athletes call this latter state 'the zone'; dancers (and psychologist Csikszentmihalyi) call this state 'flow': the ability to be fully engaged and effortlessly performing at peak.

While adrenalin gets us going and acetylcholine enables us to recover, it is the relative levels of cortisol and DHEA that dictate *how* we get going and *how* we recover and whether we are in a state of flow. Too much cortisol drags down levels of the four 'feel-good' chemicals – dopamine, oxytocin, serotonin and testosterone – whereas DHEA boosts them.

If you doubt yourself, worry, feel anxious, frustrated or overwhelmed, or often wake up on a Monday feeling low, yearning for more sleep and wishing it was Friday, then cortisol is running too high. If you are enthusiastic, motivated and passionate as you get going into your day and are content and receptive when you relax and recover, then DHEA levels are high and you are in great shape to take on new challenges.

Physical Intelligence will be an important part of your own personal transformation to enable you to spend more time in the high DHEA state that will come by applying and habit stacking the Physical Intelligence techniques in this book.

The body is a complex system with many chemical interactions that we can't and wouldn't want to influence. However, the more we understand about the neuroscience that underpins our behaviour, the more we can exercise control over the balance of chemicals that we *can* influence, increasing the impact we can have on our strength, flexibility, resilience and endurance.

With this foundation in place, we are ready to take a closer look at the first of the four elements of Physical Intelligence: strength.

PART 1
STRENGTH

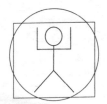

Introducing Strength

I'd like to be like a rock that the waves keep
crashing over. It stands unmoved and the
raging sea falls still around it.

—ANONYMOUS

It is Saturday afternoon and John has rented a small sailboat to take his family out sailing in San Diego Bay. Suddenly the water becomes dangerously rough where the bay meets the ocean. To keep the boat under control, John knows he needs to bring the boom around immediately, but his five-year-old daughter is hanging precariously over the side of the boat looking for dolphins, his eight-year-old son is playing pirate, shouting as he pops in and out of the hatch, and his ten-year-old son (an amateur sailor) is standing on the edge of the bow, looking like he's ready to leap. John's partner is in the back of the boat preparing lunch – facing in the opposite direction, oblivious to all of this. Despite the imminent danger, in a clear, confident voice John rapidly calls each family member by name and gives each person specific instructions: directing his partner to grab their five-year-old away from the edge of the boat and sit down; telling the eight-year-old to close the hatch and sit down; and instructing the ten-year-old to quickly bring the boom around while John himself remains at the helm. Crisis averted – thanks to John's *strength*.

Strength, with regard to Physical Intelligence, is the fundamental physical, mental and emotional capacity to keep a cool head under pressure, to hold our ground and act and speak decisively and wisely in complex, high-risk situations, *without feeling threatened or needing to threaten others*. This enables us to *look* and *feel* confident. Without strength when we are threatened, cognitive function diminishes and we become preoccupied with fight, flight, blame or saving face. The hallmark of strength is the ability to maintain and improve cognitive function while making quality decisions under pressure. Thankfully, not all situations that require strength are a matter of life and death, the way John's was. In many situations, the pressure or threat comes from changes in our jobs, our health, or the actions of other people. In more complex personal, social and professional situations, if we are to be constructive, we need to manage our threat response, build confidence and feel empowered.

Being physically 'grounded' is important for strength – feeling the weight of the body on the ground, or in the chair; feeling rooted rather than 'uptight'. Our stance and breathing patterns are critical, and we need a robust approach to generating confidence and tolerating risk – and building those qualities in others. In this section, we will learn how to create the inner feeling of strength and confidence, how to be positively assertive, independently minded, astute and highly productive, and able to increase our capacity for achievement.

> **LIFE HACK:** Have you ever not spoken out when you wish you had, and kicked yourself afterwards? Next time, STOP, feel the weight of your body in your chair and speak out.

THE WINNING COCKTAIL FOR STRENGTH

Testosterone
We all need to access testosterone to be able to assert ourselves positively, stand our ground and have our voice heard. When testosterone levels are where they should be, we feel like we have a driving force inside us and are powerful and influential.

DHEA
We can't actually feel short-term shifts in DHEA – but we *can* feel the long-term shifts in our underlying state over weeks, months and years. People with 'full tanks' of DHEA will feel enhanced confidence and an appetite for a challenge. They will compete strategically, approaching life more like a chess game than a boxing match.

Cortisol
High cortisol, with its feelings of anxiety, can lead to defensiveness, aggression or retreat. For strength we need to be able to achieve a balanced, stable, low baseline cortisol level so that we can *act* rather than *react*.

Dopamine
We need the right amount of dopamine – not too much, not too little – in the brain so that we can concentrate well on tasks without being distracted and enjoy ourselves. Impulsive, risk-taking, ruthless behaviour indicates too much dopamine; feeling demotivated and joyless indicates too little.

All of these chemicals and hormones interact. For many years, researchers believed that testosterone alone was the chemical that makes us aggressive; however, we now know that it is the *combination* of testosterone and high cortisol that triggers aggressiveness and unsociable, selfish actions.

Balance is key. When cortisol rises against high testosterone, we enter 'hyperarousal'. We are over-controlling, appear arrogant or overly critical of situations and people, uncaring and dominating. We are pushy and try to conquer the pace of life. When cortisol rises against low testosterone, we enter 'hypoarousal', becoming over-compliant, self-blaming, covering up weakness with bravado, nervous laughter, talking fast, pretending confidence but giving ground. We are intolerant of risk and collapse under pressure.

> **LIFE HACK:** To discover if you tend towards hyper- or hypoarousal, ask yourself: Under pressure, do you . . .
>
> 1. Go straight into action – dishing out orders, demanding answers, becoming provocative and testy? This is hyperarousal. Remedy: STOP – slow your breathing pattern, bring your focus to the front of your mind, calm thoughts, one by one, and prioritise.
>
> 2. Freeze, hold emotion in, contain frustration, feel inner turmoil, collapse on the inside, but keep smiling on the outside? This is hypoarousal. Remedy: MOVE – remove yourself to somewhere private – shake out vigorously, punch the air, thump a cushion, then take action.

The cocktail of high testosterone/high cortisol/high dopamine is a state of heightened powerfulness, and can send us into a dangerous overdrive in which we may be careless and take unmitigated risks. Cortisol also has a crucial relationship with dopamine. When we feel happy, positive about something or someone, wanting to engage, we are having a 'towards' response in which dopamine rises and cortisol settles to optimal. We feel rewarded, which makes us want to engage more, do more, be more in the situation. When we feel disappointed, demoralised, lacking motivation, angry or unhappy about something, we are having what has been termed an 'away' response; a primary threat response in which cortisol rises and dopamine drops. We feel unrewarded by the situation – therefore, we instinctively move away from it or resist it.

It is now recognised that the primary threat and primary reward circuitry, known to be activated by our basic animal needs for food, water, shelter and the opportunity to procreate, is also triggered by *social domains*. These social domains include status (being recognised in society as valuable); certainty (anticipation of needs being met in that society); autonomy (ability to make choices and own decisions); relatedness (being well-bonded, stable, safe and included in the group/tribe); and fairness (equal distribution of work, challenges and resources between people in the group). (See reference to David Rock's SCARF model in Research and Resources chapter, p. 441, for more on this.)

This knowledge is important for strength in two ways. First, if we start to see situations, demands and expectations for what they are – triggers of our primary threat (away) or primary reward (towards) responses due to elevated cortisol and diminished dopamine levels – then we can be less reactive and more constructive in our response. This puts us in a stronger, more realistic position to act.

Secondly, when working in groups, managing people or bringing up children, if we know what people need in order to feel fully engaged – e.g. being valued for their input (status), having clear boundaries and expectations (certainty), having the ability to prioritise and make their own decisions (autonomy), being included (relatedness), knowing that participation is spread evenly across the team/family, and that they can be honest in communication (fairness) – then we can speak and behave in such a way that draws people together, by creating and fostering the chemistry of a 'towards' response.

Developing strength is a lifelong journey that underpins our ability to assert ourselves, develop and demonstrate confidence, and perform consistently. By creating stability in our nervous and endocrine systems we can develop deep-seated, sustained strength, leading us to believe in and reach successful outcomes for ourselves and those around us, while being realistic and seeing situations clearly. Our strength and the ability to use it wisely enables us to support our own progress and that of others, creating an environment where there is an appetite for challenge and the capacity to achieve more. Let's begin our journey towards Physical Intelligence and learn some fundamental techniques to develop our overall strength.

2

POSTURE

How our stance and seated posture builds our confidence

Today's mighty oak is just yesterday's nut
that held its ground.

—ROSA PARKS

The way we 'hold' ourselves is very powerful because it changes the way we think, feel and make an impact. Parents instinctively want their children to be strong and confident. Most of us can remember being told to stand up straight, chin up, shoulders back. In fact, coachees often say to me, 'My mother would have loved you!' Well, your mother knew what she was talking about. Good posture enables you to feel and portray confidence and readiness for action. It also makes room for the lungs to fill and the breathing mechanism to function effectively, which is why we will address posture first.

THE ANATOMY OF POSTURE

The *spine* (or backbone) is a miraculous and complex flexible structure. It runs from the base of the skull to the pelvis and serves as a pillar to support the body's weight and to protect the spinal cord. There are three natural curves in the spine relating to the three sections: cervical (neck and upper back), thoracic (shoulder and chest) and lumbar (waist and lower back). The curves give it an 'S' shape when viewed from the side and help distribute the weight of the body from front to back, so that we neither fall forwards nor fall back. (If the spine was straight down the back, we would be sure to topple backwards. In fact, the spine is nearer to the central line of the body, not really a 'back' bone but a 'central' bone.)

The spinal column is made up of vertebrae separated by discs of fibrous tissue and contains the spinal cord, including the central

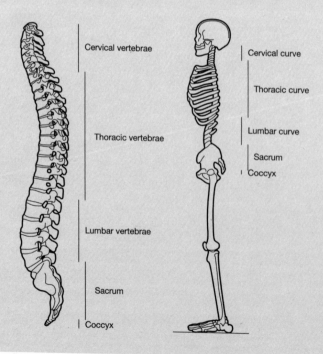

Cervical vertebrae

Thoracic vertebrae

Lumbar vertebrae

Sacrum

Coccyx

Cervical curve

Thoracic curve

Lumbar curve

Sacrum

Coccyx

nerves and a column of spinal fluid. The spinal fluid keeps the brain and central nerves buoyant in a pressurised system.

The very *top vertebra* is called the atlas, from the mythical figure of Ancient Greece who balances the weight of a globe on his shoulders. This vertebra facilitates a 'yes' action with the head. The *second vertebra* in the spine is the axis, enabling the head to turn from side to side in a 'no' action.

At the other end of the spine is the *sacrum*, a triangular bone that sits into and is flanked by the two sides of the back of the pelvis. The weight of the spine, the thorax (rib cage and organs) and the neck and head are distributed throughout the pelvis and down through the hip joints to the leg bones and feet.

The *pelvis* sits on top of the legs. The ball-and-socket joint of the hip is a strong joint with the bone held in by suction, but it is mobile and needs to move freely in walking and be lightly held in standing.

The *tailbone* or coccyx is the remains of an ancient tail, used for balance. It should be neither tucked under nor stuck out. It is helpful to think of it extending down to the floor behind you, balancing you in the way a kangaroo's tail does.

The *legs* are for stability and locomotion, with joints at the hips, knees and ankles. It is important that the muscles of the calf, thigh, hamstring and gluteus maximus (buttocks) are not rigidly held so that the leg joints can absorb shock and enable us to move fluidly. Skiers and golfers know how vital unlocked knees are to stability and experiencing 'flow'.

The *feet* are a miraculous complex jigsaw of bones that distribute body weight into the ground and enable us to make tiny adjustments of balance every second. While the spine extends us upwards, the feet extend us down into the ground like roots of a sturdy tree.

The *arms* hang from the 'coat hanger'-like structure formed by the collarbones in the front and shoulder blades in the upper back. They reach out for things we need and want and communicate through our gestures.

The *head* is very heavy. The protective skull contains the dense, compact brain matter. The head balances on the top vertebra of the spine. The atlas and the alignment of the head enable us to look around at our environment and be in a position to make eye contact with each other.

The *lower jaw bone* is jointed to the *upper jaw* just in front of the ears. It needs to be free to move so that we can chew food, make facial expressions and speak. A clenched jaw creates tension and causes the cervical curve in the neck to shorten, taking the head out of alignment. When the jaw is released, the back of the neck and throat area find their balance, and this affects how our voice sounds.

The *core muscles* should support the spine effortlessly when the bones are well-aligned. Strengthening core muscles is needed if there has been a history of misalignment and they are weak, or to engage in more strenuous resistance work or sports.

The winner pose

Using your height is an important factor in how you feel. A short person can appear empowered and a tall person can appear defeated depending on how they position their spine and head. In fact, research from the universities of Washington and Cornell in 2012 found that how powerful we feel can dictate how tall we think we are.

If we are competing or doing something new or risky, standing tall is an important part of withstanding the emotional and mental pressure. England rugby player George Kruis described what it felt like to face the New Zealand haka. He said, 'It's odd, because you feel like you are being challenged without being able to fight. You know there is tradition and obviously lots of culture behind it so there is no insult, it's a privilege, but you find yourself standing up an inch taller than you normally would to show that you are not afraid of what's about to come.'

It is not just using your height that is important, but also breadth, expansion and striding out. Masai hunters watch a lion make a kill, then stroll up to the feeding lion, spreading their arms, owning the space. The lion runs off until it realises it has been duped. Meanwhile, the Masai have cut away some prime cuts of meat to feed their families, ensuring their survival.

Spreading and opening our arms, stretching out into the space around us and taking a wide and open stance with our feet and legs (making a shape like a starfish) helps build confidence and risk tolerance. At Companies in Motion we call this the 'winner pose' because a 2008 study showed that both blind and sighted athletes equally strike this pose on achieving competitive wins – it is an innate expression of pride and confidence.

A 'winner pose' is a type of 'power pose', the concept coined in 2010 by Amy Cuddy et al. in what later became controversial Harvard University research. While endocrine effects of the Harvard experiments have not been replicated, fifty-five studies demonstrate a link between expansive postures and feelings of power, and Cuddy's own research on this passes the statistical p-curve test.

LIFE HACK: Think back to a moment in your childhood when you were outdoors, perhaps running down a hill with your arms stretched open, or standing and leaning into the wind. Expand your posture and your whole body in the same way now. You can have that confidence whenever you like by triggering that feeling with your body posture.

With coachees, I find that the winner pose is particularly effective at reducing the symptoms of nerves created by high cortisol and adrenalin levels. A young salesperson came to Companies in Motion because he was flushing red at the start of every sales call. In a shared office, this was causing him embarrassment, and the situation was getting worse. A winner pose in the bathroom combined with a breathing technique (see next chapter) prior to calls sorted the issue out straight away.

Expansive posture also changes how others perceive us. With open body language and making our presence felt, we show the world we are secure and confident enough to take action. A few years ago, I worked with a distinguished permanent secretary in the British government in his early sixties who transformed the impact he had on his department when, over the period of a year, he changed his posture. When I met him, he was rather hunched over. However, when he learned to release tension in his legs and hips, enabling his lower spine to better support his upper spine, he was able to open his shoulders, lengthen his neck and raise his head, appearing strong and connected, rather than disengaged and detached. It's a great example that it is never too late to change.

LIFE HACK: Put your feet flat on the ground, lengthen your spine and notice how your thoughts become more clearly focused.

The relationship between posture and leadership

Posture plays an important part in leading people. Research from Stanford University in 2010 showed that the act of taking the lead in a critical situation tends to be by people who use open, expansive body posture, *rather than by people who have been assigned a leadership role.* Look around the room to the person with the most open, expansive body posture and often you will see them step in and rally the team.

MANDY LEADS HER TEAM TO SUCCESS...

It is 3pm on Thursday afternoon. Mandy and her team are in a conference room engaged in the final preparation for a major sales presentation to be made the following morning. Unexpectedly, the client calls to say they are also considering working with a competitor. This competitor is not only a market leader, but the key decision-maker at the client company used to work for the competitor and still has friends there, which poses a significant threat to Mandy and her team's success.

As Mandy feels that threat, her cortisol spikes, taking her heart rate and her body temperature up. She knows she needs to rally the team and build their confidence. She calls a short break and while everyone is out of the room she walks away from the table and stretches her arms wide. This open, expansive body posture will help dial down the effects of cortisol and dial up her courage. Within a matter of seconds, she feels the chemical tide of emotions turning. She feels her mental state shift from deflated and defeated to confident and assertive.

It occurs to her that not long ago the team were successful in a similar situation and she intends to remind them of that. The visual picture of this rewarding event triggers dopamine release in her brain and she immediately feels more focused and able to move towards the challenge. When they reconvene, Mandy stands at her full height with broad shoulders at the front of the room; she takes charge of the situation, owning her role as leader. She shares with the team why she still believes in their pitch and how, by adding a short sentence to the introduction, they can ensure that the client understands their unique value proposition, differentiating their pitch from the competitor's. After a couple of minutes, the mood changes and the confidence of others returns. They make a minor adjustment to the pitch, find their flow and win.

What if, when the team were out of the room, Mandy had sat slumped in her chair with narrowed, hunched shoulders, letting the threat overwhelm her instead of thinking about what to do? What if she had let the thought take hold that the competition may indeed be better placed to win? What if, when speaking with the team, she had faked confidence and let underlying doubt creep in? The team may well have lost confidence in the value of their approach. They most likely would not have found their flow in the pitch. Thankfully, Mandy changed her body's response to this stressful situation and it helped her team change theirs. They stood their ground and raised their game in the face of competition.

Focus, mood and posture

The level of focus and the mood in a room is often affected by the posture people adopt, which is contagious. Have you ever sat in a meeting where most people were slumped back in their chairs the entire time, or hunched forwards over their laptops, or leaning heavily on the table while a kind of creeping death took over the room? When first learning posture techniques, many people say to me, 'But it feels so comfortable to sit back and fold my arms ...' While that may be true, these are only habits and muscle memories, which can be replaced with an alert stance that helps you be fully present and aware.

LIFE HACK: Next time you meet other people, experiment with using your posture to positively influence the pace and tone of the interaction. In time you will find others join you in more alert, open posture.

We come in all shapes and sizes

No two bodies are alike, and it is our diversity that makes the world an interesting place. People of all shapes and sizes can equally own a room. For example, think of people with shorter stature: the performer Sammy Davis Jr; the actor Daniel Radcliffe; Simone Biles, the American gymnast who won Olympic gold – all, and many more, are able to command a large stage or an arena.

In 2002, I choreographed a dance work for CandoCo, an integrated dance company of international renown. Some of the performers are disabled, some are not, and the company includes dancers shorter in stature, those dancing in wheelchairs, and dancers who have lost or have paralysed limbs. Each dancer owns the stage entirely, using their unique body. I travelled globally with CandoCo to progressive countries, and also to countries where people with disabilities were hidden away from the public eye.

Without fail, the ovations for CandoCo's performances were not only for the appreciation of the dance, but for the shattering of preconceptions about disability.

LIFE HACK: Think about a moment when your body helped you achieve something significant – delivering an important presentation, standing up for something you believe in – or when your body helped you do something positive – helping someone across the road, running or walking for charity. Nobody is perfect, so appreciate and make the most of the body you have.

Posture is not a fixed, rigid state, and we can all develop the ability to be easy in our own unique body. If we *think* openly and expansively, *act* openly and expansively, then we will *appear* open and expansive and will fully own a room.

Screen time and posture

Many of us spend extensive time in front of screens and find that our eyes and head pitch too far forwards – ahead of the spine, supported by the cantilever action of the neck and shoulder muscles. This puts enormous strain on these vulnerable parts of the body. We need to find a point of balance for the head to sit on top of the spinal column without putting strain on the neck and shoulders.

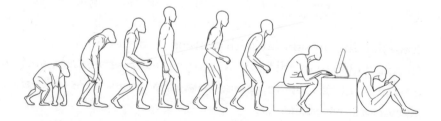

Dopamine, the reward chemical, is produced in greater quantities when we are working online because we are able to achieve more and reach our goals faster. We are constantly experiencing novelty, and this keeps us engaged, if not addicted, over extended periods of time.

However, the amount of time spent hunched over, with jutting chin and curved spine, also reduces the amount of space there is for the lungs to expand, raising carbon dioxide levels in the blood, which in turn elevates cortisol levels. High baseline cortisol reduces the quality of our cognitive function and mental and emotional performance. Many people carry a lot of muscular tension in their shoulders, partly because we spend so much of our time at screens. This can deeply affect how we think and feel while we work. Research from Hildesheim and Ruhr-University in Germany in 2014 revealed that even subtle changes in seated posture affect how we interpret and remember events.

If we use hunched posture all day, we shape our bodies into the position of defeat or avoidance. We need to be aware of jaw and neck tension as we work because the jaw connects with the cervical region of the spine and if it is tense it restricts the spinal column and interferes with information processing, memory retrieval and the collection of data by the insular cortex in the brain, which means we cannot sense or feel what is happening in our bodies.

Let's train: Posture

Exercise: Experimenting with posture

Imagine the email that you were dreading has just dropped into your inbox. Collapse your spine, slump your body a little; adopt your favourite 'losing the will to live' body position. Now, attempt to say the following words out loud: 'I feel confident and optimistic!' (Don't worry if you feel silly, it's just an experiment.)

How does that feel? Not very convincing? Perhaps this is

because, in this body position, we simply *can't* feel confident and optimistic – it doesn't make sense to our physical, mental and emotional system to voice those words while assuming that posture.

Now, instead, sit upright, put your arms out to the side, slightly above shoulder height, open your hands and spread your fingers, then open and expand your whole body into a winner pose. Say the words, 'I feel demotivated and depressed.' How does that feel? Again, it doesn't make sense, does it? It is *almost impossible* to feel demotivated and depressed in this body position or to have that kind of thought or voice those words while assuming that open, expansive posture. It feels paradoxical.

Let's work on the idea of expansion using a visualisation, aligning our thoughts with our bodies.

Imagine you are standing or sitting in front of a powerful floodlight and you want to let the light pass through your body from back to front. Let as much light travel through the space between each and every one of your bones so that you see on the wall in front of you the shadow of a perfect skeleton, with each bone distinctly spaced, as if the bones would float away from each other if they were not contained by muscle and skin. As you think about this, your brain is sending messages through the kinetic chain of nerves and muscles instructing your body to open and expand itself.

Now, let's work with the idea of being 'grounded'. Think about what happens when you are standing on a train or on the tube or subway with your knees locked. Are you more or less likely to fall over? If you are too tense and rigid, it is easy to topple over, so unlock your knees (by releasing calf, thigh, hamstring and buttock muscles) while maintaining your height. That will keep you from falling over.

You are now 'standing your ground' and using an open, expansive stance. Let's train this in more detail.

Exercise: Posture technique for standing and walking

Posture is an important foundation for your Physical Intelligence. At first, you may need a room that is quiet to help you to concentrate. For the first week of your Physical Intelligence practice, take ten minutes each day to go through the following exercises, taking the steps slowly, one by one. Learning the standing and walking posture first will help you understand the positioning of your spine when you work on seated posture. Have a chair at hand so that you can move straight on to seated posture technique afterwards.

Step 1: Unlock joints

- While standing, check the placement of your hips/pelvis over your legs and your feet. Notice whether you tend to bring your pelvis forwards, tucking it under too far and making the spine collapse or whether you tend to puff out the chest and stick the bottom out. Find a comfortable balance point in the middle. Remember your imaginary tail – picture it touching the ground behind the heels, balancing you in the way a kangaroo uses its tail.
- Let the thigh muscles and gluteus maximus (buttock muscles) relax so that the knees can be 'unlocked'. Your legs don't have to be bent; just relax them and soften the joints. How does that feel?
- Let the ankle joints feel as free as possible. Find the position in which the body weight can fall freely down through the ankles into the feet. Experiment with your balance; move your weight front to back and side to side until you find the position in which the ankle can just be poised, ready to fold on walking, rather than tense and rigid.
- Try standing tall with all your joints free, as if at any

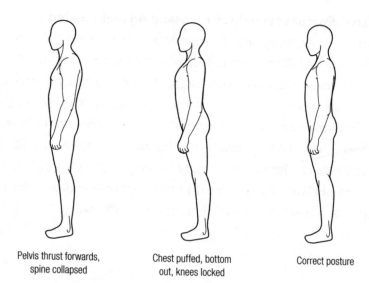

Pelvis thrust forwards,
spine collapsed

Chest puffed, bottom
out, knees locked

Correct posture

moment you could quickly sit in a chair by folding at the hips, knees and ankles.

Step 2: Feel the ground

- The ankle, knee and hip joints need to be free and unlocked, so that the feet distribute your weight into the ground. Take a walk and feel the feet contact the ground, heel to toe each time, relaxing from the hip, letting the knees relax and bend as you pick up the next leg for the next step, letting the ankle joint relax. Enjoy the swing-through of the lower leg using gravity just before you place the heel down.
- Each time you put your foot down, feel the weight of the body distributing through the bones of the feet into the ground, down into your 'roots'. Notice if this physical state accompanies any changes in your emotional or mental state. You are exploring your state of authority and 'gravitas'.
- Come to a standstill with both feet on the ground in parallel, feet underneath the hips, not too wide or too

narrow. Imagine you have a triangular base in each foot: two points on the ball of the foot; one on the heel. Feel the weight distribute through that triangular base, making sure there is equal weight between the balls of the foot and the heel.

- Take another walk around the room where you are. Imagine you have a fine thread emerging from the crown of the head right at the top of your skull suspending you from the ceiling as you walk, while, at the same time, imagine that you have the gravitational pull through your body and you feel the triangles in the feet contact the ground with each step.
- Walk slowly and feel the ground under you – feel how the slower pace provokes feelings of confidence.
- Become used to using both the feeling of expansion and the feeling of grounding. They are two parts of the whole and they happen simultaneously all the time, with every step and every movement.

Step 3: Stand tall and wide

- Adopt a winner pose for a moment. Open and stretch your body into a starfish shape: your widest, tallest stance – feet wide, arms open, hands open, fingers spread, eyes open looking into the distance, using peripheral vision. Breathe deeply. Hold for a few seconds, not rigid, not static, but open and expansive.
- Keep the feeling of expansion. Imagine you continue to take up that much space while you slowly bring your feet back in underneath the hips and your arms down by your sides until you are in a more natural standing stance. Still remember the floodlight shining through the bones of your skeleton.

- Make sure your feet are directly under your hips, feet parallel to each other.
- Imagine that between each vertebra of your spine there is a space.
- Now place one hand on the very top and centre of your head/skull and gently press down as if you could compress the curves of the spine very gently. (Do not tip the head backwards or forwards.) Keep pressing down for one minute. Now release the pressure by taking your hand away – can you feel your spine extend and grow taller? Do you feel taller, lighter, more vertical? You should feel a renewed space in the spine between the vertebrae as a result of removing the compression. As you focus on the next instruction, keep that height you have found.
- Focus on how your head sits on top of the spine, aware of the atlas (the top vertebra) – nod 'yes' a few times – and of the axis (the second vertebra) – shake your head 'no' a few times. The head balances effortlessly on the pillar of the spine so that the throat and the back of the neck are equally relaxed and long.
- Drop your head forwards, creating a stretch and a relaxation in the back of the neck. Breathe deeply and hold for ten seconds.

Step 4: Bend forwards to lengthen your spine

- Slowly let the weight of your head drop forwards and lead you into a forward bend. Roll down through the spine, relaxing the weight of your shoulders and arms, letting them hang forwards as you roll down and end up with most of your spine upside down, stretching the back of your legs (hamstrings) and your lower back. Feel free to bend the knees a little. When you reach your comfort limit for your hamstrings, take a few deep breaths and hold for five seconds.

- Then slowly reverse the journey of your spine and head. Roll up gradually, rebuilding your spine vertebra by vertebra as if you were rebuilding a wall brick by brick.
- Finally, rebalance your head on the top of your spine, not lifting or dropping the chin and eyeline, but lengthening the back of the neck and remembering to release the jaw. Find the position where you can use the least amount of muscular effort to maintain the upright position of your head and spine.

Step 5: Open shoulders

- Lift both of your shoulders up as high as they will go, hold for five seconds and then drop the shoulders. Repeat three times.
- Pick the shoulders up and rotate them in a forward circle and then a backward circle. Repeat forwards and backwards circles three times.
- Widen the shoulders, then squeeze them in to make them narrow, then widen them again. Repeat three times.
- Roll your shoulders again in a circle backwards and clasp your hands behind your back. Stretch and open the front of the chest – you can look up slightly at this point. Hold the position in the stretch for a slow count of ten while breathing deeply, then release.
- Let go of the hand clasp, and let the shoulders find where they now want to be – don't push or pull them into place, just let them find their new alignment. You'll find the stretch has helped open them. Can you feel that the shoulders are more open? Imagine that they could float outwards away from you and touch the sides of the room you are in.

- Think broad and wide shoulders. This should feel pleasurable unless you have painful tension in your neck and shoulders. If so, you may want to repeat Step 5 again very gently and very slowly making only small movements. This can be a very effective way to release tension.

(NB: If you have high blood pressure, back pain or pain in any area of your body, or you have any other condition that may be affected by doing a forward bend or shoulder-opening exercises, please consult a medical practitioner, osteopath or physiotherapist before embarking on exercises involving these parts of the body.)

Now, let's learn how these principles translate to seated posture.

Seated posture

When sitting down, good posture can be difficult to apply consistently. I know I still occasionally want to wrap my legs around my chair legs or cross my legs, or I suddenly realise that a challenging thought has made me hunch my shoulders.

Saying that, you should sit tall with your feet on the ground as often as you can. Be aware of when your body needs a change of posture throughout the day and vary it, giving yourself a break to sit back and curve the back or stretch the spine or neck when you need to do so.

Exercise: Seated posture technique

The principle of seated posture is the same as for standing posture. You can use it every day at your desk, in meetings while speaking or listening to others and while relaxing at home. Being open and expansive is the key.

Good seated posture requires enough flexibility in the lower back and the hip joints to be able to sit tall. If the following causes strain, then build up your practice slowly, maintaining it first for two minutes, then a few days later for three minutes etc. Always consult a medical practitioner or osteopath if you experience back pain.

Sit on the front third of your chair so there is a space between you and the back of your chair and you are in a position to support your own spine.

Feel your feet flat on the ground.

Sit firmly on the bones at the very bottom of your pelvis – your 'sitting' bones. Your buttocks create a nice cushion, so settle your weight down into that cushion.

Think of a long backbone/spine with the three vertebral sections – lumbar, thoracic, and cervical – active and lengthened, rising up out of your pelvis.

Have your knees spaced hip-width apart (unless you are wearing a skirt, in which case bring them slightly closer in). If your knees press together, there may be tension and tightness in the lower abdomen that will impact your breathing and if they are too far apart you may not feel aligned or very dignified.

Balance your head on your spine without projecting the head forwards or tilting the chin up or down – apply the same principle as standing – find the equilibrium.

Check that your jaw is released and your facial muscles are relaxed. As mentioned earlier, the jaw is connected to the cervical area of the spine; therefore, tension in the jaw brings tension to the neck, which limits the flow of impulses to and from the brain.

Seated posture choices

If you are working at a screen, make sure it is at eye level and that you can see well – that you have good light, proper glasses etc. Avoid frowning, because this action causes an elevation in cortisol levels and the proliferation of negative thoughts.

If you are working at your desk, alternate how you sit; sometimes bring your chair close to the desk so that your abdomen is touching it and your pelvis is right back in your chair. In this position you can lengthen the spine and balance the head while the back of the chair provides full back support. Sometimes, sit on the front of your chair with your feet firmly on the ground supported by your core muscles.

If you experience discomfort, use a straight-backed chair and sit right at the back of it with a cushion or rolled up towel in the curve of your lower back.

Drop your shoulders and let your arms rest lightly on the desk; ensure your fingers move lightly on the keyboard. The height of your chair should be such that when the shoulders are relaxed your forearm is at a right angle to your upper arm, with a ninety-degree bend in your elbow.

If you are speaking at a meeting, whether on a phone/video conference or in the meeting room, place both feet firmly on the ground. Your core muscles will engage, and you will feel more confident in your interactions.

Avoid leaning on the table or slumping towards the desk in front of you. Rest your arms lightly on the table or desk.

If you are the speaker or leading the agenda, sitting on the front third of your seat – upright and alert – will signal your full engagement and communicate confidence all around the table.

If you are actively listening and receptive, you may sit back in your chair for a while if you would like to, but remember to keep the principle of open and expansive posture.

If you are having a quiet or challenging conversation, it is natural to lean in and mirror the other person's body position for a while. Return to open, expansive posture when it feels appropriate, and feel free to change again.

If you are sitting on the sofa relaxing or cuddled up with a partner or the kids, enjoy! But make sure your back and neck are well-supported with cushions, particularly after a busy day. Enjoy sprawling and relaxing, but don't spend too long in an asymmetrical position (e.g. legs tucked under you to one side or legs crossed on a stool, spine slumped in the sofa) because the pelvis may become misaligned and the spine blocked in key areas; this in turn can affect diaphragmatic breathing (see next chapter).

EQUIPMENT

Many people favour standing desks, or adaptable-height desks, so that they can vary their position during the day. If you do stand at a desk, ensure that your knees are not locked and that your weight is balanced between the balls of the feet and the heels.

Kneeling stools are not very good for the spine and can put pressure on the knees; you have to be careful you don't hyperextend (arch) the lower back.

Pilates sitting balls are very good for working and for meetings because as you move towards and away from the screen, or as you think and talk, the ball rolls with you and the whole spine shifts, rather than only the head and neck pitching forwards. You can also bounce on them, which increases the movement of your cerebrospinal fluid in the spine and the brain, enabling toxins to drain away more effectively.

While technology can negatively impact posture, it can also help us. There are numerous apps and gadgets now available to help embed positive habits for our posture. (See the Research and Resources chapter, p. 449, for more information.)

How empowered you feel is greatly impacted by how you use your posture. Good posture enables you to feel simultaneously stronger, more present, alert and more at ease as you walk, stand and sit. The more you use your new posture in everyday life, e.g. while you walk to the train station or push your trolley around the supermarket, the faster you will create new muscle memory. In Chapter 8, we will help you plan your posture practice by integrating your new understanding of posture into your day through habit stacking.

Once you have learned and are applying correct posture, observe how others start to behave around you. Don't apologise for who you are; use your full height to create fantastic first impressions. Posture and breathing go hand in hand because posture enables us to find the physical space for our lungs to fill with breath and fuel our body and brain. Let's move on to learn how we can use our breath to build strength.

3

BREATH

How to find emotional and mental stability through breath practice

If I ever doubted myself, my mum would say, 'Take a breath . . . There, you see what you can do for yourself? You don't need nobody to breathe for you, do you?'

—WILL.I.AM

We breathe in and out 25,000 times a day in an orchestrated miracle of diaphragm, ribs, lungs and abdominal muscles without giving it a thought. Our breathing patterns mirror our emotional, mental and physical state, and they change depending on our feelings, thoughts and the type of activity we are engaged in. Stability and consistency under pressure rely on robust nervous and endocrine systems supported by good breathing. As we will discover, breathing technique is a critical bedrock for achieving our best.

The Ancient Greeks thought that breath contained the spirit or soul and was a spiritual life force. The Latin root of the word 'inspire' is *spirant* – breath. Business leaders *inspire* employees to believe in the success of a business. Parents *inspire* children to do their best. The breath, therefore, is not only a physiological necessity, it is a social currency.

LIFE HACK: Take a large lungful of air through the nostrils, then breathe it out through the mouth. Literally 'inspire' yourself!

If we are breathing effectively, air enters the lower two-thirds of the lungs and we take in enough to fuel the body and the brain, breathing diaphragmatically. When we breathe poorly (clavicular breathing), the collarbones (clavicles) move up and down, breathing is shallow and only the top third of the lungs fill. When this happens, our thoughts, feelings and actions become more erratic; we can't think as clearly under pressure or balance our emotions as easily. We are far less stable.

HOW DIAPHRAGMATIC BREATHING WORKS

The diaphragm is a sheet of muscle stretching horizontally across the body, dividing it into two sections: the thorax and head; and the lower abdomen and legs. It's like a domed tent sitting under the lungs, the edges attached all the way around the bottom ribs and at the back to the spine. It has muscle strands (diaphragmatic crura) connected vertically all the way down through the lower abdominal muscles to the pelvic floor. Breathe in and the diaphragm moves down, inverting the dome and creating a vacuum that is immediately occupied by air in the rapidly filling lungs. Breathe out and the diaphragm moves back up into its domed position, helping to expel air from our lungs. This movement is part of a complex and miraculous muscular action that includes various abdominal muscles releasing and contracting. We cannot directly control the diaphragm muscle, but we can allow an efficient and full breathing action by the conscious release, use and toning of the muscles that support our breathing.

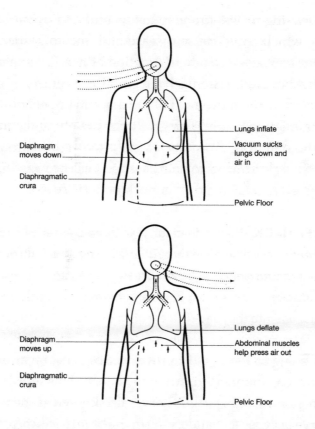

Lungs inflate

Vacuum sucks lungs down and air in

Diaphragm moves down

Diaphragmatic crura

Pelvic Floor

Lungs deflate

Abdominal muscles help press air out

Diaphragm moves up

Diaphragmatic crura

Pelvic Floor

The Greeks also believed that thoughts themselves originated in the lungs. They had made an important link. A thought we intend to share triggers our body to breathe in, and the out-breath carries our thoughts into the world, so thought and breath are profoundly connected. Movement of the diaphragm ensures we have enough breath to speak our thoughts with energy so that our voices are heard. All verbal communication relies on this.

In addition to keeping us alive by supplying oxygen, the action of breathing makes us healthier. Every time we breathe, the stomach, intestines, liver, spleen and kidneys are displaced by the movement of the diaphragm and the expansion of the lungs, leaving us less prone to toxins building up around our organs, which could cause disease and poor digestion. Also, the solar plexus – a spaghetti junction of nerves situated near the spine behind the stomach (an emotional centre) – becomes stimulated by the movement of the diaphragm, enabling us to feel our emotions more strongly. If our breathing technique is poor, the diaphragm becomes locked too tightly around the solar plexus, leading us to hold back feelings, procrastinate and perhaps even delay making important decisions.

> **LIFE HACK:** Procrastinating? Take three deep stimulating breaths, drawing air in through the nose and out through your mouth, sending your in-breath down into your lower abdomen so that it expands, and blowing it out through your lips into the space in front of your mouth. And BEGIN!

Just as going to the gym improves *muscle* tone, breathing in a steady, paced manner improves *vagal* tone. This term refers to the functioning of the vagus nerve, also known as the wandering nerve because it 'wanders' from the brain to the heart, lungs and stomach. The vagus nerve is part of the parasympathetic nervous system (our recovery and renewal system). It releases acetylcholine, the calming chemical that counteracts the effects of adrenalin and brings the heart rate back to normal after intense effort, enabling balance, renewal, a cool head under pressure and *coherent*, rather than *chaotic* patterns of thought and behaviour. With paced breathing, it is possible for all of us to achieve *coherence*, the state where physical, mental and emotional systems are aligned and we function effortlessly at our very best. Clarity and quality of thought improve if we breathe well, and we achieve superb emotional self-regulation, too, enabling us to improve our vitality and perform at the top of our game regardless of our role.

Clever biology underlies this. Our hearts beat 100,000 times a day in a rhythmic choreography co-ordinated with our breathing. Our heart rate speeds up while we are breathing in to pump oxygen around the body and it slows down while we are breathing out. Via the vagus nerve, the heart and the brain are in constant communication with each other about levels of threat.

Under pressure, an individual's heart rate will speed up and slow down, ideally, in a smooth manner, putting less strain on the heart muscle and sending more *coherent* signals to the brain. This enables them to take a build-up of pressure in their stride. Remember John and the sailing incident? He was in a coherent state when the sea became dangerous. A less confident, anxious individual's heart will speed up and slow down erratically, sending more *chaotic* signals to the brain, leading them to respond negatively when pressure builds. The *rate of change* in the heartbeat as pressure builds is the critical factor for stability and high cognitive function. This is called our heart rate variability (HRV). To improve our HRV and become more mentally and emotionally stable and confident, we need to use paced breathing (see exercise on pp. 60–4), which regulates our breathing pattern. This improves the production of the steroid chemical DHEA, produced in the adrenal glands, so that when we are under pressure we are more likely to be able to handle the situation with clarity, balance and control.

In the first graph overleaf, the subject's breathing pattern is paced. As a result, the heart rate is speeding up and slowing down smoothly. In the second graph, the subject's breathing pattern is anxious at the start, jumping up to a high number of beats per minute, then suddenly crashing down. It then transforms from anxious to paced as soon as the subject starts paced breathing; their heart rate speeds up and slows down in smooth increments. The smoother and taller the wave, the higher our HRV. HRV and DHEA production are biomarkers of age, health, fitness and nervous system function, and they measure regulation of emotion and cognitive performance.

In a 2012 study by Dr Justin Kennedy of the University of Pretoria, eighty bankers (male and female) were taught to use paced breathing as part of their performance coaching. After just three coaching sessions and twenty-one days of practice, they achieved an average of 62 per cent improvement in cognitive capacity on complex decision-making tasks. They had

Good HRV during paced breathing

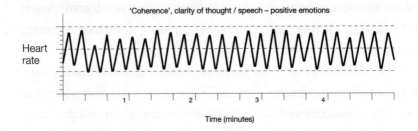

Bad HRV and effect of breathing

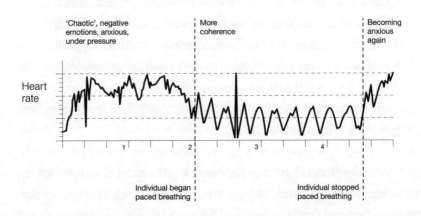

become more *coherent*. Biofeedback technology was used in this study. Subjects wore sensors, linked to a computer, giving them a real-time read-out of the effects of their breathing on HRV, similar to those in the graphs above.

If we were to scan the brains of the South African bankers when their breathing was erratic, we'd see low activity in the pre-frontal cortex (PFC), the decision-making part of the brain, and high numbers of chaotic beta waves in the rest of the brain. Practising paced breathing increases activity in the PFC and the quantity of alpha, delta and theta brainwaves in the brain, associated with clarity and focus. In addition to boosting DHEA, testosterone levels become optimal as unhelpful cortisol and adrenalin drain away. As a result, the bankers are transformed from making lower-grade decisions in survival mode to being astute, productive, competitive and *coherent*.

You can train your HRV, improving breath control and brain function, with a simple piece of biofeedback kit and software (see the resources section). Even after many years of practice, I come back to this training time and time again because you can see the impact of breath control on your physiology in real time, and you can measure your progress.

> **LIFE HACK:** Think of a situation in the near future that you'll find challenging and that you want to go really well. Breathe in and out and picture yourself doing well, with your heart speeding up and slowing down smoothly as you respond to the pressure. You have primed your muscle memory so that when you come to it your performance will be enhanced.

But you don't need to use technology for effective breathing practice. Sarah, a busy mum and businesswoman I recently coached, found that she had far better clarity of thought during the day when she set aside the newspaper and spent part of her train journey to the office practising paced breathing. My partner Adam is an aerial director of photography, filming movie scenes from helicopters. Often, he has only one take to get a difficult shot. He uses paced breathing before each shot to gain focus and get it right the first time.

There are many fit-for-purpose breathing techniques for yoga, meditation, martial arts, rugby, archery, acting, dancing, singing, trumpet playing and so on. But for everyday life we need a straightforward technique that can be practised anywhere and integrated into our lives, so that it gradually becomes the norm.

Become aware of your breathing as you read this. Is it fast or slow, shallow or deep? Many of us hold our breath while we are thinking, snatch breaths while writing emails, and breathe too shallowly in business meetings or while cooking supper or watching TV. Life interferes with breathing in ways that were not intended, to the detriment of our cognitive function, emotionally stability and our productivity. With that in mind, let's learn how to power up our brains and stabilise our emotions with paced breathing.

Exercise: Paced breathing

In paced breathing, we aim to breathe diaphragmatically, smoothly and regularly, in and out through the nose (or if blocked, the mouth). We recommend that you commit to ten minutes a day, though if you are very motivated, you can practise this breathing technique for twenty minutes in the morning and twenty minutes in the evening for three weeks. By doing this, you will get close to the improvement achieved by the South African bankers.

Prepare: Drop your shoulders, relax your abdominal muscles and remember the spaciousness of posture technique.

Breathe . . .

Diaphragmatically

- While seated, ground yourself and breathe all the way out.
- Now relax your abdominal muscles – don't hold your stomach in – breathe in, observing how your lower abdomen expands in the front (your belly gets rounder) and your lower ribs expand to the sides (you get wider).
- Then breathe out and observe how the lower abdomen and ribs move inwards.
- Try not to lift the shoulders or collarbones or puff out the chest when you breathe in, and there is no need to force, push, pull or hold the breath.
- It helps to try this in different body positions. First, lean forwards and rest your forearms on your thighs, spine long and free. In this position you can feel how the deep low diaphragmatic breath moves the lower back, spine and ribs. Another option is to lie down on your stomach with your arms out in front of you, rest the forehead on the floor or turn the head to one side and rest on a cushion. It should feel easier to breathe deeply. You can also try lying down on your back, knees bent up, soles of the feet on the floor, with a book on your navel area and use the breath in to raise the book, letting it lower as you breathe out.
- Notice how you feel. If you feel lightheaded, you are over-breathing; use less effort, let the breath happen to you.

Smoothly, with even flow

- Find a smooth, consistent flow of breath in and out, as if you were pulling a thread through with a needle.
- Don't rush or snatch at the beginning or end of the breath; just let the breath turn, like the tide on a beach.

- At this stage, some breaths may be longer than others and, occasionally, extra-big breaths will come.
- For now, keep the flow even and let each breath find its own length.
- Don't worry if your heart starts to jump about a bit as you do this part of the technique; your breathing and heartbeat will want to synchronise and sometimes the heart rhythm resets itself.

Regularly

- In a relaxed, focused manner, start to be aware of pacing.
- Measure the length of each breath as you breathe in by counting quietly in the back of your mind.
- Start exploring the counts your body feels comfortable with today. The numbers do not need to be even (e.g. four in, four out); they could be different (e.g. three in, five out). The numbers and pace of counting are up to you.
- Some people like to create a visualisation to go with the count (e.g. climbing upstairs on the breath in, and downstairs on the breath out; walking to and from the water's edge at the beach; playing up and down the piano keyboard; running to the goal and scoring, then taking your applause) or you may prefer to simply count and quieten your mind. The in-breath is like an injection of fuel for your body; the out-breath is your exhaust.
- Repeat the pattern in and out for the duration of your practice.

You will find that the more you practise, the easier it becomes to slip into a paced rhythm. I suggest practising for ten minutes a day so that your body gets used to this rhythm over time. If the counts change, that's fine; just find a new rhythm.

Strive to automatically start paced breathing upon waking and incorporate it into your day at other times through habit stacking. This way your breathing becomes a foundation for your performance and your days will start turning out better, provided that you practise. Going about everyday life you will not *always* be *actively* aware of your breathing rhythm because your mind will be occupied with other things, but if your body starts to *know* the rhythm, then it becomes part of your established muscle memory. At any moment, when you begin to experience pressure or stress in your life, use your paced breathing pattern. You now have the most powerful tool there is to sail through demanding situations.

Exercise: Pace variation

Your pace may vary for different purposes and different situations, for example:

If you feel sluggish and would like to pump your energy up with your breath pattern, then choose a faster pace, briskly filling and emptying the lungs, counting, for example, two in and two out. If you would like to relax, then choose a slower pace; for example, four in, five out.

If you tend to be indecisive, bottle things up and not always express yourself easily (*hypoarousal*), you may benefit from 'powering up' with a shorter count in and out, i.e. a quicker breath pace. Try to gradually shorten the count in and out by one or two. Experiment with what works for you.

If you tend towards overdrive and *hyperarousal*, you will need a slower breathing pace to stabilise your nervous system. Without putting yourself under strain, gradually lengthen the count in and out by one or two, slowing your breath pace. Do this by relaxing and letting go of your abdominal muscles even more on the in-breath.

Most people like to practise on trains, flights or sitting quietly at home, but you don't necessarily *have* to be sitting still. Many coachees like to add to their practice by pacing their breath while walking, counting their steps with their in-breath and their out-breath. This takes a bit of practice, but soon you'll find a rhythm you enjoy.

Breath is life, so enjoy your breath practice and the additional focus and energy it gives you. Be creative with it. Use these principles and experiment.

Now, let's build on this by developing the ability to be 'centered'. We will learn how to instantaneously focus and hone our approach to bringing our best selves to a variety of challenging situations.

4

CENTERING

How to develop inner strength and focus

> At the centre of your being you have the
> answer; you know who you are and you
> know what you want.
>
> —LAO TZU

Busy schedules packed with important commitments, critical decisions, an ongoing effort to try to achieve everything, all while being a super partner or parent, can push and pull us in many directions. The sheer quantity of information and need for multiple forms of effort and communication can make it challenging to find clarity and focus in our lives. We can achieve that focus, developing the ability to think, act and speak clearly while withstanding enormous pressure, by learning to center* ourselves and also to build inner strength in a process we call 'Finding Your I'.

What is centering?

The process of centering results in a physical, mental and emotional state in which you know who you are, where you are,

---

* We've used the US spelling for this technique as it seems more clearly to communicate the core idea.

and have everything around you in perspective; seeing and experiencing your changing environment in high definition accompanied by feelings of great confidence and inner strength. When centered, thinking takes no effort and focus is sharp.

> **LIFE HACK:** You are far more attractive when you find a 'still point' inside yourself, because you maintain your authority while being relaxed enough to truly listen to others. Think about this when you go on a date or are in a job interview or negotiation.

Centering provides a way of preparing, a protocol you can use to find inner balance and set yourself up for success – for example, before an exam or a job interview, or prior to serving in a tennis match or taking a putt on the golf course. Secondly, it gives you a way to turn fear into focus when there are sudden or dramatic changes in circumstance. If you are affected by changes at work, then centering can be a lifeline.

The anatomy of centering

The 'centre' is both a helpful concept of mind and an actual location in the body – in the abdomen, just behind and below the navel. Imagine drawing a vertical line from between your feet to the top of your head, dividing your body in half. Then imagine drawing a horizontal line through your body so that half of your weight is above, and half is below the line. This will be approximately just below the navel, and is the location of your centre of mass.

When we actively think about this point and breathe deeply down towards it, we stimulate the very ends of the vagus nerve that reach the gut, and further enhance the interaction between the sympathetic and parasympathetic nervous systems, balancing adrenalin and acetylcholine. If we also apply the grounding principles that we learned in Chapter 2 (p. 31), deep core muscles become engaged for action without the need to tense up the outer layer of abdominal muscles that would inhibit breathing and ease of movement. This way, our movements and gestures can be relaxed and skilful, and we are less likely to bump into things or knock over that glass of wine on a first date.

Centering reinforces the chemistry of high testosterone and low cortisol, and it supports our dopamine function, ensuring efficient firing of neural pathways that enable us to focus and co-ordinate our physical and mental energy to achieve and win. With dopamine at optimal levels – not too much, not too little – our movements, gestures, speech and behaviour feel like they originate from our 'centre', giving us time and space for considered action, communicating competence and self-control.

The physics of centering

The laws of physics also offer a way of understanding being centered. Gravity and centrifugal force are the two physical forces that exert pressure on us, and our bodies are held in balance in the middle ground between the two.

While maintaining a centered state of mind, your physical centre of *gravity* may differ depending on the activity. A tennis player receiving serve needs to be more aggressive and alert, their centre of gravity forwards, with weight on the toes. When preparing to serve for the match, the centre of gravity is lower and the demeanour is calmer. In a pirouette, a dancer finds the central axis of rotation using deep core muscles that draw in towards the spine. A negotiator protecting his interests will need to drop his centre of gravity to the lowest possible point, to appear and feel immovable and maintain status. An actor playing an anxious character will create a higher centre of gravity in their body, most likely in the chest, because anxiety typically focuses tension around the chest and shoulders. Wherever the centre of gravity is, centering as a protocol brings the right kind of focus for whatever it is you are trying to achieve.

CLAIRE TAYLOR RELIES ON HER CENTERING PROTOCOL...

Claire established her basic centering protocol early on as a young hockey player. She said, 'We learned to center step by step; release tension, find balance, breathe, focus. Then, with practice, we speeded it up so that you didn't have to spend sixty seconds preparing; it was just there. I got to the point where I just looked at a certain point on my hockey stick, and that was the trigger. I was immediately there, ready.'

As a cricketer, Claire did a great deal of psychological and technical work to identify how to center herself to achieve her optimal performance state. How roused should she be? How calm should she be? What she was looking for was a relaxed yet alert state, irrespective of what was happening.

As Claire described, 'The ball is coming at you at 80, 90 miles an hour and I center myself for every ball, enabling me to consistently bring my best technical performance under match pressure.'

LIFE HACK: Do you tend to rush from one thing to another, one meeting to another, sometimes without properly preparing your focus? Centering is effective when done immediately prior to the action you wish to perform well, and can be used as a transition, to regroup between one event and the next.

Finding your centre and practising the routine to get you into that state of awareness and readiness is exciting. It is a technique you can rely on to give you strength whenever you apply it, and it will set you up for success. Let's discover how.

Exercise: Centering

To center ourselves, we need to release tension and find our balance, breath and focus.

Step 1: Preparation

- Standing or seated, release unnecessary tension all the way down the centre line of your body – eyes, jaw, tongue, throat, chest, neck, shoulders, core, diaphragm, pelvic floor.
- Release jaw and tongue tension by separating the upper and lower back teeth and letting the back of the tongue lie heavily down in the back of the mouth. You cannot be centered with jaw and tongue gripped and tight; further tensions will cascade down the body, and you will be less effective in your action.
- Throat and chest, neck and shoulders are not braced, but dropped and open, core muscles are released enough so that the diaphragm can move up and down freely, freeing the breath.
- Feel your feet placed firmly on the ground, aligned below the hips or anchored on the floor in front of you if you are seated.

Step 2: Centering

- Find your balance; place your centre of mass where you need it.

Notice whether you feel balanced right now. Move your weight forwards, backwards and to the side and find the optimal central point. Whether you are trying to maintain your balance on a moving train, talking with your team, negotiating with your teen about chores or dancing the leading role, finding and re-finding your physical balance dictates how emotionally and mentally balanced you are. Life has a habit of taking us off-balance. The question is, can you find your inner balance even when under pressure or threat, e.g. awaiting critical feedback or when a reorganisation at work threatens you with redundancy?

- Feel the force of gravity.

Thankfully, gravity is anchoring you to the surface of our planet, preventing you from floating away. You have already learned to ground yourself in the Posture chapter. Apply that again now. Notice that if you get lost in thought or worry, you will cease to feel the grounding effects gravity.

- Feel centrifugal force suspending you.

The planet is spinning, and we are suspended in the atmosphere. Notice how you can use this force as well by feeling effortlessly supported by the air around you. When working hard in life, constantly driving towards your goals in a busy, competitive world, just the thought of being supported by centrifugal force can enable us to take things more lightly. Try experiencing that now. Remember how it feels to spin on a fairground ride? You spin so much that you can't fall down – you become weightless. Be aware of the spinning force of the earth and, while thinking about that, release more muscular tension. You may find that the more you let go of muscular tension, the lighter you feel and the more you can experience being supported by centrifugal force.

- Combine finding your centre of mass with finding the point of support between gravity and centrifugal force and you will immediately find inner balance.
- Breathe down to below the navel.

It helps to imagine the breath reaching a specific point just below the navel so that, with practice, you can center yourself with one breath. The breath goes directly to that point, and when you breathe out you can release unnecessary tension. Some people like to imagine the breath reaching an area the size of a tennis ball below the navel, filling with warm light.

- Focus.

Soften your gaze slightly so that you can use more peripheral vision, taking in more information but with less effort. Do you tend to grab at things with your eyes or not see the world around you because you are so intensely focused on your task or because you are lost in thought? For your preparation routine, see what intensity works best. We suggest a soft focus. In everyday life you may be focused on one thing or one person or using peripheral vision (as you would use to welcome a group of people to your home or to a meeting). Choose an appropriate intensity in your eyes for your action/situation. Experiment with centering and observe how being centered changes how you see the world.

> **LIFE HACK:** If you need to read a document or an article quickly, soften the focus of your eyes, center your breath, let your eyes skip along the line while you also have a sense of the whole paragraph. You will be able to read faster.

Now practise your protocol slowly three times – taking at least one minute on each stage the first time you do it, then speeding up a little as it becomes familiar.

Balance, Breathe, Focus
Balance, Breathe, Focus
Balance, Breathe, Focus

How does that change how you feel? How does it change your perception of the environment around you?

Now think of a situation where you would like to apply this regularly. Maybe you want to use centering to

- Prepare for important meetings or conversations;
- Improve your preparation in the sports you play; or
- Apply it in a particular type of interaction that often doesn't go so well.

Practise centering and observe the impact it has on your relationships with others. Can you listen better? Are you more clear and discerning? At the end of the strength section, you will have an opportunity to create centering habits and integrate them into your daily life.

> **LIFE HACK:** Start thinking about one trigger point each day at which you will center yourself, e.g. when you take your seat for a meeting. Start today.

Building inner strength

Centering enables us to achieve a high level of confidence and control in every type of challenging situation. Feeling centered relies on being comfortable enough with our selves, knowing and accepting our strengths and weaknesses. If we are not comfortable in a particular situation, then our outward behaviour will be partly motivated by the need to reduce the discomfort. This may be at odds with what the situation requires of us. We may give up, give in, not speak out or take action when we really need to.

At Companies in Motion, we have devised a super-charged form of centering that builds inner strength and motivation. It is a visualisation called 'Finding Your I'. When life around you is challenging and there is very little extrinsic reward, your 'I' enables you to find intrinsic reward and motivation by enabling dopamine release when you imagine it.

Dopamine, the reward and focus chemical, is closely linked with the visual cortex of the brain, which means that when we visualise potent imagery, dopamine production and uptake increases. By imagining a central 'I' built into our bodies, our strengths are described in mental images and metaphors, giving us a resource to draw on as we work towards achieving our potential.

There are many different ways of thinking about your 'I' or your 'self'. Wherever it derives from for you, it is a driving force. Your unique 'I'-dentity is based on your beliefs about who you are, what you are good at, what you are here to achieve and how you play your part in society.

Imagine that you are on jury service and you are the only member of a jury who believes that the accused may be innocent, or at a work meeting with more experienced team members where you want to raise a concern that you believe has been missed. Thinking of your 'I' at the moment when you doubt yourself, such as deciding whether or not to speak out, can help you remember who you are, why you believe what you do and what strengths you bring so that you can do your best to influence others from a position of power.

If you don't access your strength, you may swallow your words and avoid the uncomfortable situation of being the sole voice – going along with the majority opinion even though you have doubts. We may not always be popular when we speak out, but if we rely on feeling rewarded by external events – whether that be the approval/recognition/praise of others, or having the nice car or the new shoes – then we are dependent on the need for *extrinsic* reward, in which case the dopamine supply will inevitably run dry. If, however, we can connect more with the *intrinsic* reward that comes from within, from our 'I', we can access that dopamine at any time and will subsequently be more motivated and robust.

VISUALISATION TAKES CLAIRE TAYLOR OUT ONTO THE PITCH WITH CONFIDENCE...

Before batting in an England match, Claire could often feel cortisol spiking and fear and anxiety threatening to take over. Claire handled it by using powerful imagery the coaches had given them: 'greyhound' to engage core muscles and center the body psychologically; and 'angel' to engage the shoulders and prime the upper body for power striking. In a critical match in the 2009 Twenty20 World Cup, Australia had won the toss and scored 163 runs, but as she walked out onto the massive field after the fall of the first wicket, she imagined huge angel wings unfurling, boosting testosterone and dopamine. At the crease, she repeated her stance protocol, imagined the 'greyhound' to engage her core and felt the cortisol drain away. It was a T20 match, she scored seventy runs off fifty balls, England won the game and went on to win the World Cup a few days later. It was the most important innings of her career.

Exercise: 'Finding Your I'

Preparation

- Find a quiet place.
- Read the instructions below, then close your eyes and center yourself – take a few moments to settle.

Step 1: Creating your 'I'

- Turn your mind to imagin-ing a capital letter 'I' that fits in your body.
- Begin by imagining a simple structure as in the illustration. (Some people feel a kinaesthetic sense of the 'I' in their bodies, other people create a pic-ture of themselves and their 'I' in their mind's eye and focus purely on that mental picture. Some people with a condition called aphantasia cannot visualise at all. If that applies to you, then please use words to describe your 'I' or experiment with drawing it on paper in front of you to discover what it is like.)

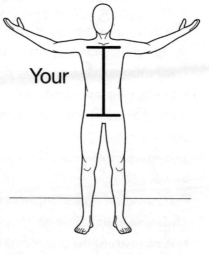

- Now, let your creative imagination join in. If you could choose any material that comes to mind, natural or man-ufactured, liquid or solid, or combinations of these, what would your 'I' be made of? Explore various options. You are the architect and engineer.

- Let the ideas, the image in your mind's eye, evolve. Your 'I' may remain simple or may become elaborate. Your 'I' may evolve structurally to become very different from the initial simple form. It may stretch, or contract, or grow wings ... let it develop in any way you choose.
- Finalise the picture of it. It should make you feel powerful and strong when you think of it. Zoom in and see the detail. Are there any special features? How is it engineered? Are there any attachments or accompaniments needed? For example, with your 'I', what are the joints like? How are parts of it connected – with what materials and mechanisms? If there are parts of your 'I' made with organic matter, how is that kept alive? Does it need a water supply or nutrients? This gives you more detail within the visualisation so that the image is as strong and powerful as it can be.
- Open your eyes and draw, or describe it in words on a blank piece of paper or on the illustration in your book.

Step 2: Interpreting your 'I'

- What sense do you make of why you chose the particular materials and design?
- Which strengths of yours does this 'I' represent?
- In which situations could you use these strengths more?
- Who in your life needs to see more of this 'I'?
- How can your 'I' help you face specific current challenges?
- When will you need to use your 'I'? For example, when do you want to positively assert yourself, manage upwards, be in control, use silence, make a greater impact on others around you, feel composed and competent, believe in yourself?
- You can keep this exercise private or you can share it with friends and compare notes. Have them question you more deeply and share with you their interpretation of your 'I'

in relation to your strengths and qualities. You can then reciprocate. It is fun to analyse why we made certain choices for our 'I'.

One 'I' does not usually last for life. I have a note in my diary every month to review it and I instinctively know if it has changed or if I need a new one. Some people create a wardrobe of 'I's for different occasions. I have witnessed the creation of thousands of 'I's over the years made of all sorts of substances: steel, titanium, carbon fibre, Lego, silk, bamboo, rubber/metal combinations, water fountains, oak trees, iron decorated with living flowers, and many more creative choices.

One businessman I coached, who was quite introverted, had to do a lot of networking in his job and he hated it. He created an 'I' for himself specifically to bolster his sociability for networking events. It was made of a tower of champagne glasses overflowing with bubbly! He said that it immediately made him smile when he thought of it and he felt more like meeting new people. It replaced the severe discomfort he used to experience prior to working on his 'I'.

The relative strength and vulnerability in our 'I' imagery always relates to our strengths and vulnerabilities in life. The images come from our creative imagination and although they are playful, a little like our dreams, they often hold messages for us from our subconscious.

You can visualise a specific 'I' for parties and presentations, crises and celebrations, or use it as the final stage of your centering protocol, making the four stages: balance, breathe, focus, and 'I'. I encourage you to use this exercise to continue to identify your strengths, augment them in situations where you want to stand your ground, and acknowledge new strengths as they emerge. We are all unique and have the ability to make a positive impact on the world.

ANGUS'S 'I' MAKES HIM RUN FASTER...

My son Angus used his 'I' to get himself through gruelling athletics training sessions one winter. I remember sitting in the car watching Angus and his teammates running around the track. It was dark and pouring with rain and they all looked bedraggled. Then, suddenly, I saw a change in energy and pace – they started to run with more purpose and I saw Angus pull to the front of the group. Later, when he climbed into the car, I asked him what had happened. He said, 'Well, I put in my "I" and suddenly I felt like running again – the others came with me.'

When we gain in-depth knowledge of our physical body and use its intelligence, we can't help but make an impact on our voice – how we say what we say and how we project our thoughts and ideas into the world. Let's now learn more about vocal strength and how to create it.

5

VOCAL STRENGTH

How to convey authority and confidence through our voice

It took me quite a long time to develop a
voice, and now that I have it, I'm not going
to be silent.

—MADELEINE ALBRIGHT

When we speak, our breath moves across the vocal folds in our
voice box, creating sound waves that vibrate in the cavities of
our body and head. Sound resonates differently depending on
our unique anatomy and bone structure. Therefore, the sound
we make also will be unique. In 2012, the skeleton of King
Richard III was found in a car park in Leicester, UK. From
analysing his bones, we can now get very close to recreating
the actual sound of his voice. However, it is not only bone
structure that impacts the unique quality of our voice; how
we use muscle tension, breathing and articulation also play a
large part.

Have you noticed that when you deeply relax, the pitch of
your voice lowers? After a massage, for example, as you speak
to the receptionist on the way out, your voice may sound
deeper. Muscles in the shoulders, throat, upper spine, jaw, and

around the voice box and vocal folds have released, enabling vibrations at lower frequencies. Opening up the pitch range in this way, to access the lower register, tends to build confidence in the listener.

A voice coming from a body held in a state of muscular tension will make a dull, tight sound, as would a guitar packed with tissues, because the resonant spaces are constrained and the sound is muffled. When we center ourselves, creating musculoskeletal balance, our body is instantaneously in a more resonant state. The sound of our words then resonates in our own unique way, giving us our own personal authority and authenticity.

> **LIFE HACK:** To give your voice instant authority and authenticity, imagine that your words originate in your 'I' (created in the previous chapter). Try saying 'good morning' as if the sound comes from your head. Then try saying it as if the sound comes from your 'I'. Do you notice a difference? The first may sound rather disconnected from you, the second will feel more ... 'you'.

Breathing down into your centre ensures that the lower two-thirds of the lungs fill with air. The in-breath, as we have already discovered, also known as the 'in-spiration', is a relaxation of abdominal muscle and a movement down of the diaphragm to create a vacuum in the lungs that naturally fills with air. For our voices, this is a critical action that provides enough breath to commit to what we are saying. Also critical is the out-breath; the breathing muscles in the front, sides and back of the abdomen need to be fully active in order to provide good 'breath support'. An 'unsupported' voice will quickly run out of power on the out-breath, trailing off at the end of a sentence, or the sound will break up mid-word. It may sound thin in tone, breathy, or gravelly in the throat and will not be heard across a meeting table, at a family meal or in a noisy bar or restaurant.

When there is inadequate breath and breath support, we struggle to create the additional volume needed to emphasise key words, which lets the listener(s) know which words are more important than others – one of the basic requirements of a strong speaker.

MARION FINDS HER VOICE...

I recently trained a group of managers at a leading fashion house. On the first day, all eight of us had lunch together in a restaurant. Marion sat on my right, and when we ordered our food it took her three attempts before the waiter heard her clearly. She turned to me and said, 'That often happens to me. I always have to repeat myself.' I explained that I thought it was because she needed more breath support and forward placement of her voice. Back in the training room that afternoon, Marion found that when she breathed in diaphragmatically, then directed her out-breath and her words towards their destination (the waiter's ears) she could be heard; the issue wasn't volume, it was projection. The next day at lunch, the waiter heard her request first time round.

I gave Marion some daily practice. After cleaning her teeth in the morning, she was to stand back from the bathroom mirror and say to her reflection ten times: 'My words come forwards out of my mouth' (breathing diaphragmatically between each repetition). She did this every day for three months, to strengthen her vocal support muscles. She was also conscious of projecting her voice at other times, and it soon became second nature.

LIFE HACK: When you order your morning coffee, practise breath support. Breathe in to your centre, then direct your voice to its destination (the ears of the assistant) on the out-breath, as you say, 'I'd like a cappuccino, please.'

Our vocal stability is impacted by our emotions. A powerful emotion or even a minor threat response is accompanied by a rise in cortisol and adrenalin. These chemicals cause muscle contraction and are responsible for the tightening of the throat, including the muscles around the voice box. Our diaphragm seizes up, judders and jumps and our abdominal wall pulses when emotions are heightened, which is why it can be challenging to read a eulogy, for example.

Pat experienced this first-hand a few years ago. While working on a high-profile project with a challenging senior executive, she received negative feedback on what she had created, despite meeting the brief. Negative feedback is never pleasant, but this challenge was exacerbated when the primary contact lied to the senior executive, stating that she had asked Pat to produce something different. Politically, it was an impossible situation. Pat knew she couldn't contradict her daily contact and continue to work effectively with her. She and the team had to apologise and accept the blame for missing the mark. As they worked through the changes to the project over the next month or so, there were a number of calls with the senior executive and the primary contact. On the first of these, Pat, who is a trained voiceover artist and frequent public speaker, told me:

I opened my mouth and my words just squeaked out. I immediately realised that the stress of the situation had constrained my voice. Concerned that lack of vocal strength would further undermine my credibility, I knew I had to get it back under control fast. From that point on, I stopped assuming that my voice would automatically be there for me. I immediately applied centering and relaxation techniques to open my throat in order to get through that call and continued to use those techniques prior to and during subsequent calls until that project was completed.

Smooth, paced diaphragmatic breathing releases acetylcholine, the renewal and recovery chemical that counteracts the pace and tension created by adrenalin and provides a crucial balance, keeping the muscles around the voice box relaxed and the thoughts clear enough to communicate through difficulty. In addition, the dopamine boost Pat achieved when she centered herself enabled her to refocus, control and co-ordinate her voice and behaviour.

> **LIFE HACK:** When emotions run high, the throat tightens. If you begin to feel tension in your throat prior to a presentation, find a private space, center yourself and say out loud three times, 'My throat is open and relaxed.' If you are in company, say it in your head.

When Pat was attending Emerson College, every first-year student was required to study 'Voice and Articulation', regardless of their specialism, and these classes were taught by giants in the field of oratory. That training has served her well throughout her career in business. While it may be obvious that for actors and singers their voice is their instrument, and articulation and clarity are especially critical, the same is true for all of us. Resonance, tone and shaping of the mouth on vowel sounds enable the audience to register the emotional components of the voice. Articulation of the mouth, forming consonants with the lips and tongue, structures the sound into words that enable the audience to understand the meaning.

DAWN MARIE FLYNN SIRRENBERG TALKS
ABOUT THE POWER OF CONSONANTS...

A classically trained singer and vocal coach, Dawn shared that, when singing, the consonants should be energetic, present and bright. Some consonant sounds are made at the front of the mouth (e.g. M, P, B); others are made behind the front teeth with the tip of the tongue (e.g. S, Z, T, D, L); and others are made at the back of the mouth (e.g. K, G). To articulate any consonant clearly, there should always be space before or after it to maintain roundness of tone. For example, instead of just a *p* sound, you want a *puh* sound.

For clear articulation, we also have to pay special attention to end consonants and ends of words or phrases. Clearly articulating end consonants makes you expel air from the lungs. The vacuum this creates forces your body to take a new full breath, energising the next thought. When singing, many people often drop end consonants and phrases. As Dawn tells her students, 'You are not finished singing until the entire piece is over.'

The same is true when speaking – many people tend to trail off at the ends of words or sentences. Whether singing or speaking, pauses are connections to the next thought. You need to maintain your energy through pauses. If you shut them off and lose connection between phrases, you also lose connection to the audience. Physical Intelligence exercises will help you to awaken the muscles of articulation, particularly if you tend to mumble. Give it a try. Strong, muscular consonants are confidence-building if you start to use them.

As director of Companies in Motion and in my work with RADA Business, I have helped literally thousands of people find their breath, vocal resonance and clarity, giving even those with quieter voices the tools to speak out with confidence.

> **LIFE HACK:** To improve articulation, learn this tongue-twister and recite daily: 'I'd like a proper cup of coffee in a proper copper coffee pot, if I can't have a proper cup of coffee in a proper copper coffee pot, I'll have a cup of tea.' Speed up, but keep every word clear.

Whether you want to persuade your family that an adventure holiday is a better summer activity than playing on a beach, or you want to argue for more resources at work, vocal strength comes from being centered, having breath support, creating resonance and articulating clearly so that your argument carries weight and impact. If you communicate using the techniques that follow, people will believe and trust in you.

Let's train: The centered voice

A centered voice enables you to sound clear and genuine as opposed to adversarial or defensive. It also helps you maintain credibility when you are required to answer a difficult question or one where you do not know the answer. With a centered voice, your natural authority shows through.

Exercise: Relaxing the throat

- Loosen your neck and shoulders by rolling the head forwards and sideways.
- Stretch the mouth by yawning, focusing on opening the throat.
- Try speaking this sentence out loud: 'I am speaking through a tight closed throat.' Notice where you feel tension.

- Now relax the throat and jaw, breathe in and feel how this relaxation of throat and jaw allows the in-breath to pass directly down to the area below the navel.
- Try this sentence now: 'I am speaking through an open relaxed throat.'
- Repeat it three times with a new breath each time, noticing how your voice changes as you relax the throat and jaw. It is likely that your pitch has dropped and your voice is naturally more resonant. You may also notice that your pace of speech slows down.

Exercise: Breath support

To stabilise your diaphragm and train your breath support and control muscles, try long, sustained sounds.

- Take a deep, diaphragmatic breath in. On the out-breath, make a long *fff* sound. Try to keep the air flow constant, neither forcing breath out, nor holding breath back. Repeat three times.
- Take another breath in, add the voice and make a long *vvv* sound. Again, try to keep the air flow constant. Repeat three times.
- Repeat with an *sss* sound, then with a voiced *zzz* sound.
- Repeat with a *shhh* sound, then with a voiced *zh* sound.
- Repeat with a *thhh* sound (as in 'thistle'), then with a voiced *th* sound (as in 'this').

This exercise will help you develop muscular support for the out-breath – enabling you to sustain your vocal strength through longer sentences and more complex ideas and ensuring that you will have enough breath in reserve when you need it.

Exercise: Forward placement of your words

- Focus on a specific point about 2 metres in front of you.
- Speak out loud ten times the phrase, 'My words come forwards out of my mouth.'
- Imagine the words flying out of the mouth on the breath, and arriving at the point you are focusing on. (You can also try this in front of the mirror, as Marion did.)

Exercise: Finding resonance

Your voice needs to feel and sound as though it comes from your body (not your throat). The abdomen, chest, back, face, head and mouth all vibrate when we talk. Depending on the sounds, i.e. the combinations of consonants and vowels, the vibrations will move from one body area to another. You can feel this happening.

- Try putting one hand on the crown of your head and then one hand on your chest, then say the days of the week: Monday, Tuesday, Wednesday etc. You will feel the vibrations of the sound move between head and chest resonance.
- Now move the hand from your head to the bridge of your nose. Repeat the days of the week, and see if you can feel the resonance shift between the nose and the chest as you practise this. Notice how *m* and *n* sounds particularly resonate in the nose.
- Now move one hand to the lips, rest the fingertips there, and say, 'Monday'. Notice how much vibration there is in the lips and front of the face on an *m* sound.
- Pick up a newspaper or a book and read a passage out loud. Notice the resonance in your head, face and chest and how it moves between them.

- Read to or speak to a friend while experimenting with your resonance. Get their feedback.
- Ask them to describe how your voice sounds.

Achieving clarity

Our articulation can become less clear if we haven't limbered up our articulation muscles or if we are hesitant or unsure of what we are saying. These classic articulation exercises will help. Although they may not look very attractive and seem rather strange, they are very effective.

Exercise: Shaping the mouth and limbering the tongue

- Stick your tongue gently out of your mouth, laying it over the lower lip like a duvet hanging out of a window to air.
- Now speak out loud as clearly as possible the months of the year: January, February, March etc., leaving the tongue out as an obstacle to work around. Make your very best attempt at making the words understandable. Exaggerate the movement of your lips and the shapes your mouth makes.
- When you reach December, allow the tongue to come in. Now recite the months without the obstacle in the way. You will notice more clarity of articulation.
- Wine lovers may want to save the corks and try the same exercise – but instead of having the tongue out, place a cork lightly between the upper and lower front teeth, then try to speak. This exercise improves our shaping of the mouth to create clearer sound.

Exercise: Crisp consonants

Consonants give structure to desires and emotions. Young babies let their desires be known using open vowels sounds – a wail or cry for food, or an 'ah' of wonder. Then they burble, accidentally happening upon consonants until they learn to speak full words, using consonants purposefully to communicate. As adults, mumbled consonants reduce impact; crisp consonants drastically improve it.

- Articulate your consonants fully. Practise: *ptkt* – *ktpt* – *bdgd* – *gdbd* – *th-ss-sh, sh-ss-th* – *the-ze-j, j-ze-the* – 'Red lorry, yellow lorry', 'She sells sea shells on the sea shore', 'Peter Piper picked a peck of pickled peppers' etc.

Exercise: Emphasis

Emphasis is essential in order for others to understand us.

'It is the responsibility of the speaker to let the audience know which words are more important than others.'

- Speak the above phrase and, the first time, put the emphasis on the word 'responsibility'.
- Now say it again, but put the emphasis on the word 'speaker'.
- Notice how the meaning of the sentence changes depending on where you place the emphasis.

Exercise: Pace and pause

Clarity of thought leads to clarity of speech. Verbal punctuation and speaking with a sense of structure require the effective use of the pause. A pause is not 'nothing', it is alive with thought, and provides a transition between one thought and another, giving the listener time to process what has just been said and prepare for what will be said next. When a speaker connects with (thinks about) their next thought before they speak it, two things happen: 1) a pause is created that gives more value to their thought (than if they had rushed on), and 2) miraculously, they take the right amount of breath to sustain the full length of that thought. 'Think, breathe, speak' is our motto at RADA Business, and the following exercise enables you to practise creating pauses, connecting mentally with your next thought before speaking it, and being able to control your pace. We will use simple numbers, building up from 'one' to a full count of one through ten. Avoid speaking in a monotone, automaton fashion. When you speak these series of numbers, feel free to vary the pace and pitch as you would in normal speech.

- Connect mentally with the word 'one' (let that concept 'one' flash up in your mind), breathe in, then speak 'one' on the out-breath. *Pause while you* ...
- Connect mentally with the word 'two' (let that concept 'two' flash up in your mind), breathe in, then speak 'one, two' on the out-breath. *Pause while you* ...
- Connect mentally with the word 'three' (let that concept 'three' flash up in your mind), breathe in, then speak 'one, two, three' on the out-breath. *Pause while you* ...
- Connect mentally with the word 'four' etc.

... and so on, until you find that you can support the entire count, from one to ten, on one out-breath and enjoy the thoughtful silence of the pause in between speaking. Notice how the breath comes in and fills the lower abdomen fairly quickly when we are breathing for speaking compared to the paced breathing to boost DHEA etc. we practised earlier in Chapter 3 (pp. 60–4).

Practise this exercise daily, while driving to work or in the shower perhaps. It will enable you to slow down, be comfortable with silence, and find the punctuation points, commas and full-stops in your speech. Giving your speech structure builds confidence and certainty in the listener. Their cortisol levels will become optimal for listening as they settle into the rhythm of your speech, and their dopamine levels will boost as they become fully engaged in what you are saying.

Exercise: Committing to your message

When we have a tight jaw, it can seem as if we are holding something back, and when our face is expressionless we can be monotone and appear to lack commitment (cortisol also rises in the listener and they begin to doubt the speaker).

When we relax the jaw, the sound can come out of the mouth with ease, and it indicates that we want to share our words with others, that we are openly communicating with them.

- Relax the jaw by opening your mouth and using the heels of your hands to massage and smooth down the chewing muscles in your cheeks. Count to ten, letting the sound of your words out into the room.
- Use your eyes, face and body to inject meaning into your words – to commit to your message.
- If you are asked a question that takes you out of your depth, that you don't know the answer to, rather than shrinking back in your body and voice, commit to a confident answer, with energy and forward placement of the words. For example, you may say, 'We absolutely can help you address that. Let me arrange a call with Bill,' or, 'Let me take that question back to the team.'

You can use these exercises every day to train your voice. Car journeys, loading the dishwasher or while preparing food all provide perfect opportunities to practise. The shower is also a brilliant option because the bright acoustic quality of tiled surfaces will make your voice sound strong and confident. Your voice will bounce back at you and you can shower in your own vocal vibrations as well as water. Always rehearse speeches and presentations out loud, especially the opening and closing statements.

Our voices are incredible. They are part of our identity and express our personality. Yet, we so often take the incredible gift of language and speech for granted. I encourage you to spend time developing your vocal strength so that when you speak with confidence you start to *feel* more confident too. Your confident voice will release chemicals of confidence in other people, empowering them, just as using confident posture does. Let's now find out more about confidence.

6

THE CHEMISTRY OF CONFIDENCE

How we prepare, take risks and succeed

No one can make you feel inferior without your consent.

—ELEANOR ROOSEVELT

Confidence is not a static state, and no one feels confident all the time. New and challenging situations are often accompanied by a dose of self-doubt, whether we are asking someone out on a date, competing in a school sports day, applying for promotion, speaking in public or making a career change. There is always risk, always the hope that things turn out well, and always the chance that they won't. So, what can we do to create sustained confidence with only small doses of self-doubt and large doses of risk tolerance? How can we best handle the risk of failure? What part does humility play? Can 'swagger' be helpful? And how can we avoid overconfidence, arrogance or aggression, yet compete with a healthy desire to win?

The basic chemistry of high confidence is derived from well-functioning adrenal glands. We need high testosterone, plenty of DHEA, cortisol at an optimal low level, managed dopamine levels and plenty of available adrenalin (the accelerator) and acetylcholine (the brake), so that we can apply effort and recover as needed. With this cocktail we are emotionally and mentally stable, yet able to take risks; we are motivated to achieve our goals, but not obsessed; we feel excitement, but have the ability to relax before that excitement turns to fear.

Low confidence, on the other hand, is caused by low testosterone, high cortisol and low dopamine, with too much adrenalin and too little acetylcholine. With this chemical cocktail we underestimate what we are capable of achieving, want to retreat or escape, and often feel nervous. We may try to act confidently, but all the while there is that nagging self-doubt in the background, hoping that this time the 'fake it till we make it' principle will turn out to be true.

What, then, is the purpose of self-doubt if it can be so debilitating? Humans have a built-in negative bias that means that we see threat before opportunity. The threat centre of the brain is always alert to danger and one of the ways it tries to keep us safe is through the mechanism of self-doubt, usually relating back to our personal histories. The problem is that the threat centre can be over-vigilant, so we have to make sure we accentuate the positive where possible.

Pat grew up in a working-class, blue-collar neighbourhood in Philadelphia in the USA. At the age of six, after her parents unexpectedly divorced, Pat and her mother and two brothers moved into her grandmother's home where they all had to share a spare bedroom. As Pat says, 'We had a lot of love, but not a lot of anything else – although we never felt we lacked for anything.' Thanks to a good education, hard work and family support, Pat has built a solid reputation in her field and a life that is worlds away from that shared back room. She is one of the most trustworthy, committed and competent people I know, and yet when asked to join the board of trustees at Emerson College in the USA (Pat's alma mater), for a moment she found herself thinking back to that humble childhood, surprised that they had picked her.

A small dose of self-doubt is useful to ensure that we prepare well and maintain an engaging level of humility, but a larger dose leads some people to give up too easily and they often live unfulfilled lives, never feeling confident enough to try to achieve what they want to deep down, or, if they do try, 'choking' because cortisol rises too high and testosterone drops too low when the pressure builds. Sadly, this means that talented people may not ever realise their potential, contribute fully to society, or may be overlooked for roles in which they are more than capable of succeeding.

On the other hand, while a bit of swagger on the tennis court might help you communicate or regain confidence in the eyes of your opponent, arrogance and high-risk behaviour can be destructive and set us all back. The combination of high testosterone, high cortisol, high dopamine and high adrenalin generates feelings of greed, entitlement and omnipotence, driving us to win at all costs. In everyday life, this is the chemistry of someone who seems always to prioritise their own needs, continually interrupts others, doesn't listen well, or takes a phone call right in the middle of what for you is an important discussion. Gamblers, financial traders and negotiators can become addicted to the powerful feelings associated with winning and start to believe that they can never lose, which of course is not true. The financial crashes of the past 100 years are testament to that. Traders in those situations get carried away on a winning streak, and when the inevitable first signs of losing come, cortisol and adrenalin levels rise and, like gamblers, they take ever-greater risks to try to maintain the dopamine and testosterone high, believing they can't lose in the long run. Finally, they are so far into risk that nothing matters anymore, and they risk everything. Such highs are followed by lows, when the levels of all four chemicals drop, leading to a loss of energy and drive all round.

Humility is endearing when it comes from someone who already respects themselves. They play down their achievements, thereby including us and making us feel that we could do it too. We love them more for it because they appear centered. But when someone *always* plays low status, even slightly underestimates themselves, apologises for entering a room, minimises their language with, 'Can I just . . .', or 'Can I quickly say . . .', it is easy for others to also underestimate them. Perpetual humility is a high cortisol state and will not build confidence in you or in others.

WAYNE MCGREGOR STANDS HIS GROUND WITH THE DANCE CRITICS...

We all face criticism – in appraisals, 360-degree feedback and comments from colleagues, friends and family – and sometimes it can drain our confidence just at the time when we need it most. Wayne has a refreshingly grounded approach to handling the critics that we can all learn from.

Unlike some artists, Wayne reads all of his reviews and has discovered that not every critic fully understands his approach to modern dance. Occasionally, reviews can be personally wounding; some he reads in disbelief when they apply an outdated lens to his progressive work. Rather than remaining silent (and misunderstood), he gets into dialogue with those critics, inviting interviews with them, some of which have been published and broadcast in the press. His confidence, humility and open attitude enable him to stand his ground and generate debate that is educational for everyone. He says, 'You have to look inside yourself and ask yourself what you were trying to create – did you achieve it in your own terms, does it have integrity, did you do it with passion, and what did you learn?'

He works to his 'Personal Best' (see p. 100) with a learning mindset. This is exactly the kind of approach that we encourage people we train to adopt when receiving feedback. Be confident and centered, ask questions and push back appropriately – to communicate your perspective – where necessary.

To develop our confidence – not too much, not too little – we need to pay attention to three As.

1. *Attitude.* How do you approach what you set out to achieve? Do you know what success will look like? In a moment, we will learn two 'attitude' exercises – 'Ideal Self-Image' and 'Personal Best' – that will help you put your confidence levels in your own hands.
2. *Achievements.* Achievements create new opportunities, giving us status and confidence to achieve more. Do you celebrate your achievements actively so that you get used to how it feels? Using the winner pose and doing what we call a 'lap of honour', we'll learn how to bolster our belief in ourselves.
3. *Analysis.* Uncertainty is one of the killers of confidence. If we *prepare* and *learn* in every situation, we keep cortisol optimal, preventing us from 'choking' and boosting acetylcholine, which brings us more certainty and clarity of thought.

Attitude

Think about a child learning to walk: trying, falling down and trying again. The chemistry of confidence is about trying again and improving each time, building towards our 'ideal self-image' by working on what athletes call their 'personal best' or 'PB'. Out of a field of runners, there can only be one winner. If your focus is only on winning the race, competing is likely to become a demoralising activity. If you lack confidence unless you receive acknowledgement or praise from the people around you, or frequently compare yourself with others, then developing a 'personal best' attitude will enable you to develop a new level of inner confidence. Ballet dancer Mikhail Baryshnikov says, 'I do not try to dance better than anyone else. I only try to dance better than myself.'

Exercise: 'Ideal Self-Image'

> There is a law in psychology that if you form a picture in your mind of what you would like to be, and you keep and hold that picture there for long enough, you will soon become exactly as you have been thinking.
>
> —WILLIAM JAMES (1842–1910)

We can all nurture a self-image of confidence and success and prepare for the positive feelings associated with these successes. This helps us break through to new levels of achievement. Do not misinterpret the word 'image'. This is not about conforming to stereotypes of how you 'should' look; it's about making choices about how you want to *think, feel* and *behave*, and working towards that.

- Find a private space. Close your eyes. Breathe and center yourself.
- Imagine yourself displaying the skills and qualities that

you would most like to have, such as greater happiness and ease, more assertive communication skills, a confident posture, an ability to manage emotions during high-pressure situations, more clarity, better focus, being more thoughtful towards others, achieving better fitness or health.

- Imagine when and where this is happening – the specific moment in a specific place. Notice how you feel in your body. Do you feel the dopamine boost?
- Compare this with your current self-image and see how the behaviours differ.
- Identify the specific changes that you want to make and decide how you will practise towards them. If it is something you want to practise daily, then find a trigger and you can habit stack it in the next chapter.
- Complete the table below:

Current self-image	Ideal self-image	What needs to change	How I will change	Practice

(Give this exercise ten to fifteen minutes per sitting. It takes a bit of time for the mind to settle, to clear away unhelpful judgements and play through some options for the imagery you want to settle on.)

Exercise: 'Personal Best'

The 'Personal Best' process applies to any situation in which you want to achieve more, e.g. timekeeping, holding your ground in challenging meetings, a big competitive event, improving an aspect of parenting or a specific relationship, tidying your desk, presenting your ideas, working towards a significant goal at work or in a competitive sport etc. The 'Personal Best' exercise is particularly useful at times of review, after an appraisal or a heart-to-heart with your partner or coach, or when you have received some critical feedback. You will require a quiet, private space.

- Set open, expansive posture, pace your breathing and center yourself.
- Identify an aspect of your life/your performance that you want to improve.
- Note your personal best on this so far, appraise yourself fairly and honestly.
- Bring up your calendar and look ahead for an opportunity to improve your personal best. (It may be within a few days, weeks or months.)
- Identify what training, mentoring or practice you need in order to improve.
- Plan a schedule for how you are going to train and develop your skills.
- Diarise it.
- Get to it.

What do I want to improve?	Personal best so far	Training/ mentoring available	Practice needed

Achievement

Confidence is built through past achievements because success creates new opportunities. Yet we often forget to let success soak in. I remember many times when I would arrive home having had great things happen that day, and yet I wouldn't mention them to my family because I took my achievements for granted. I would, however, mention what went wrong and want a shoulder to cry on sometimes – allowing a negative bias to take over.

When we succeed, testosterone, dopamine and adrenalin levels rise, creating a surge of elation. We want to repeat that experience and win again, so we double our efforts for next time. This is not the time to underplay the achievement. If we allow ourselves the pleasure of acknowledging our success, elevated testosterone levels mean that we are more likely to succeed again – the chemistry of the 'winning streak'.

Taking my lap of honour . . .

The winner pose that we learned about in Chapter 2 (pp. 34–5) is very useful to generate the surge of chemicals and elation with regard to success. At my brother's fiftieth birthday party, I had some fun with this. A group of embarrassed teenagers were judging a dads' dancing competition and my husband attempted 'the caterpillar', diving onto the floor then rippling through his body head to toe. (I thought, *Ouch – he's going to be suffering in the morning!*) Despite these efforts, my brother was the one who strutted to victory. When it was announced he had won, he put his arms in the air and took his lap of honour (around the dining room), revelling in his winning moment. It looked fun. Then it was the mums' turn to compete. I strutted my stuff and won (the teenagers were very kind). I thought to myself, *I'm going to try it.* I put my arms in the air, laughing, and stomped my lap of honour like Tina Turner. It felt great. When things do go well, we need to find a moment in private or in public to put our arms in the air and metaphorically, or literally, do our 'lap of honour' and let testosterone and dopamine boost our confidence for next time.

A word of warning here: After a win, when testosterone and dopamine levels are elevated, people can experience 'winning highs' that can often lead to arrogance, which can be dangerous, leading us to skimp on preparation or cut corners on training. Instead, it is important and advantageous to reset and regain humility. George Kruis and Jarrod Barnes both commented on this. George said that in any sport, after an easy win a team can become too relaxed, not prepare as well and therefore not perform at their best in the next game. Jarrod highlighted the importance of setting a specific period of time for celebration followed by a disciplined return to the routine, preparation and analysis that led to the win in the first place. It's not just the art of winning, but the art of winning after winning that counts.

Exercise: Winner pose and lap of honour

The physicality of collapsing the spine, narrowing the shoulders, dropping the gaze, kills the chemistry of achievement that makes us want to achieve again. In this exercise, we'll use the winner pose and make a lap of honour a private ritual where you celebrate your achievements, using that feeling to boost confidence for the future. The lap of honour takes about thirty seconds and you should really sense the feel-good chemistry surge through you.

- Think of a recent achievement, even if it's a small win.
- Put your arms in the air in the winner pose.
- Walk around the room, doing your own private lap of honour.
- Allow yourself to feel happy, proud, elated and good about your achievement.
- Continue to celebrate your success for twenty-four hours – congratulate yourself, enjoy the feeling, share the joy with friends, family and colleagues – then move into analysis and preparation for the next challenge.

Cautions:

- After a big achievement, defer making important decisions about the future for a couple of days. Your risk-taking profile is high, so you may take a gamble and regret it. At the very least, be aware of the feeling of hyperarousal in your body; bring it down using breathing practice and think things through carefully.
- If you know you get a bit too big for your boots sometimes, notice your behaviour. Celebrate fully as above, then make sure you cap your testosterone and re-center yourself.

Analysis

To support our confidence, it is important to analyse what we need personally to perform well at specific events, especially challenging ones. The exercises below can be applied to any walk of life, in many different situations, by parents, partners and performers. When established into routines that are repeated regularly, they all contribute to keeping cortisol at the optimal level: where we are fully engaged and alive in the moment – not clamming up, choking or going into overdrive. They also boost acetylcholine, which balances adrenalin, giving you a clear head under pressure.

Exercise: Prepare

Use the following questions to help you analyse how you prepare for important events. We build certainty through preparation, and if we have done everything we possibly can to prepare, it enables us to be carefree in performance and find more ease and flow.

To achieve well, to what extent do you:

- Thoroughly research the context and people?
- Keep up with your training, working daily on the skills you need?
- Rehearse as if you were doing it for real?
- Visualise success?
- Detach from the outcome? (If 'choking' thoughts arise, such as 'Will I get it right?' or 'This would mean so much . . .', say to yourself firmly, 'STOP'. Then detach from the outcome and focus on your personal best.)
- Prepare your body, voice and energy levels?
- Prepare equipment/materials/pack your bag early?
- Ask yourself, 'What is missing?'

Spend five minutes with this question: to better prepare, I need to ...

LIFE HACK: To build confidence for a pitch, speech or important conversation, rehearse well. A dress rehearsal in which you speak out loud enables you to feel that you have already achieved it – so you will have more certainty during the real thing.

Exercise: Psyche up

This exercise takes as long as you'd like it to; approximately two to five minutes with practice, but more time if you wish.

- Close your eyes.
- Imagine yourself walking down a dark tunnel to a door that leads into a room. It is a very comfortable and pleasing room, designed exactly as you would want it.
- The room is sealed, and special air is piped into the room that creates precisely the type of energy that is needed for your situation.
- Feel yourself become more energised or relaxed with each inhalation.
- Feel the increase in focused intensity or relaxation.
- Continue breathing until you feel appropriately energised. Now walk back through the tunnel feeling relaxed focused, centered and confident.

You now have an imaginary place that you can go to in order to create optimal energy for any situation. The room becomes a 'go-to' place in your mind to manage your pre-performance arousal levels.

TOP TIPS FROM OUR PANEL ON PREPARATION...

Wayne McGregor:
- Get clarity on what your role is and what is expected of you.
- Use breath, posture and centering to be in a state of preparedness – physically, mentally, emotionally.

Jarrod Barnes:
- Establish your personal preparation rituals and routines.
- Get fully engaged in practice – be attentive, absorbed and focused.
- Sometimes practise while tired (you may have just got off a plane when you actually have to perform).
- Leave thoughts of outcomes or winning behind.
- Out-prepare yourself compared to last time – 'You're only as good as your last preparation.'

Alessandra Ferri:
- Create a detailed schedule of rehearsal. DON'T squeeze it in at the last minute. Each rehearsal builds up to performance, so that when it arrives you can be free and enjoy it.

Claire Taylor:
- Study the approach of others.
- Use mental rehearsal to visualise your options in response.

Dawn Marie Flynn Sirrenberg:

- Don't forget the non-vocal work. In performance, tell the story and allow the emotion to come through.

Joan Beal:

- Use sensory imagery. (Joan says, 'By envisioning all aspects of what I know I'll experience, I remove the fear of the unfamiliar. I imagine the wooden floor under my feet, the warmth of the spotlight, the smell of the stage, the hushed silence before I sing, the vibrations of the instruments. Then, in performance, I have a calm sense that comes from familiarity. Confidence can come from muscle memory and mental preparation.')

Karl Van Haute:

- Repetition is key. Attaching a physical motion to a mental exercise connects the two and establishes a routine so that, whether you perform a standard procedure or act smoothly and quickly in the event of an emergency, the muscle memory is there.
- '*Perfect* practice makes perfect.' Simply practising a skill isn't good enough; ensuring that you do it exactly right each time and not accepting less is what effectively establishes the skills.

Learning from every single experience gives everything a purpose, settling cortisol at an optimal level. It is pointless to get too caught up in winning or losing, success or failure; it's better to focus our efforts on learning. We need to analyse accurately, sometimes with the help of others, before we can learn. Avoid rumination at all costs. Carry out the following exercise for situations that go well and for those that don't go so well.

Exercise: Learn

Think of an event/situation where you performed and want to learn from the experience. Now take ten to twenty minutes to work through these questions.

Ask yourself:

- What exactly was the result?

- What did you do that contributed to that?

- Where do you stand on your personal best?

- What environmental factors were there?

- What evidence do you have for that?

- What aspects were out of your control?

....

....

- What aspects are in your control for next time?

....

....

- What have you learned?

....

....

- What do you plan to do about that?

....

....

- How do you want to adjust your practice/training accordingly?

....

....

- What are the next opportunities to practise performing?

....

....

Using our physical bodies and our Physical Intelligence, we can transform feelings of fear and doubt into feelings of confidence

and empowerment. Confidence is learned and earned by boosting the chemistry of confidence and taking charge of our
personal growth. In this chapter, we've learned to use
our resources and to achieve our personal best with regard to
building confidence, both to take risks and, even more crucially,
to learn from our experiences.

Food and fitness also have an impact on our nervous and
endocrine systems' balance, and play an important part in our
emotional, mental and physical strength. Let's take a look now
at some key principles for nutrition and how to build a fitness
programme for strength.

7

NUTRITION AND FITNESS FOR STRENGTH

How to build inner stability through diet and exercise

> Strength is the capacity to break a chocolate
> bar into four pieces with your bare hands
> and then eat just one of the pieces.
>
> —JUDITH VIORST

In this chapter we will look at the key aspects of food and fitness that contribute to our physical, mental and emotional strength, as well as the underlying stability of our nervous and endocrine systems, our muscles and our bones.

Nutrition

- Water is vital for every process in every function in the body. If we want to feel strong and have energy available, women need approximately 1.5 litres a day; men 2 litres, more if you are exercising. To make sure you're drinking regularly, use one of the many 'Drink Water' apps that notify you throughout the day, or schedule some reminders yourself.
- Coffee is a powerful drug. One good-quality coffee in the morning, after a good night's sleep, is great for brain function, particularly short-term memory. Caffeine stimulates

the production of adrenalin and dopamine, making signals in the brain fire off in all directions and accelerating movement and speech. If you are feeling anxious, stressed or overwhelmed and your heart rate is already up or erratic, or if you are sleeping poorly, don't drink caffeinated drinks. Drink water or herbal tea instead.

• Dark-green, leafy vegetables contain iron, which is vital for the production of haemoglobin in red blood cells and therefore transportation of oxygen around the body. Peas, beans, seafood and red meat are also good sources of iron.

• Proteins are also fundamental to our strength. They are the building blocks of every single tissue in the body. Units of protein are amino acids that are also essential in the production of many of the neurotransmitters and hormones that we address in this book. The nine essential amino acids cannot be manufactured in the body; we have to get them from our diet. They are present in good-quality protein, whether from plant or animal sources. All types of fish, meat, dairy foods, pulses, soya and green vegetables like spinach contain protein.

• Too much sugar can be our kryptonite, sapping our strength if we eat too much in one go. We get twenty minutes of energy buzz, then suddenly it's all used up. Blood sugar levels drop along with our mood, though the adrenal glands continue to pump out cortisol, making us light-headed and jittery with reduced brain function. Low glycaemic index (GI) foods like avocado, nuts, grains or a piece of wholemeal bread help to re-balance blood sugar. (The glycaemic index is a rating for carbohydrates indicating how much blood sugar [glucose] they release into the bloodstream when eaten alone.) Low GI foods release glucose gradually, keeping blood sugar levels in balance.

• Eat fresh fruit for its natural sweetness but *always* along with a handful of nuts or seeds to prevent a blood sugar low. The sugar (fructose) in fruit gives us immediate energy and the protein and fat in nuts and seeds gives us sustained energy, stabilising our blood sugar levels.

• Taste your food fully. If you eat quickly or while on the move, your body believes that you are in 'fight or flight' mode and produces fewer digestive enzymes. That means fats are only partially processed and stay stored in the liver or are dumped locally around the vital organs and the waist area. Take time to look at food, taste it, and chew properly. When you do that, you release the correct level of digestive enzymes to do the job thoroughly and take advantage of all the nutrients.

Fitness

When we exercise our bodies to build muscular and functional strength, we promote the release of steroids – testosterone, DHEA and human growth hormone (HGH) – in both women and men. These steroids make us stronger and more confident all round. The robustness of the nervous system and heart–brain function relies on our physical fitness. This is logical; if we know in the back of our minds that we can't run very fast or lift obstacles, then our survival is less certain. As soon as we start exercising and feel our muscles gain strength and tone, we immediately feel more able. Body movement enhances brain connections and function in a variety of ways, which means mental focus also improves.

Whether you're in the gym, in your local park, even in the kitchen between stages of cooking a meal, you can build your own personal strength-training programme, exercising three times a week for ten minutes. These exercises require no equipment; instead you use your environment.

Core stability is vital for overall strength, and I find doing core exercises has a *big* impact on how strong I feel mentally and emotionally. Here are two of my favourites:

Crunches

- Lie flat on an even floor – wooden or with a mat or carpet.
- Clasp your hands together behind your head.
- Bring both shoulders off the floor.
- Bring your left knee up and twist your upper body to bring the right elbow towards the left knee as close to touching as you can.
- Straighten out, but keep the shoulders off the ground.
- Repeat four times.
- Relax both shoulders down to the floor and release the neck for a two-second pause.
- Lift both shoulders off the floor again. Repeat the exercise with the right knee and left elbow coming towards each other four times, keeping the shoulders off the ground.

- Relax both shoulders down to the floor and release the neck for a two-second pause.
- Repeat the whole exercise. See how many repetitions tire you and then add one more. Add repetitions gradually as your strength develops.

Planks

- Place your forearms on the ground, shoulder-width apart, palms down or making fists. Your shoulders must be above the elbows.
- Put weight onto your shoulders and arms, then step the right leg, then the left leg back until they are fully extended, toes tucked under, ankles together.
- Retract the muscles just below the shoulder blade to stabilise the shoulder joint.
- Keep the hips in line with the shoulders, so that your body forms a straight plank.
- Transfer the body weight onto the right elbow.
- Slowly pick the right arm up, rotate the torso, hips and legs to the left and extend the left hand and arm up to the ceiling. The outer side of your right foot and the inner side of your left foot will now be in contact with the ground. (You can put your right knee down to begin with as you find your strength.)
- Slowly bring the left arm down and control your return to your starting plank position.
- Transfer your body weight onto the left elbow.
- Slowly pick the left arm up, rotate the torso, hips and legs to the right and extend the right hand and arm up to the ceiling. The outer side of your left foot and the inner side of your right foot will now be in contact with the ground. (Put the left knee down to begin with as you find your strength.)

- Slowly bring the right arm down and control your return to your starting plank position.
- Keep the movement slow, smooth and controlled.
- Repeat three times each side to begin with, depending on your current fitness level. Add repetitions gradually as your strength develops.

For your personal programme, choose five resistance movements (see below for examples), then put them in a sequence, alternating upper and lower body, and repeat the whole sequence four times. Always work with correct postural alignment and muscle engagement. For example, with lunges, keep the spine long and shoulders easy; with chest presses, retract the muscles just below the shoulder blade to stabilise the shoulder joint, always engage the core to support the spine throughout. Movements with the correct focus work a lot more of the body than just the target area. Here is my favourite sequence:

Squats

- Stand with the feet slightly wider than hip-width apart. Have your toes pointing forwards or slightly out, arms down by the sides of your body.
- Retract your shoulders (which activates the core muscles and buttock muscles).
- Bring the arms forwards and out in front of you for balance to allow you to safely put weight on the heels while you bend the knees and move your pelvis back as far as you can, moving into a squat in which (eventually, with practice) your thighs will be parallel with the floor. Imagine you are going to sit on a stool/step.
- Only go as low as you can while keeping your shoulders back. Knees should never be further forwards than the toes, and heels must stay on the floor.
- Keep the core engaged and, breathing out, come back up to the original starting position, legs and arms arriving back at the same time.
- Repeat this process five times to begin with, spending two seconds squatting, two seconds standing, then gradually increase repetitions.

Push-ups

- Use either a vertical wall, the end of a bed, a sturdy chair/coffee table or the floor (depending on your level of fitness and strength).
- Place both hands on the surface in front of you. Rotate the hands slightly outwards.
- With shoulders in line with the hands, drop the chest towards the support. Your shoulders should now be back and down. Engage the core muscles.
- Step the feet back one by one until you are fully supported by the wall, furniture or floor.
- Keeping the core engaged, with the body in one line and the elbows in line with the chest, close to the body (not out to the sides), slowly lower your weight towards the support.
- Pause.
- Push your weight away from the support while breathing out.
- Repeat five to ten times depending on fitness and add repetitions gradually as your strength develops.
- If you are doing this horizontally with hands on the floor you can make it easier by putting the knees down. Just remember to keep the body in one line, and knees, hips and shoulders in line.

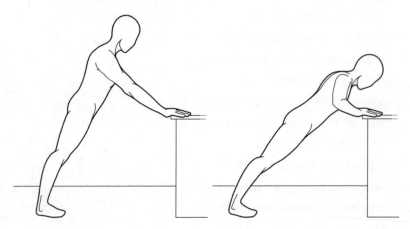

Lunges

- Stand tall, feet together, your arms down by your sides.
- Shoulders should be back so that you engage the core muscles.
- Take a large step forwards on whichever is your non-dominant leg and bend the front knee until the back knee is as close to the ground as possible (or touching it lightly). Your legs should be making a series of right angles. (Don't make the step too big or you will turn it into a stretch.)
- Keep the spine erect and shoulders relaxed. The movement should be slow and controlled.
- Using the front leg, push up and bring the back foot to the front foot and place them together.
- Repeat the above sequence with the dominant leg lunging forwards.
- Now reverse the process by taking a large step *back* with the non-dominant leg.
- Bend the front knee until the back knee is close to the ground or lightly touching it.
- Push from the front leg to bring the front foot next to the back foot and place them together.
- Repeat using the dominant leg.
- Remember to keep the shoulders back and core engaged at all times.
- Repeat the whole pattern of four lunges (two forwards, two backwards) three times to begin with and add repetitions gradually as your strength develops.
- Take two seconds to go into each lunge, two seconds to come to a standing position.

Shoulder Presses

- Stand tall, arms by your sides and shoulders back, which naturally engages your core.
- Bring your non-dominant arm up in front of you with the palm up to shoulder height, as if you were a waiter holding a tray.
- Place the heel of the other hand over the heel of your non-dominant hand.
- Push vertically up with the non-dominant arm while resisting with the other arm, finishing the movement just before the elbow locks.
- Lower the left arm, maintaining resistance.
- Repeat five times with the left arm pushing up (it is like a battle of the arms).
- Change sides to push up with the dominant arm and repeat five times.
- Add repetitions gradually as your strength develops.

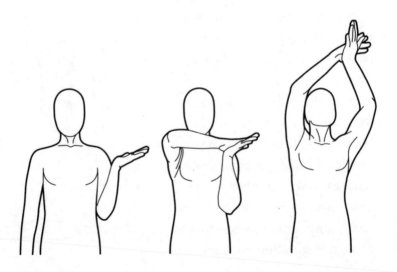

Step-ups

- Find a stool (without padding for better balance), a large step or a low wall outside that is no higher than knee height. It should feel manageable to step up onto, yet still give you a bit of a challenge.
- Stand tall, arms to the sides, with shoulders back to engage the core. Look directly ahead and keep the spine straight.
- Lift the foot on your non-dominant side up to the stool or step, placing the whole foot on it, with 2 inches to spare behind the heel. Step up slowly using the front leg, then bring the other leg up to meet it.
- Step down, leading with the non-dominant leg, but using the front leg to control the movement. Bring the feet together.
- Repeat stepping up and down with the non-dominant leg five times, taking two seconds to step up and two seconds to step down.

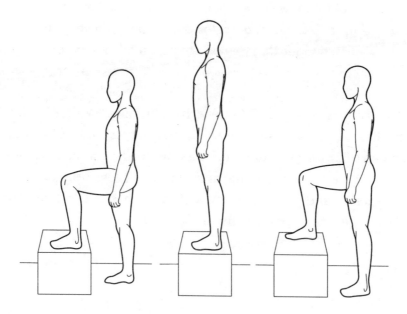

- Repeat another five times, this time starting with the dominant leg.
- Add repetitions gradually as your strength develops.

During any exercise, always remember to breathe. By doing so in a regular pattern to fit with the particular exercise you are doing, you will find a rhythm and increase natural DHEA while training. Remember, too, that simply taking the stairs is a great workout for your thighs, calves and gluteus maximus (bottom) muscles.

> **WARNING:** *Do not buy or take synthetic DHEA as a supplement.* DHEA supplements are available on the American market, but not in the UK. The only DHEA we are interested in is that which we make naturally through breathing technique and muscle strengthening. If you take synthetic DHEA, you risk creating more of either oestrogen or testosterone. Unfortunately, there is no way of telling which it will be. Synthetic DHEA will force levels of oestrogen or testosterone up way beyond the natural nudges that we need to be confident and tolerant to risk.

That completes the set of strength techniques. With attention to these aspects of strength, you can support the chemistry that is vital for your decision-making, focus, confidence, and performance at work, home and play. Now, let's find out how to rehearse and perform our new strength habits effectively by weaving them into our daily life.

REHEARSE AND PERFORM: STRENGTH

Now it is time for you to take action. Unless you work in the performing arts, rehearsal may not be something you have given very much thought to before. Rehearsal is the exploration of how something works, and the practice of it using repetition of actions to create reliable muscle memory. You can apply this principle to anything you want to get better at doing in life. We'd like you to spend a week experimenting with practising strength techniques to find what works for you, then you'll be ready to perform with strength every day.

Performance is the execution of something you have practised. Learning the piano as a child, there was no bluffing – if I hadn't done the practice that week, I couldn't play the piece. Performance doesn't 'just happen', no matter how easy that other parent at the school gates makes it look or how effortless that 'high performer' at work makes it seem. Practice is what makes performance possible and it is an amazing thing when you can effortlessly perform what you have practised.

Here's how to get started:

Choose five of the strength techniques that you particularly like.

Rehearse them for one week to explore the best way to integrate them into your daily life and what the right triggers are.

(Take a look at our habit-stacking ideas and suggestions for triggers below if you need some inspiration.)

Now perform them daily for the rest of the month until they become second nature.

(In time you can go back and choose more to rehearse, then perform those too.)

Here is a reminder of all the techniques we learned in the strength section. Think of this as a menu. You won't order everything on the list the first time you visit, so select what you feel like applying first. Go down the list and mark the ones you feel will be most beneficial to you. Then you'll put them into a programme.

- ☐ POSTURE – Apply posture technique. Ground yourself and stand/sit tall.
- ☐ BREATH – Use paced breathing in a regular ratio in and out.
- ☐ CENTERING – Balance, breathe, focus – release unhelpful tension: find *balance* on the feet or chair; *breathe* down to below the navel; *focus* your eyes appropriately.
- ☐ YOUR 'I' – Remember visualising your 'I'? Recall what your 'I' is made of. Picture it now, remember the strengths that it represents. Do you feel the dopamine boost?
- ☐ CENTERED VOICE – Support your voice with your breath and use its unique quality to communicate. You can imagine that your voice originates in your body from your 'I', your authority.
- ☐ IDEAL SELF-IMAGE – Know what you are aiming for. Visualise how you want to be performing, what it looks like and feels like in your body and behaviour.
- ☐ PERSONAL BEST – Note your current personal best and your development aims.
- ☐ WINNER POSE – Be ready to meet the day confidently and celebrate success.

☐ LAP OF HONOUR – Leverage your success. Take a private lap of honour, arms out in a winner pose, whenever you succeed.

☐ PREPARE – Make decisions about how to improve your preparation.

☐ PSYCHE UP – Imagine walking into your energy room. It has just the right air quality for you to breathe to give you precisely the right levels of adrenalin and cortisol, focus and excitement you need; in one breath you are in the zone.

☐ LEARN – Schedule time to reflect on what you are learning.

☐ NUTRITION – Improve hydration, blood sugar balance and check protein and green vegetable consumption.

☐ TASTE YOUR FOOD – Take time to let your digestive enzymes do their work and enjoy the taste of food.

☐ FITNESS – Execute your ten-minute core and muscle strengthening fitness workout.

Now, let's habit stack:

ON WAKING

- Drink 500ml of water (have it ready by your bed).
  Trigger: The alarm goes off.

- Switch into a regular, paced breathing rhythm.
  Trigger: Putting the glass/bottle of water down.

- Note your intentions to attain a personal best today in one specific aspect.
  Trigger: Completing five paced breaths.

- Complete your strength fitness training programme: ten minutes on core strength and your chosen five resistance exercises.
  Trigger: Exiting the bathroom.

AT BREAKFAST

- Strike a winner pose and/or do a lap of honour to celebrate your last achievement and build confidence.
  Trigger: Putting the kettle on for your morning tea/coffee.

- Eat a nutritious, low-sugar breakfast, to ensure your blood sugar level is set steady for the day ahead.
  Trigger: Opening the fridge door.

IN THE BATHROOM

- Project your voice on the phrase: 'My words come forwards out of my mouth' or simply count to ten. Use long s-z, f-v sounds etc. to activate breath support for your voice.
  Trigger: After cleaning your teeth or while taking a shower.

ON THE JOURNEY TO WORK

- Set and use open, expansive body posture (imagining light between the bones of the skeleton).
  Trigger: If leaving the house, closing the front door. If working from home, as you walk towards your office/ workspace, perhaps.

- Spend ten minutes practising paced breathing (pp. 60–4) and centering (pp. 69–72).
  Trigger: The train doors close or you get stuck at a red light or in a queue while driving.

- Psyche up with the energy room exercise (p. 105). What kind of energy is needed to be particularly effective today?
  Trigger: Finishing paced breathing technique or opening up your schedule for the day.

- Use the 'Ideal Self-Image' visualisation (pp. 98–100) as you mentally prepare for the day.
  Trigger: Closing your schedule for the day.

ARRIVING AT WORK

- Apply seated posture technique (pp. 49–50).
  Trigger: Fingers pressing the keys that log you into your computer.

- Apply breathing technique alongside posture set-up.
  Trigger: Setting posture.

DURING THE DAY

- Before meetings, think about your 'I' to give you a boost of confidence and a sense of your authenticity. Center your voice.
  Trigger: A five-minute pre-meeting alert, set on your phone or computer.

- Use centering for presentations or key meetings.
  Trigger: Picking up the slide clicker or opening the file you will share.

- Drink water.
  Trigger: Reminders given to you through your 'Drink Water' app.

- Pace your breathing.
  Trigger: Walking to meetings/to get a snack.

AT LUNCHTIME

- Register wins and achievements from the morning's work.
  Trigger: Walking out the door of the building.

- Center yourself.
  Trigger: Joining the queue to buy lunch.

- Make nutritious lunch choices.
  Trigger: The sight of food choices in front of you.

- Take time to taste the food.
  Trigger: Taking the first bite.

ON THE JOURNEY HOME

- Set your paced breathing pattern and do something you enjoy for the rest of the journey as a reward.
  Trigger: The train moving out of the station/key being inserted into ignition of your car.

- Register wins and achievements and note personal best progress.
  Trigger: Practising paced breathing pattern.

IN THE EVENING

- On arriving home, center yourself; enjoy the feeling of returning to your base and connect with the people you share your space with (family members/flatmates).
  Trigger: Placing the key in the front door.

- Ten-minute strength-training programme (if not done in the morning).
  Trigger: Your suit or work clothes have been hung up, or the dinner is on.

- Take a lap of honour; celebrate your achievements.
  Trigger: Taking the first sip of a drink of water, tea, juice, wine or beer.

- Prepare adequately for the next day by getting clothes/food/documents ready etc.
  Trigger: Finishing your evening meal.

It would be impossible to integrate all the strength techniques in one go. Five is a manageable number to start with. Do make sure to include breath (pp. 60–64) and posture techniques (pp. 41–50), however, as they are fundamental.

Once you have chosen techniques, find crystal-clear triggers – moments in your day when you can purposefully integrate them. Triggers are precise occurrences – often ones you can visualise, e.g. your hand on the silver latch closing the white front door. Whatever they are, they need to be simple and immediately applicable.

Without these triggers, despite good intentions, you are likely to forget to practise the techniques and feel disappointed at the end of the day. The trick is to identify habits you *always* do at clearly defined moments in your day (triggers) and place your strength habits right alongside them (habit stacking).

Make a note of your own strength programme and triggers here:

Technique	Trigger

Rehearse: Seven days

Take the first week to explore the techniques, giving yourself time to learn how to practise them and find your own personal way of integrating strength work into your life. At the end of seven days, you will have a good working knowledge of the techniques and will have adapted them to fit into your routine. Adapt the routine to suit you at the weekends.

Perform: Strength

Once you have settled on what works, the rest of the month is easy, because you will have a plan. Every day you practise you will be taking better charge of your body. Enjoy building your strength. Stand up for what you believe in, be unerring in your focus, and inspire others to be the same. Quietly perform your strength habits every day, knowing that you are taking charge of your physiology and becoming more and more physically intelligent every day.

Now it is time to turn to flexibility. In this next section we'll discover how we can release tension and move more, be more flexible in relationships, develop our ability to engage with others with a flexible voice and presence, and find out how to be more creative and innovative. You can then marry flexibility techniques with your strength techniques at the end of the next section to become more agile and versatile, or you can skip to resilience or endurance if either of those are priorities for you.

PART 2
FLEXIBILITY

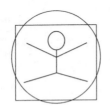

Introducing Flexibility

The measure of intelligence is the ability
to change.

—ALBERT EINSTEIN

A high degree of flexibility is required of us today. Flexible working hours, flexible working environments, working globally across time zones, languages and culture, the rate of change in technology, the amount of information we process daily, the varied responsibilities of parenting and living in diverse communities – all make demands that require us to be increasingly flexible.

The type of flexibility we need is not the 'go whichever way the wind blows' kind, but that which is underpinned by strength and self-assurance; not threatened, but discerning and creative, joyous and resourceful, open-minded, generous and life-affirming.

In this section on flexibility we will learn how to roll *with* change, becoming increasingly aware of emotions, able to expertly manage ourselves and view the world from perspectives other than our own, creating the conditions in which we can innovate.

To achieve this, we need first to become more alive to changes in our bodies, especially physical tension and the visceral aspects of emotions. When anything changes in our environment, our bodies change too, and because change brings uncertainty, our natural human response is to brace, tense up or collapse. A rigid body can lead to blinkered and narrow thinking and inhibits creativity, while a collapsed body leads to low self-esteem, giving up, and a loss of buoyancy and hope.

The 'winning cocktail' for flexibility is created when we consciously adapt and boost our levels of the four key flexibility chemicals: oxytocin, dopamine, DHEA and serotonin. When we do that we can increase the *ODDS* for success.

Oxytocin

An important part of flexibility is being able to work with and live alongside diverse groups of people and create excellent relationships and collaborations. We can *always* get better at 'loving thy neighbour', and a growing consciousness about oxytocin will enable us to use its incredible bonding power to greater effect. When we share stories that let people know a bit about us, show that we understand others and are able to negotiate and compromise for the greater good, oxytocin – created not only in the brain but by *independent* neurons in the heart – is released in ourselves and others, building trust.

Dopamine

Dopamine is released when we are creative, and when we feel rewarded by our environment and the people around us. It is also concerned with homeostasis (the body's inner balance in changing circumstances). In times of change, when homeostasis is harder won, dopamine stimulates creative thinking, ingenuity and innovation to problem-solve so that balance can be re-attained. There is a strong link between dopamine, creativity and survival and yet, for the most part, in peaceful regions of today's developed world we do not need to be creative to survive because most things (i.e. food, shelter) are easier to come by than they used to be. There is a different kind of urgency now that so many of us are innovating in situations where we have plenty of what we need rather than scarcity. In this relatively new context of abundance, dopamine enables the kind of brain connections that make us ingenious at enhancing life with high-tech gadgets. We are becoming designers and consumers of novelty and pleasure.

On the darker side, dopamine is also the chemical of addiction. Addictive things are pleasurable, but we need more and more of them to release the same amount of dopamine – to get a 'hit' – which leads to consumption that increases until it is out of control. Just enough but not too much dopamine enables us to be flexible and creative and to enjoy life's pleasures.

DHEA

This fundamentally important chemical underpins flexibility as well as strength because it provides a strong platform for emotions such as excitement and happiness rather than fear or depression, making us more flexible, curious and open. We can think in a wider variety of ways, see and consider various options, and think divergently (creating many options from one stimulus) as well as convergently (choosing from a set range of options). It is also a marker for the flexibility of the heart muscle; the more we have, the more supple the heart is and the more likely we are to live a long and healthy life – able to quickly adapt to changes in pace and intensity.

Serotonin

Created in the brain and by *independent* neurons in the gut, serotonin gives us well-being, balance, self-esteem and status; our sense of place in the world. When serotonin is at an optimal level and we have enough serotonin receptors to take up this vital chemical, we feel at ease. It also keeps the connective tissue in our musculoskeletal system flexible, literally creating more space between the bones of the skeleton. Muscles are long and smooth rather than contracted or collapsed and knotted into balls of tension (common when cortisol levels are too high). Space in our bodies gives us more mental and emotional space. Our insular cortex functions better, the quality of data is more refined, our perceptions tend to feel wide and deep and we may feel 'whole' rather than bothered by conflicting thoughts and feelings.

Where our sense of place in the world is concerned, our serotonin levels are vital. We can own our place at the table confidently without feeling we need to fight for it; we can breathe, expand and open up dialogue. We have more capacity to connect with others and discuss rather than fight or defend our stance on issues. Where testosterone enables us to be risk-tolerant, to compete and stand our ground, serotonin enables a flexible presence that peaceable leaders in our times have had. (Gandhi and Nelson Mandela come to mind.)

Oxytocin, dopamine and serotonin together enable us to be socially responsible, creative and happy. DHEA creates a background of vitality and energy that makes boosting the other three possible. We can change and adapt with grace and can flex to others' styles of behaviour. Our ability to learn new things increases, giving us greater versatility. We move expansively and freely, using bigger, more fluid gestures, and speak with greater vocal variety. Movement of all kinds – physically, mentally, and emotionally – becomes more fluid, enabling us to transition easily from activity to relaxation, from action to rest.

For example, imagine you get together with friends to discuss going on holiday together. You all have different ideas before you start; discussion takes place, people express themselves freely and respectfully and new ideas emerge. Compromises are made and everyone, using their creativity, makes an effort to ensure that each other's needs are met. In this situation, you have all four flexibility chemicals released at one time, delivering a peak experience of social interaction.

When you clash with someone, there is tension in the air and you find your cortisol rising. If you smile and let them know you see their perspective and that you have a different view, rather than arguing in a series of 'No, but . . .' responses, you up the *ODDS* of success for you *and* the other person.

Developing flexibility enables us to find true flow and ease in ourselves and with others. We become someone others want to be around because we know how to transform difficulty into options, adversity into advantage. If we learn how to access our flexibility, releasing the chemicals that enable us to change and adapt, we can inspire others to do the same – leading by example, creating cultures built on kindness, trust and creativity. So, let's get to it.

8
MOVE MORE – MOT (MAP OF TENSION)

How to release tension, find flow and boost happiness

I move, therefore I am.

—HARUKI MURAKAMI

A dripping dog emerging from a river shakes energetically because it feels the weight of water in its fur. When it's cold we shiver and hunch, and when the sun shines we open our bodies and bathe in its warmth. Our bodies move all the time in response to the external environment, but we are less responsive than we could be to the internal environment of our bodies.

When it comes to your car, how do you know when something is wrong? An unfamiliar noise? A strange vibration? Or worse, when the engine blows a gasket? It should be the same with the body, but we tend not to notice changes in tension and sensation that call us to consider our well-being until it is too late.

> **LIFE HACK:** Right now, are your shoulders gripped? Let them go. For the next ten seconds use only the essential muscle effort you need to sit and read the words on the page – leave every other muscle group alone.

The perception of changes inside our bodies (called 'intero-ception') provides an important set of data that underpins our Physical Intelligence. If tensions in our muscles become habitual responses, we may become less flexible and find that we are less collaborative and creative, less able to be authentic and adapt to new things.

For example, how might we interpret a 'gripping' or 'clench-ing' state in the jaw, shoulders or stomach? Are they familiar sensations or are they new? When did they start? What might be the cause?

Overuse of muscular tension uses up valuable energy to no effect and often creates discomfort and pain caused by high cortisol and low oxytocin, dopamine, DHEA and serotonin levels. Improving physical flexibility changes the internal chemistry, lowers cortisol and improves mental and emotional flexibility, transforming the feeling of being 'in the grip' of stressors to feeling open and adaptable to them.

A large-scale study from the University of Surrey, UK, in 2004 showed that, in the working environment, low reward, role ambiguity and job future ambiguity tended to show as neck, shoulder, elbow, forearm, hand/wrist complaints. Taking on too much responsibility and role conflict appeared as lower back complaints. Raising self-awareness, taking charge, moving more and understanding the underlying causes prevent such complaints from becoming serious conditions.

Movement keeps us 'fluid' in so many ways. After all, we are made up of 60 per cent water, the base for all the fluids in the body (blood, spinal fluid, digestive juices etc.) and the trans-mission fluid for hormones and neurotransmitters. All feelings, thoughts and actions are the result of impulses, chemical or electrical, passing through these systems of fluids. We need to be well-hydrated in order to be flexible, but we must also move our bodies. In nature, non-flowing water becomes stagnant;

it's the same in the body. When we move, the fluids move too, releasing toxins from cells, transforming static chemical states into more adaptive states and 'flushing' our system. Our bodies are designed for locomotion and movement and doing so enhances our health, our mood and our mindset.

> **LIFE HACK:** Stand up. Picture Usain Bolt preparing to race for the 100m gold medal in the Olympics. Shake out your arms and legs like he does for ten seconds. Notice how you feel now. Tension causes static states; movement creates change.

We should be standing/moving/walking for between two and four hours of our day according to a 2015 paper commissioned by Public Health England. Those who sit all day have a 13 per cent greater risk of cancer and 17 per cent greater risk of mortality than those who spend time moving. A revolution in the way we work is needed. Consider walking to talk to colleagues rather than emailing, using stand/sit desks to keep us mobile and flexible and setting reminders for movement routines using our devices and apps. At Companies in Motion, we are passionate about encouraging and supporting this transformation.

TOM BECOMES MORE FLEXIBLE AND HANDLES A DIFFICULT MERGER...

As the new CEO of an organisation going through a merger, Tom had a lot of responsibility on his shoulders. When I met him, his mother was also in ill health, his house was being renovated, and he had a long commute home each weekend. He had become so tense that his throat, neck and shoulders were rigid. As someone who always pushed on regardless, he had not realised how the build-up of physical tension and the build-up of emotions were linked. Over the course of just three coaching sessions, Tom was able to release years of tension that had built up in his body. A few tears were shed, and we laughed a lot, too. Once Tom found his own way of releasing tension, he was able to meet the challenges of the merger by thinking creatively and better understanding the needs of all stakeholders.

Now, Tom is more aware when tension builds in his neck and shoulders. He uses alerts to remind him to get up every hour to stretch and walk around and do his sequence of flexibility movements. He is also much more aware of his overall Physical Intelligence and can feel the chemicals change in his body when the pressure is on. When that happens, he breathes freely, goes for a walk and stretches to release tension and be more open. It doesn't completely stop the feelings from coming, but they no longer create blocks in his body and he can process them.

LIFE HACK: Don't hold back the tears. When we cry, the diaphragm pulses, moving strongly up and down. This stimulates our vagus nerve to trigger the release of acetylcholine, the chemical that brings us back into balance (homeostasis). Cortisol levels drop, serotonin, oxytocin and dopamine levels rise, physical tension dissipates and we feel 'relief'. Crying has a physiological purpose.

Let's explore how breath and movement improve the chemistry of flexibility, enabling us to be happier and healthier.

Let's train: Move more

Exercise: Free breathing

Just as paced breathing (pp. 60–4) helps us build stability and strength, free breathing gives us flow and ease, which is especially important if we spend long hours focusing intensely on our work or other things. A sigh of relief is an important mechanism for releasing tension and lowering cortisol. The out-breath expels toxic carbon dioxide and boosts acetylcholine and serotonin, eliciting a feeling of 'relief', while the end of the out-breath stimulates the new in-breath so that we also get a plentiful supply of oxygen.

Inspire (breathe in freely)

- Expand the lower abdomen
- Feel the lower ribs swing out sideways
- Fill the chest cavity to stimulate the solar plexus

'Sigh' (breathe out freely)

- Let tension go
- Feel the lower ribs swing in and settle down

Feel relief

- Notice that you can generate a real feeling of relief at will by using your breath
- Enjoy the next in-breath; the 'inspiration'

Explore this now, repeating the technique a few times, pausing in between breaths and finding the feeling of relief as you do it. Don't force it, find a pace that works for you and let it happen.

Practise free breathing to release tension at any time – as you finish the morning's work and stand up to get lunch, or at the end of your day as you leave the workspace, for example.

(NB: This is a sigh of relief for your personal benefit, not a sigh of exasperation or weariness that makes your feelings known to other people. Be aware of how you use the sigh in public as it could be misinterpreted.)

Having freed the breath, let's explore and learn how to identify and release tension in specific parts of our bodies, balancing muscular contraction and expansion. We will also become skilled at interpreting physical tensions from an emotional and mental perspective.

Exercise: MOT (Map of Tension)

In the Physical Intelligence curriculum, MOT stands for 'Map of Tension'. Creating your own physical MOT is a powerful technique for monitoring tension in yourself and understanding its mental and emotional significance.

- Notice exactly how your body feels right now. Don't change your position, but scan through your body. Are there areas of your body or specific muscle groups that are overly tense, held too tightly for no apparent reason or purpose? (Most people have at least two or three 'hotspots'.)

COMMON TENSION HOTSPOTS

- Jaw tension is often linked with frustration, being in the grip of something or holding back on communicating something of importance.

  Remedy: Move the jaw gently side to side, forwards and backwards, and stretch your mouth into a wide yawn.

- Stomach knots can accompany performance worries, feelings of personal anxiety, insecurity or guilt.
  Remedy: Twist to the left and to the right (see p. 152). Identify the specific location of knots of tension and imagine sending your breath directly to the knotted area.

- Neck tension or shoulders raised or tense is related to the effort of carrying the weight of our head and brain as we strain forwards towards the screens in front of us or the people we are in conversation with. They are also classic signs that there is general stress in our system.
  Remedy: Regularly realign your head on your spine using seated posture technique from Chapter 2 (pp. 49–50) as well as the exercises 'Shoulder Stretch and Drop' (p. 151) and 'Freeing the Neck' (pp. 160–61).

- Lower back tension can indicate a lack of postural core support or support from family members, peers and bosses. Ask yourself: Are you taking on too much responsibility? Are you communicating with others, asking them to step up and play their full part?
  Remedy: Use posture technique from Chapter 2 (pp. 41–2) and strengthen the core by balancing on one leg, slowly lifting the knee towards the chest, then gradually lowering and repeating with the other leg. See also the 'Torso Twist' (p. 152), 'Golf Swing' (p. 153) and 'Freeing the Hips' (p. 160) exercises.

- Arm and leg tension can result from clenched fingers, toes bracing and frequently making fists. This often indicates that you are bracing against your environment and feeling the need to fight a battle.

Remedy: Loosen your limbs by gently shaking your legs one at a time and your arms both together like Usain Bolt does before getting into the starting blocks; imagine you want to loosen the muscles' grip on the bones, releasing tension. Also use stretches (pp. 162–5), 'Shake Out' (p. 154) and 'Free Breathing' (pp. 144–5).

- Chest tension may indicate accumulated containment of emotional reactions.
  Remedy: Try stretching into a diver's pose – head up, arms out to the side and pointed back, chest out and forwards and breathe into your sternum/chest.

- Hamstring and spine tension may be associated with a mindset or approach that is too fixed, or being bored or under-stimulated, e.g. always walking the same path with no stretch of the hamstrings in different directions.
  Remedy: Stretch the legs in multiple directions – see what feels good. Practise 'Shake Out' (p. 154), taking care to stretch hamstrings gently first.

- Mark on the graphic overleaf with a cross or a circle the key areas of tension you have noticed.
- Move your body now; stand, walk, bend and stretch. Are there any additional hotspots you notice? Mark them on the graphic and number them.
- Carefully explore the first hotspot by moving that specific area of your body slowly, giving the movement your full attention. If you have been given restrictions or instructions by medical practitioners, osteopaths or physiotherapists or any physical therapist as to how you should move that part

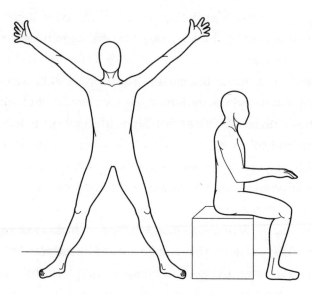

Mark your tension 'hotspots' on these figures.

of your body, then please adhere to those instructions completely. If you have pain in that area of the body, then work with the smallest of movements to start with before you try any bigger movements. Do not carry out any movements that might exacerbate any medical conditions you may have.

- Now, find a movement – tiny, small, medium or large – that alleviates the tension. Experiment slowly and gently to find exactly what feels most beneficial. If you experience discomfort, sit still and simply focus your mind on that area with the aim of releasing the tension.

- Sometimes focusing on a painful body area can make it temporarily more painful. If this is the case, do not try to move that body part. Instead, take three breaths, imagining that the breath could reach the area directly, then focus on another, less painful, body area.

- Create your own movements or adapt stretches/movements that you already know help, but try them with a renewed focus and attention. Work carefully and precisely using your body's intelligence to tell you what it needs.

- Make a note of the movements you have chosen on the chart below.
- Bearing in mind that each hotspot sends data (sensation or pain) to the insular cortex of the brain that communicates with many other brain areas to enable us to interpret and find solutions, ask yourself these questions: What are each of your hotspots telling you? If they could speak, what would they be saying? What requests would they make? What advice would they give? What insights into your patterns of thought and feeling does this exploration provide? What do you want to do differently?
- Now go on to the second hotspot and work through the same process.

My MOT movement	Why am I holding this tension? What is my body telling me?

Well done, you have made a great start on upping your *ODDS* by creating your MOT movements and listening to your body. You are taking charge of your chemistry and of how you think and feel.

SYLVIA LINKS GUT TENSION TO WORKING-MOTHER GUILT, AND RELEASES IT . . .

Sylvia is the head of a business unit in a financial services company. She used to hold extreme tension in her abdominal muscles – manifesting as a knot in her stomach, associated also with digestive problems and IBS. Through coaching, we helped her interpret this tension. She did her MOT and we asked her: 'If you could give it words, what is this tension saying? What does it need from you? What advice does it have for you?' She voiced the associated thoughts and feelings and discovered that this tension was related specifically to a twist of guilt she felt in relation to working full-time and being a mum of two young boys. She was the main breadwinner, but this came at a cost to her.

Many women in full-time roles identify with this, and, for some, guilt may be something they acknowledge and learn to live with, while others may feel differently. Sylvia hadn't made the connection until she did her MOT. She identified her hotspot and explored her interpretation. The words that came to mind were, *Don't make it worse; don't punish me.* She created her own MOT movement – a version of the 'Torso Twist' and 'Free Breathing' – and used it every day for a month. Sylvia found that she was better able to live with a feeling of guilt, which in time turned into a more occasional mild regret. She would regularly remind herself that she was a good mum; she was providing for her family and doing the very best for them that she could. Sylvia's career is going from strength to strength and her boys are growing up resilient and independent.

Let's look now at how to maintain and develop your repertoire of flexibility movements both at and away from your desk.

Exercise: Flexibility at your desk

Use the following movements at work, at your desk or in a more spacious private space, whenever you want to free yourself of tension.

Shoulder Stretch and Drop

This movement is easy to do at your desk.

- Begin by using the seated posture technique we learned in Chapter 2 (pp. 49–50).
- One by one, lift the shoulders up in eight steps so that by the eighth step the shoulders are up by the ears.
- Tip the head back and squeeze the neck and shoulder muscles.
- Breathe in, hold for a second and then drop the shoulders down, simultaneously breathing out and balancing the head back on the vertical spine.
- Repeat as needed.

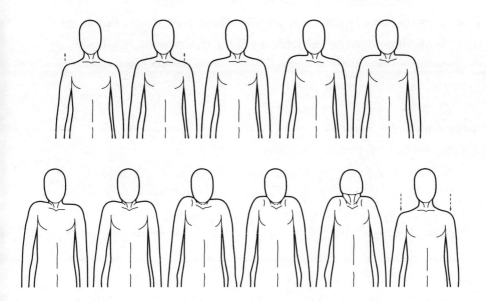

Torso Twist

- This stretch can be done inconspicuously at a desk at work because it appears to others as if you are just looking behind you.
- Begin in correct seated posture (see pp. 49–50).
- Keep the knees and hips facing forwards.
- Cross the left hand and arm diagonally down across the body, so that the back of the left hand/wrist presses against the outside of the right thigh.
- Straighten the left arm and press the back of the hand/wrist gently but firmly against the outside thigh while twisting the whole torso to the right.
- Turn your head to look over the right shoulder. Your hand and arm create leverage so that you can gently increase the range of the twist. Do not lever yourself to the extent that you cause any pain.
- Breathe in and out. Lever yourself further into the twist depending on the flexibility of your spine.
- Breathe again, release the position, then slowly face front.
- Repeat to the left with the right arm crossing the body.

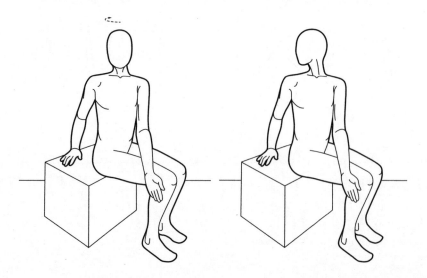

Exercise: Flexibility away from your desk

Golf Swing

Even if you've never played golf, the golf swing action is a great way to release tension. Don't worry about the perfect stroke.

- Bring the arms back to prepare and then swing them through freely, letting the movement come to a natural end.
- Repeat on the left side and right side, breathing out while you swing through.

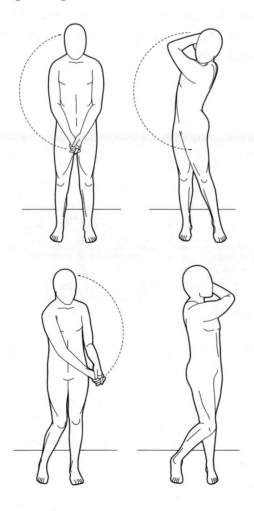

Racket sports and golf are a great way to up the *ODDS*. They are social (oxytocin), sometimes out in open space (dopamine is released when our visual cortex is stimulated by seeing landscapes), and because they involve swing and twist movements the adrenals receive a detox (supporting DHEA production) and independent neurons in the gut are stimulated (releasing serotonin).

Shake Out

To be done in private, the 'Shake Out' is important when there is a build-up of negative emotion and you want to choose a different emotional response, or when you feel overwhelmed and can't think straight.

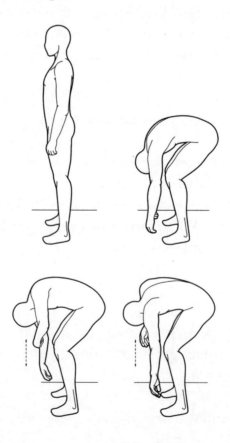

- Flop forwards from the waist, relax the upper body, especially the neck.
- Take a deep breath in.
- On the out-breath, vigorously shake the shoulders and torso while making an *ah* sound.
- Repeat and enhance until all tension has gone.
- Slowly roll up with the head coming up last. You will feel different, better and will be more able to focus. The inversion and vigorous movement around the spinal column shakes up spinal fluid, like mixing a cocktail. The catabolic chemicals created after a cortisol spike drain away. It is like pressing 'refresh' on your computer.

(NB: If you have high blood pressure, the 'Shake Out' exercise should only be done briefly and gently. Always consult your doctor before making any significant changes to your health protocol.)

Exercise: Flexibility movement sequence
This sequence of flexibility movements enables you to release tension and feel 'free'. They can be done at the gym, at home, or outside in the park – wherever you exercise. Do them as a warm-up alongside your strength fitness training or at any point in your day. With practice, one movement links onto the next to form a seamless sequence.

Free Twist

- Anchor the feet to the floor and lengthen the spine.
- Twist your shoulders around to look over your right shoulder – wrap your arms around the right side of your body, as follows: the left hand should touch the right hip and the right arm will fold naturally at the elbow and should

lie across your back so that the back of your right hand touches the back of your left hip. Feel the full twist.

- Now, allowing the arms to be relaxed, heavy and free-flowing, twist your shoulders around to look over your left shoulder, letting your arms follow along until they wrap around the left side in a mirror image of the placement above.
- Breathe freely while you do this.
- Repeat eight times.

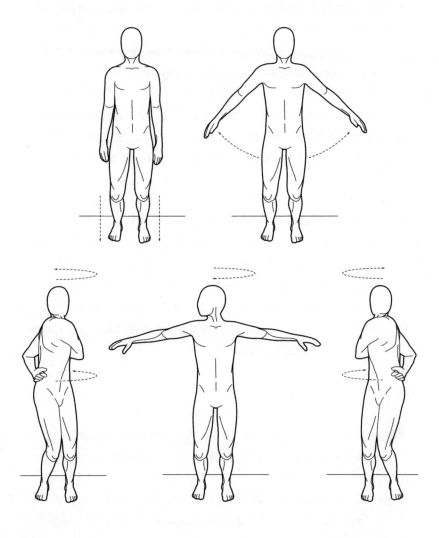

Butterfly

- Anchor the feet and lengthen the spine.
- Use the same free twist action as opposite, but instead of letting the arms flop and wrap around the body, when twisting to the right, straighten the right arm to just above shoulder level, palm down, looking behind you towards your right hand. Keep the right shoulder down.
- At the same time, bend the left arm and bring the left hand to the right shoulder, palm down, and perch the hand lightly on the shoulder as if it was a butterfly landing softly.
- Take a slight pause, then sweep both arms forwards at waist height and round to the left side to arrive with the left arm straight, just above shoulder level, palm down, looking behind you towards your left hand. Bend the right arm and perch the right hand on the left shoulder lightly.
- Pause and sweep the arms around to the right again.
- Repeat eight times and find relaxation, swing, and a pleasurable twist of the spine and opening of the shoulders.
- Keep the neck free and without strain.

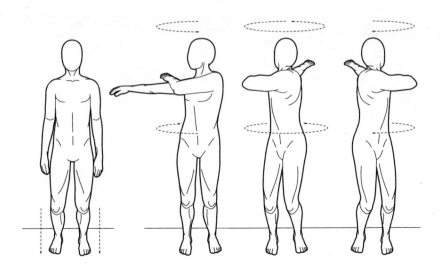

Figure of Eight

- Center yourself with flexible knees.
- Swing the arms down towards the floor on the right side of your body, then swoop them back and up high towards the ceiling on the right side of your body.
- Swoop the arms down on a diagonal from high on the right side, to low on the left side of your body.
- Swoop the arms back and up high on the left side of your body, then down on a diagonal from high on the left side, to low on the right side.
- Find the swing and the rhythm in this movement as you swoop from one side to the other.
- Imagine you are drawing a big figure eight with your arms as they swoop through the air in front of you.
- Release the neck and let the head follow the movement of the arms.
- Repeat eight times.

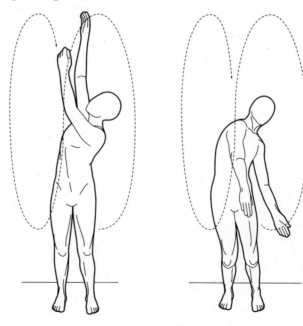

Flow

- Imagine you are holding a large ball in your hands.
- Move it to the right, the right hand leading.
- Move it to the left, the left hand leading.
- Find the flow in this movement, swaying side to side.
- Repeat eight times fully, then let the movement slowly die down.

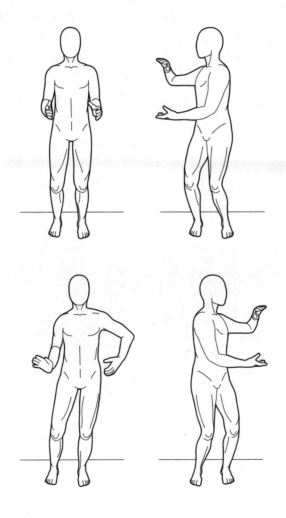

Freeing the Hips

- Move your hips freely by drawing a horizontal figure of eight with the hip bones. Start slowly and increase the pace as you become familiar with the movement.
- Repeat sixteen times.

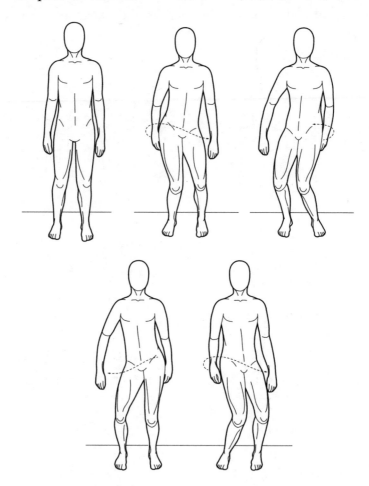

Freeing the Neck

- Roll the head slowly around on the neck once in each direction.

- Draw a figure of eight with the nose – tipping/turning the head from side to side.
- Release the jaw.
- If you feel comfortable with it, let the movement grow in size and the figure of eight get bigger.
- Repeat sixteen times.

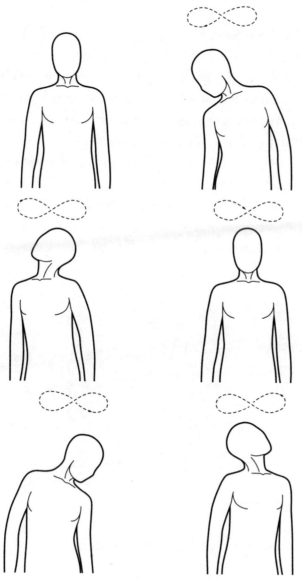

Exercise: Flexibility stretches

When you stretch, always elongate the body and lengthen out into the space around you; imagine the limbs and body parts extending farther than the body. You can do these stretches after a workout, or in short windows of time during your day.

Lunge/Hip Flexor Stretch

- Come forwards into a lunge on the right leg, find your balance and bring both hands to rest on the front thigh. Stretch by straightening the back leg – stay for a minimum of thirty seconds. Change legs and repeat.
- Next, repeat the lunge on the right leg, but put the back knee down on the floor and put both arms up in the air. Lean over to the right side, feel the stretch deep into the hip flexor (most lower back pain is caused by tension in the front hip flexors, not back strain).

Forward Bend (for hamstrings, lower back, spine and gluteus maximus)

- Stand with feet hip-width apart.
- Take your arms up over the head and fold them to grasp the opposite elbows.
- Lengthen up through the spine.
- Fold forwards from the hips as far as you can go.
- Breathe and hold/relax here for thirty seconds.
- (Optional: Stay forward, drop the arms, let them dangle. Breathe and hold/relax here for a further thirty seconds.)

Kerb/Step Stretch (for calves and Achilles tendon)

- Stand on a step or kerb and let the heels reach gently lower than the toes.
- Hold for thirty seconds.
- If very stiff, do one calf muscle at a time.

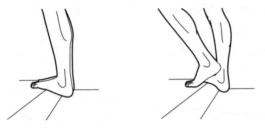

Torso Twist

- See earlier in this chapter (p. 152).

Neck/Head Rolls and Side Stretches

- Drop the head forwards; relax the neck and hold for ten seconds.
- Roll the head to the side, relax and feel the stretch between ear and shoulder. Hold for ten seconds.
- Roll the head forwards again and hold for ten seconds.
- Roll the head to the other side, relax and feel the stretch between ear and shoulder. Hold for ten seconds.

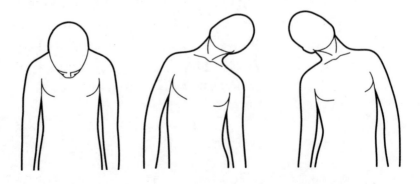

Yoga

- You cannot beat the ancient systems of yoga for offering complex, challenging stretches that benefit all the systems of the body, including vital organ function, stability in structure of muscle and bone, nervous system, lymph system and cardiovascular system function.
- If you have a busy mind, learn Iyengar Yoga (a series of stretches in still poses).
- If you hold too much tension, try Hatha Yoga (breathing and gentle movement).
- If you live a static life and want a dynamic yoga class, try Ashtanga Yoga (powerful breathing, stretching and movement sequences only to be tried under guidance as they can be very intense).

Dance like no one is watching (secret dancers – don't hold back!)

- Play some great music through your headphones and dance freely, making sure you don't get repetitive by continually changing your moves.
- Let go and enjoy the movement. This unlocks creativity.

Strategic use of flexibility movements will benefit your entire physical, mental and emotional functioning. Movement has a profound effect on us, changing the way we think and feel, releasing energy if we feel tired and calming us down if we feel overwhelmed. You may already have some ideas for how you want to 'move more' in your life – so what's stopping you?

9

BEMOTION

How to recognise and manage our emotions

> Without the aid of trained emotions
> the intellect is powerless against the
> animal organism.
>
> —C. S. LEWIS

When challenging situations arise, it is easy to act impulsively based on emotion alone rather than managing those emotions and engaging in thoughtful communication. For example, if somebody challenges your thinking on a point you've made or you discover that your three-year-old has opened your nail varnish and been ever so creative with it on your chest of drawers, it's easy to react without thinking. This chapter introduces a technique that helps you develop a more highly attuned awareness of how you act in each and every moment.

'Bemotion' is shorthand for 'being aware of emotion'. Emotion means 'energy in motion'. The particular kind of energy depends on the cocktail of chemicals that are driving our behaviour at any given moment. The field of emotional intelligence has taught us that emotions, rather than reason, drive our behaviour and that impulse control in relation to emotional triggers is important for self-regulation. That is absolutely right and, thankfully, emotional literacy is taught early now in the education system in the UK, the USA and many parts of the world, with very young children now able to name their emotions and take charge of them. However, whether you are young or old, there is more mastery to be gained from being physically as well as emotionally intelligent.

Choreographer Wayne McGregor spoke about the importance of this. If he 'comes out of his body', i.e. ceases to be aware of the data coming from his body, the rest (meaning his emotional and mental connections) doesn't function. He said, 'We tend to experience an emotion, then try to understand the emotion, and only then do we become aware of the physiology, but we know it is the opposite way around. Actually, the physiology is a chemical reaction that makes us aware of how we think and feel.'

Emotions are the movement of electrically charged chemicals – neuropeptides that rush, seep, crash or permeate in and through our bodies. Different emotions have different electrical charges and exert different pressures on our bodies in different ways. It was American neuroscientist Candace Pert, working from 1980 to 2013, who discovered that emotional messages are carried by neurotransmitters called peptides. She is well-known for her ground-breaking research on the chemistry of emotion as presented in her books *Molecules of Emotion* and *Everything You Need to Know to Feel Good*.

Neuropeptides have either a negative or positive charge, and when we experience an emotion or a change of emotion, it is these neuropeptides travelling throughout your body and your brain that are literally changing the chemistry of every cell in your body.

You can think of the body as the instrument through which each emotion plays. A swell of oxytocin is felt as pride; a drain of dopamine as disappointment; a tsunami of high cortisol and testosterone as rage; the crest of the wave of adrenalin and dopamine as excitement.

If we don't act on these waves of emotion, the charged molecules literally get stuck in the body like the wrong key stuck in a lock. Being aware of them, expressing them and acting upon them enables them to discharge. Both positive and negative emotions need expression.

One of our clients, Paul, a young accountant, had a habit of clenching his fists and bouncing up and down on his feet while presenting at client pitches. Through 'Bemotion', he discovered that this was suppressed excitement that he had not yet learned to process and use. He learned how to channel his excitement more wisely and appropriately in his voice and delivery. His credibility was transformed.

When negative emotional states persist, the danger is that harmful chemicals remain in our cells, inhibiting the recovery to homeostasis. A build-up of harmful chemicals makes us more susceptible to illness because the cells in our body can't function as well. When our brains are caught up in thought patterns driven by negative emotion, we cease to be able to learn new things because the past is not being processed effectively. A backlog of chemicals creates a toxic system.

Circular thinking

If negatively charged neuropeptides (negative emotions) get stuck in receptor cells in the brain and the body, this perpetuates patterns of thinking and feeling that lead to circular thinking. In Dr Pert's 1985 seminal study, 'Neuropeptides and their receptors: a psychosomatic network', we see how our entire body and brain become (literally) negatively charged as we go round and round the same set of thoughts and feelings. If something comes along to distract us, these pause temporarily, but as soon as that distraction has gone, the same old thoughts and feelings return ... unless we use 'Bemotion'.

Another client, Tony, head of legal at a large company, came to Companies in Motion because his 'circular thinking' was creating pressure, even when the issue was not a top priority. 'Bemotion' helped him avoid getting wound up in the moment. He said, 'It's helpful to have a technique you can use when you feel you might be overanalysing an irritating situation. When you visualise it and think through it, you often discover that it really is not the worst situation or person in the world. You just have to step back.'

> **LIFE HACK:** If you notice that your mind keeps running over and over a situation. STOP! Allocate five minutes in your diary later that day, e.g. on your journey home, to do a 'Bemotion'. You can then move past it and focus better on the current task.

It is important that we experience life to its fullest, using the power of emotion rather than wishing that the painful parts would go away and the good parts would last longer.

Research from the universities of Columbia and Stanford in the USA in 2011 showed that gaining psychological distance from negative events lowers the threat chemical cortisol, and literally imagining yourself closer to a scenario in which you handle the situation more positively elicits a cortisol drop and a dopamine boost, enabling learning of new behaviour. In this exercise, we will revisit a significant moment where you would like to have understood a situation and controlled your reactions better, and will use visualisation to explore alternatives, imagining positive scenarios in 'close up'.

In reality, the window between impulse and action is 0.2 seconds – a tiny fraction of time to interrupt impulsive action with considered behaviour. We become more practised at doing this in situations that we have mentally rehearsed, taking time out and re-experiencing significant moments in slow motion and in close up.

Exercise: 'Bemotion'

Identify an event in the past that you would like to understand better, and where you want to be prepared to respond differently when similar situations arise in the future. For example, you responded sarcastically to a boss, you took a unilateral decision and fired off an email to a key stakeholder without consulting team members, or you stayed quiet when you saw an injustice and should have spoken up.

- Remember how your *body* felt and what the physical changes were. Did your heart rate increase? Did your posture or breathing change? Did you get hotter, tense up, go cold, use facial expression, experience feelings in the chest/gut? Write these down on a piece of paper in lower case next to the word 'body'.
- Name the *emotions* you felt. Did you feel regret, excitement, disappointment, frustration, pity, pride, constraint, courage, anger, fear, temerity, powerfulness, optimism, hopelessness? Write these down in lower case next to the word 'emotion'.
- Having identified the emotions, describe the features of them fully in your body as you remember them. What were the directions, pace, sensations and special features of each emotion. How did the charged neuropeptides move in your body? Write these down in lower case next to each emotion you have noted.
- What *thoughts* do you associate with these feelings? What statement(s) concerning this situation went through your mind? Write these down in lower case next to the word 'thought'.

- What did you say and do? What *action* did you take? Be precise, factual and honest with yourself about what happened. Write these down in lower case next to the word 'action'.
- Close your eyes and visualise it – play the 'movie' of this moment as it happened.
- Now step back or zoom out, imagine yourself moving away from that scenario as it played out.
- From this more distant perspective, looking at the situation as a whole, what would have been a more constructive approach?
- Revisit the moments immediately prior to that significant moment again.
- Imagine having a different physical response in your body. What could it be? Perhaps you notice a less extreme physical reaction; perhaps you notice your breathing steady, that you are grounded and centered. Perhaps your eyes focus differently, or your shoulders and jaw hold less tension. Perhaps you notice your body language is more open.
- What range of emotions might you feel now in response?
- In what way can you be more flexible with this moment?
- How can you think about it from a different angle?
- What kind of actions may you now want to take?
- Visualise how you would choose to respond. Play this new movie in full close up at least three times.
- Using upper-case letters, write your new choices boldly.

Well done! You have completed the 'Bemotion' exercise.

Sometimes we have mixed emotions and it is difficult to work out how we feel. In those situations, we can habit stack 'Bemotion' at least once a week (more often if it is a situation that continues to arise) to build confidence, awareness and skill in separating out and naming our emotions. This will help us become more responsive and flexible in our behaviour, reducing impulsivity and increasing choice.

Emotions are an essential, integral and useful part of us that alert us to situations where we need to pay attention. Nowhere are emotions more likely to be triggered and emotional self-management more important than in relationships. With that in mind, let's explore how being flexible is important in relationships in order to create a chemistry of trust.

10

RELATIONSHIFT AND THE CHEMISTRY OF TRUST

How to create excellent relationships

When someone shows you trust, a feel-good jolt of oxytocin surges through your brain and triggers you to reciprocate.

—PAUL ZAK

My husband doesn't like risotto or radishes. I do, and that's fine. It doesn't have a great impact on me. But what about when things feel like they *really* matter? What about when we feel affronted by another person's views or behaviour and yet we need to work closely with them professionally or live alongside them sociably? How do we respect others and yet stand our own ground? How can we communicate with them even though we may be very different?

Creating excellent relationships requires balancing our own agendas with those of others and flexing our behavioural style to create the chemistry of trust. This depends on the balancing of the chemicals oxytocin (core to social bonding and trust), dopamine (essential to goal-orientation/ seeking and gaining reward) and testosterone (critical for independent competitive action), and the management of the threat hormone cortisol.

One of the most powerful human acts that enables us to live together in this pluralistic world is to respect other points of view. Our neuroscientific programming, however, makes this more challenging than it may seem at first glance. Our brains are wired to notice difference and to prioritise bonding with people who are the same – who think the same, who look the same.

As a parent, when your offspring brings home a girlfriend or boyfriend, you can't help but assess if they 'fit in' or if they are different. Our first assessment is made in a flash; it happens without intention before we even form a thought. Clearly, in a diverse, global world, there are many moments when we have to – and very much want to – override our basic programming, suspend judgement and respect differences.

The 'Relationshift' technique enables us to take a stark look at such situations – corporate, global or close to home – so that we can produce outcomes that are realistic and fair and negotiate effectively. Sometimes in severe situations it is about sharing the strain and the hardship equally; in others it is finding a beneficial outcome for both parties.

In businesses there can be tension between departments with different priorities. For example, an innovation department working on new product development with a critical business need to get to market and the legal department that needs to manage risk may cause each other frustration. How can the heads of those two departments work together rather than enter into a battle of wills? I have seen this kind of scenario time and time again as it takes its toll on the performance levels of well-intentioned individuals, negatively impacting their work and home lives. One appears to threaten or thwart the other, leading to a rise in cortisol. And yet both innovator and legal expert are right and have vital roles to play in the bigger picture.

Managing the feeling of being threatened – reducing cortisol, balancing oxytocin, dopamine and testosterone – is critical. This can be achieved through 'Relationshift'. The term was coined at the top of an Austrian mountain in conversation with a twelve-year-old boy called Felix, the son of friends of mine. I was developing the Physical Intelligence curriculum at the time, and I told him I was looking for the title of a technique that could shift relationships from being against each other to seeing each other's point of view. He simply said, 'Ah – Relationshift!'

Exercise: 'Relationshift'

Find a time and place to reflect on a relationship that you would like to improve. For example, if you are experiencing resistance at work or in an ongoing personal discussion. You will need about ten minutes alone for this reflection, and then you may choose to arrange a real conversation.

- Close your eyes and think about a relationship with someone with whom you get on really well. (This helps you begin the exercise with an oxytocin boost, putting you in a compassionate state.)
- Name your emotions and notice how they feel in your body. Where do they start? How do they move?
- Now think about your relationship with someone who you find it hard to understand, and who triggers negative emotions in you.
- Name your emotions and notice how they feel in your body. As cortisol rises, where do they start? How do they move? Are they feelings of frustration, impatience, dislike, anger or resentment?

- STOP. Feel the impasse; notice the specific signature of high cortisol in your body – e.g. tension, gripping, getting warmer, flushing, recoiling, stomach clenching, irritation or a feeling of giving up.
- Resist taking action; center, breathe and 'disarm' – lowering cortisol.
- Enquire of yourself: which of your values or drivers does this person threaten? Is it control, ownership, achievement, harmony, security, certainty, freedom, creativity or status?
- Move away from the impasse and metaphorically 'shift alongside' the other person; mentally switch perspectives. Move your thoughts to what it may be like in their shoes, how they might be feeling. Imagine standing side by side with them, looking at the world from their perspective. What do you see? (When you 'shift alongside' the other person, you release oxytocin.)
- Think about how you can move this relationship forwards. Think through some possible solutions where both people could get some of their needs met.
- Arrange to have a conversation in which you aim to
  - discover and respect
  - ask questions
  - share perspectives
  - stand your ground where necessary (balancing dopamine, testosterone and oxytocin in both parties)
  - agree a way forwards (boosting dopamine and oxytocin in both parties)

SUSAN MAKES A BREAKTHROUGH WITH A DIFFICULT BOSS...

Susan, a single mum and a successful head of sales for a large pharmaceutical company, knew she needed to make improvements in the sales process but was up against senior executives who opposed the changes she was proposing. She tried going into battle with her boss, and it didn't work. She applied the 'Relationshift' technique, which helped her manage herself, reverse out of a head-on collision, sit back and take control of conversations, agreeing where possible and, if not, calmly discussing areas of disagreement. She describes it as being like 'air-traffic control at Heathrow airport': 'With many messages and planes coming in, agitation and my rising cortisol levels will interfere with building trust. It is critical to remain calm and communicate openly, continuing to value the other person's message, especially if you want to change where the other person is going to land. I have been in meetings where I feel the old "me" coming out and I apply "Relationshift" immediately and say to myself, "Get back in your box, dearie," because I know that if she comes out and I go into battle, it will be counterproductive.'

The chemistry of trust

Oxytocin, the trust and social-bonding chemical, is released into our bloodstream by independent neurons in our heart and neurons in our brain to create harmony and understanding. This chemical binds families, teams and cultures together, making people feel happy and trusting. It is designed to create lasting human relationships and collectively reduce cortisol levels by making people feel safer together.

Dopamine makes us want to move towards a situation and realise our goals because we anticipate reward. If we believe that someone else will help us realise our goals, then we are drawn to them because they appear to have our best interests at heart, or because they offer excitement, danger, security, intellectual stimulation, comfort – whatever gives us pleasure.

In the first moments of meeting someone, we subconsciously weigh up whether or not we trust them by assessing whether we 'trust their body'. We look for stable eye contact, open body language, an authentic tone of voice and a responsive face. We also read their deeper emotional state through how they breathe and hold themselves. For example, if someone is breathing fast, shallow or holding their breath and has tension in their face, we will trust them less easily than if their breathing is regular, smooth and diaphragmatic and they vary their facial expressions appropriately.

In our brains, a network of mirror neurons (discovered in the 1980s by Italian neuroscientist Giacomo Rizzolatti at the University of Parma) interpret physical and emotional states. They detect threat from other people's body language and facial expression. Hidden hands (in pockets or behind back), wide stance (like a nightclub bouncer), shifty eyes, and so on, set off a low-grade threat response in others – worth noting if you regularly give presentations. We are particularly sensitive to whether someone imposes themselves on a situation or appears to hold back – neither generates trust.

Mirror neurons are also our mechanism for understanding a wider range of intentions and emotions and are believed to play a part in how we empathise. When we see a person's posture, facial expression, movement and situation, our mirror neurons fire. By comparing what we are seeing with our own embodied memories, we recognise how the other person may be feeling. If we can't identify with the other person, we feel threatened, but if we can we are more likely to feel compassion. Oxytocin is released.

> **LIFE HACK:** Play 'Name their Mood'. Look at someone pass-
> ing by and very quickly name the mood you see. An emotion
> forms in a minute, a mood over days or weeks, an attitude
> pervades over a lifetime. Which is it that you are seeing?

If we want to understand someone and align ourselves with them, we are likely to unconsciously, or sometimes consciously, mirror their body position, their breathing and speech patterns. Their mirror neurons perceive this and social harmony evolves in a dance of recognition and reciprocation. It is the same mechanism that enables one person with integrity to influence others to behave with integrity, or one cynic to influence others negatively. Behaviour is extremely contagious.

In addition to enhancing our personal life, as has been high-lighted in books such as *Good to Great* and *The Speed of Trust*, trust has a clear, measurable positive impact on our working relationships and professional success. It builds over weeks, months and years, through consistency and commitment to one another, as we grow to understand and deeply like or even love each other. Contact makes us happy and we want to work together, live together, support each other and go the extra mile together. But when that same person behaves badly, we feel uncomfortable and trust is eroded. Oxytocin and dopa-mine levels drop suddenly, and we feel deeply let down.

We are social animals. We all need to live in a society and we all also need to have our needs met. When there is change and uncertainty, cortisol rises and puts oxytocin, dopamine and testosterone out of balance. Some people will become more independent of the group and less trusting (increased testos-terone), some people will bond even more closely with the group (increased oxytocin) and may become over-reliant or compliant – smiling even when there is discomfort so as not to endanger relationships – or more protective and resistant towards forces outside the group.

When working or living remotely, especially in teams of people from different cultures with different styles, or with family members living far away, building trust is more challenging. Without physical presence it is difficult to know if we 'trust the body' of someone, or to feel that we really know someone. Shared, face-to-face experiences create better bonds and can sustain trust over months and years of remote communication. When people do come together, sharing personal stories releases oxytocin that helps teams know and care about each other more.

Rash judgements, jumping to conclusions or grabbing at solutions limit the evolution of trust and the quality of ideas that can be generated between people who want to develop trust. Whether in a personal or social setting, on a conference call or in a face-to-face meeting at work, approaching meetings thoughtfully and intentionally gives time for the chemistry of trust to build powerfully.

WAYNE MCGREGOR BELIEVES QUICK RESPONSES ARE NOT NECESSARILY THE BEST RESPONSES…

Collaborating with people across many different disciplines, from sculptors to Cambridge scientists, Wayne shared that, from his own experience as well as that of his neuroscience research, he has found that quick responses are not necessarily the best responses. In order to listen, he consciously gets 'into his body' by breathing lower, speaking more slowly and allowing more silence – more time to open up a 'listening space'. He calls it 'felt time'. Consciously creating an environment where you are prepared to listen and think deeply increases trust.

LIFE HACK: Put yourself in 'felt time' right now; breathe low in your body, raise your awareness, think about a friend and what they may be going through right now. Phone them, and see how the conversation feels.

Behaviours that build trust

Non-verbal	Verbal
• Grounded posture • Diaphragmatic breathing • Smiling • Open body language – 'showing your hand' • Maintaining stable eye contact (or eye contact appropriate to hierarchy if in parts of Asia) • Using a tone of voice appropriate to the occasion and people • Reading others' body language and facial expression • Responding and adapting in order to empathise • Taking time to respond • Not pushing in or interrupting • Being present, creating 'felt time'	• Learning and using people's names • Being curious about others' experiences • Asking open questions • Listening carefully to answers • Checking understanding • Self-disclosure • Being honest and authentic • Not feeling threatened or defensive • Being consistent • Managing expectations • Apologising when you are wrong • Forgiving when receiving an apology • Demonstrating how you have others' best interests at heart

Flexing your behaviour

An important aspect of relationship-building is being able to step towards someone and communicate well, particularly when they have a different preferred style of interacting and especially when this is causing friction.

Learning to be flexible to others' styles of behaviour and communication is a vital skill for collaboration. For example, if you have observed that someone likes to think things through, send them an email with your thoughts prior to discussing it with them – the conversation will go much better. If someone is soft-spoken and you tend to boom, lower your volume to make them feel more comfortable. This is easier said than done because it requires heightened awareness and the ability to inhibit our deep neurological programming and impulses in order to choose a different response and move out of our comfort zone.

The less threatened and more physically intelligent we are, the more awareness we have of the data coming from our mirror neurons and the better we become at adapting to other people 'in the moment'. Working out how to approach people over time also requires thoughtfulness and sustained commitment to the relationship. All relationships go through phases when they do not feel as rewarding as they once did and not as much dopamine is released as a result. It takes considerable effort to re-establish common ground.

> **LIFE HACK:** Next time you meet someone new, make it your aim to discover three things that you have in common during your conversation. Find a way of pointing out the common ground before the conversation ends.

Analysing the physical components of preferred behaviour we find that some people's movements and speech patterns are quick, direct and sudden and they prioritise action and results. Others are fast and flexible with sustained high energy, preferring collaboration and creativity. There are also people who move at a slower pace, are highly supportive of others and who prioritise harmony and consensus, as well as those who are most comfortable when they can be steady and cautious, with structure and time to think things through.

Using these guidelines as a lens to understand each other and develop our relationships enables us to accommodate each other, name differences in an objective way, and resolve conflict by flexing our style.

Exercise: Flexing your behaviour

- Think about someone who behaves and communicates very differently from you.
- Recall an interaction with them in which your differences made it difficult for you to enjoy working/living/socialising together.
- Imagine for a moment that you have changed places with them. Adopt their posture, stance, breathing pattern, and feel what it might actually be like to be that person.
- How could you slightly flex your behaviour/the way you communicate to make them feel more comfortable?
- Take responsibility for your own reactions to others; they are not the *cause* of your feelings, but rather the *trigger* for them. It is your responsibility to work out why you react the way you do and to offer ideas for how you can accommodate each other.
- Be open, humble and vulnerable when building bridges.
- Despite the best will in the world, sometimes positions are too entrenched to change at that current moment. As a last resort, you may have to say, 'This is not working. How could we do this differently?' or 'Let's come back to this another day.' It is of course important to be aware of being *too* accommodating – sometimes politely holding our ground (using strength) is the right approach.

David W. Merrill, an industrial psychologist, along with Roger H. Reid, conducted research in the 1960s to explore ways to predict success in sales and management careers. They created a model that is still popular to this day and uses rigorous psychometric techniques and analysis to help people understand themselves and develop flexibility. Their book *Personal Styles & Effective Performance: Make Your Style Work For You* provides further reading on behavioural styles.

CLAIRE TAYLOR FLEXES HER PREFERRED BEHAVIOUR ON THE CRICKET PITCH...

Claire Taylor and her teammate frequently opened the batting for England's women's cricket team. After the first over, her teammate would always come over and say, 'Well done, excellent. I really like the way you are doing x...' But the last thing Claire needed at that moment was compliments – she was focused on the task in hand, analysing the situation. Claire would be silent and her teammate would walk away deflated. Between them, this was not going to have a positive effect on the scoreboard.

After a few months of frustration, they talked about it and suddenly it became obvious. Her teammate was behaving in the encouraging way she wanted Claire to behave. Claire was behaving in the quiet and focused way *she* wanted her teammate to behave. They needed to swap responses! Once they realised this and they understood each other, they were able to flex a little. Things fell into place, their oxytocin levels were boosted, and they found far greater flow and better results playing opposite each other.

We need to be flexible in our approach to relationships and in our verbal and non-verbal communication so that we can connect with a wide range of people and have an impact on the world around us. This is as important for a parent of four children, each of whom has a very different personality, as it is for a global leader with employees all over the world.

Having established that flexibility is essential in relationships, let's explore how flexible verbal and non-verbal communication help us bridge our differences and connect powerfully with each other.

11

ENGAGING OTHERS

How to connect with people through our voice and presence

> Words mean more than what is set down
> on paper. It takes the human voice to infuse
> them with shades of deeper meaning.
>
> —MAYA ANGELOU

Meaning is largely in our *tone* of voice, rather than in the *words* we say. Ask me how I am, and I may reply, 'I'm fine, thank you.' I could use an upbeat tone of voice, letting you know that I genuinely am happy, or a downbeat or clipped tone of voice that tells you that I don't really mean it. If you try it now, you'll find that the same words spoken with a different tone have a very different meaning.

To express meaning intentionally in this way, we need to be fully present in our body, breath and voice, with our vocal 'equipment' ready to respond to the variety of thoughts that we want to express.

In the strength section, you found your centered voice (pp. 85–88) – one that communicates authority, confidence and stability. Building on this, we also need flexibility in our voice and persona, changing pitch and tone to engage others in what we are saying, inspiring them to believe and motivating them to take action.

Mobility in our facial expression is a good place to start because it helps shape the throat and the mouth to create a greater variety of sound. Try saying 'Welcome, everyone' with an expressionless face. Notice how your voice sounds dull. Now try saying it with a brightness in the eyes and slight smile on the lips. Notice the difference? Smiling engages eye and facial muscles that are connected to the soft palate (the fleshy part right at the back of the roof of the mouth), lifting it, firming it up, moving and shaping the sound. Your voice then naturally brightens, sounding more energetic and more naturally expressive.

We've all raised our voices to alert someone to danger or vocalised softly to comfort a crying child. Many of us will have read a children's story aloud and found different voices for the characters. My father-in-law, actor Jim Dale MBE, holds the Guinness World Record for creating 146 different voices for the *Harry Potter* novels he narrated for the American audiobook market. He can still produce many of them at will, which is no mean feat. With our voices comes a natural expressive range – a gift that we can utilise and enjoy.

> **LIFE HACK:** Next time you find an interesting news story and read it out loud to a partner or friend, connect to the meaning of what you are saying and use a fuller range of vocal tone and pitch.

Joan Beal is a vocal soloist and studio singer in Hollywood known for her remarkable vocal flexibility. The sounds she can produce range from an angelic English choirboy to an operatic diva, to a folk balladeer or Russian or Middle Eastern singer and more. It's a unique talent that led us to ask her about how we can all increase our own vocal flexibility. Joan shared that we all have a larger range than we tend to use and, as with muscles, if we don't use it, we lose it. She practises singing in all ranges *daily* to ensure that she will be able to manipulate her larynx as needed when called upon by a director to do so in order to evoke different emotional states. We can all benefit from daily practice in order to help the larynx be more flexible. For example, when in the shower or the car, try singing in different octaves or try speaking at different pitches – reading a bedtime story to a child presents the perfect opportunity.

Without such mobility, mumbling and monotone speech prevail. Often when a speaker is engaged with their thoughts, but not with their delivery, speech becomes flat. The complexity and volume of thoughts combined with tension in the body, breath and around the voice box can make it difficult for some people to connect with an audience.

SCIENTIST JERRY TRANSFORMS HIS VOICE...

Despite having a rich natural resonance, Jerry's delivery in meetings was so monotone and serious, his face deadpan, that people felt intimidated by him. They couldn't connect with what he was saying. Within three weeks of daily practice, using the flexible voice techniques below, he could *authentically* bring out the meaning in his message and show his natural personality through his voice. Not only did his area of research suddenly become a success story that was shared across the business, he was also quickly pulled into a more senior role and became part of more strategic discussions. People now *wanted* to listen to his opinion.

Shaping our mouths and breathing well, as we have learned to do, enables us to shape and elongate the vowel sounds that in the English language, and indeed in most languages, carry the emotion. If we clip the vowel sounds and shorten the words, it creates the impression of distance – not caring. For example, try saying 'Welcome, everyone' again, this time with short vowels, then long vowels. Which do you think makes people feel more welcome? Long, resonant vowels, spacing words out and using pauses matter a great deal when the message is serious, concerning topics where people feel strongly. At funerals or when announcing job cuts or de-escalating a crisis, the people affected need time to connect with what the words mean and the magnitude of the emotion. This is surprisingly significant because it builds trust between speaker and listener and gives people time to feel.

Other non-verbal factors that increase the audience's connection with a speaker are eye contact and open gestures. Eye contact helps people feel 'seen', indicating to them that they have status, are important and aren't being ignored, which elevates serotonin levels. Open body language indicates that we are being spoken to honestly – which boosts oxytocin levels.

HOW BROADCASTER MEGAN MITCHELL GENERATES AUTHENTICITY TO CONNECT WITH HER AUDIENCE...

Megan Mitchell, a morning television anchor and reporter, shared with us that in her role it is very important to be authentic. In morning television in particular, where people are watching you while starting their day, it is especially important to make them feel comfortable with you – as if they know you. That need for authenticity impacts the tone Megan brings to the news stories she shares.

A block of news stories generally starts with the most serious, then a somewhat less serious story, then something more fun-loving. To help with the shift in tone and to create the necessary separation, Megan will take a breath that feels longer than it should. Others will look at a different camera, look down between stories or use verbal transitions, such as 'On a separate note...' Megan also shifts her body position, which helps change her tone of voice. During more fun-loving stories, she has a tendency to lean back and be more animated. Leaning back enables her to relax and be more 'in the moment'. During more serious stories, she shifts forwards and must be less animated. Matching tone to content allows Megan to authentically connect with her audience, literally creating chemical reactions among her viewers. We can all use similar techniques to shift tone and engage the listener when communicating with those around us.

Humour releases dopamine in others; speaking passionately about the future releases adrenalin and dopamine; naming a collective struggle releases oxytocin; and a rallying talk releases testosterone and dopamine. Good speakers build trust by referring to things that really matter to the audience, letting them know they understand their challenges. Showing appreciation and telling stories draws the audience in and makes them feel part of the journey, releasing oxytocin and dopamine. Even a simple smile releases all three feel-good chemicals: serotonin, oxytocin and dopamine.

LIFE HACK: Smile to yourself, feel the serotonin boost. Smile at someone else, feel the oxytocin boost. When they smile back, feel the dopamine boost. Are you beginning to distinguish the feeling of each chemical?

At work, acknowledging contributions, departments and individuals, showing people how they are part of the bigger picture, raises their status. Research by Harland, Harrison, Jones and Reiter-Palmon in 2004 showed that the degree to which leaders in business showed confidence, articulated a compelling vision and individually valued employees led to significantly increased resilience in employees, a feature of healthy serotonin levels. In families, the way that trust, appreciation and status are demonstrated and discussed dictates how functional and well-bonded the family is.

When we speak with others, we need to calibrate our presence and how far we transmit our energy and our voice. Being able to reach a large audience by radiating energy outwards, then adapting quickly to having a quiet chat with someone is an important part of our flexibility.

Pat learned to do this when she was six years old. She was painfully shy and soft-spoken (hard to believe when you meet her now!). Her schoolteacher set her a daily practice: to read a story to her family from the top of the stairs while they listened at the bottom. It worked! We need to be able to vary our way of conversing in order to be sensitive to changing situations and to reach other people.

Being *present* has a lot to do with listening to what is coming back, too. In fact, we were built to do just that. Have you noticed how you match others' pace and tone of voice, or even accents sometimes, especially if you have a musical ear?

We are all capable of developing greater versatility as communicators. So, let's start training our flexible voice.

Let's train: Flexible voice

Unless you are a trained actor, singer or voice coach, it may seem very odd to carry out vocal drills to train and warm up the voice.

We take our bodies to the gym, but most of us don't think about exercising our voices. The drills below are designed to be incorporated into your day-to-day life, just as you would any exercise. The first exercise reminds you about breath and the next two contain a number of vocal drills. The fourth exercise teaches you to connect with people, which you can practise every time you are in company, and the fifth gives you a structure to tell stories, which you can plan to include in presentations and at dinner parties. Remember the scientist Jerry? He chose three of these vocal drills, practised them every day as part of his routine, and it really paid off for him and his company. High-profile people I have coached, including CNN anchorman Richard Quest and Sir Martin Donnelly, swear by their vocal drills to prepare them to communicate with their audiences.

All this applies even more on the phone and in conference calls. Without visual cues, the voice holds all the meaning. Our ear loses interest in flat voices very quickly, so I encourage you to overcome your inhibitions and try at least three of the drills below every day for a week. You will hear how much more flexibility your voice has by Friday.

Exercise: Remember the breath and 'inspire'
Your breath is literally the 'inspiration' that carries your thoughts out to others. Your thoughts are always driven by intentions – to encourage, to challenge, to criticise, to soothe. When there is inadequate breath, we tend to miss connecting our words with our intentions, which can lead to a lack of vocal variation, pitch movement and intonation in the voice. This variation *creates* our meaning as we speak and without it our intentions are less clear.

- Pick up any book, read a paragraph, pausing at each punctuation mark to breathe for the next thought/sentence.

- Now choose an intention for each thought/sentence. What effect are you trying to create in the listener? How do you want them to feel? Challenged, excited, sobered?
- Use your breath as the moment of clarity and the 'fuel' for your intention for each thought.
- Notice how you naturally use your voice in a more versatile and flexible way.

Connect thought, your intentions, emotion and speech so that your words are spoken in a way that is unique to you ... in your own voice.

Exercise: Develop your pitch range and create interest

In everyday speech, many people do not use the musicality of the voice to express meaning, limiting themselves to only three or four musical pitches; yet most people have a range of 16–24 possible pitches. By increasing range, pitch and tone we will be in no doubt about what you mean.

- On an *mmm* sound, sing a note comfortably in the middle of your range. Then sing your highest possible note (men may go into falsetto sound), then your lowest possible sound, then return to the middle.
- Now join the sounds up by sliding your voice from the middle to the highest to the lowest, and back again. Breathe whenever necessary. See how much more of your voice there is to use.
- Speak the days of the week using as many pitches as possible while maintaining a 'normal' pattern of speech. Notice how when you fully *connect* with the concept 'Monday', the sound is more likely to change in pitch and tone. There is more power on certain sounds *within* the word. This creates changes in tone or intonation that communicate meaning.

- Activate the face muscles. Try to say a bright 'Hello', but with nothing going on behind the eyes. When you make the eyes dull it is surprisingly hard to move the voice. Try the opposite – notice how the voice brightens.

Exercise: Lengthen your vowels – time for emotion

As mentioned earlier, in the English language, the vowels contain the emotional and motivational components. Long vowel sounds increase engagement; clipped vowels limit engagement. Lengthen your vowels as you say 'I', 'you' and 'we'. Long vowels build trust in other people; when you sound confident and open, listeners get a boost of oxytocin.

- Yawn widely and noisily on an *ah* sound; stretch the mouth open wide.
- Move and stretch your mouth, lips, tongue and jaw to extremes in all directions while you say the vowel sounds *ayyy … eee … iiii … oooh … yuuu.*
- Say the days of the week, again overexaggerating the length of the vowels. Now return to a 'normal' iteration of the words. Take the word 'Thursday', for example. Notice the difference when the *ur* sound is short, compared with when it is long.
- Now, pick up a newspaper or a book and, speaking normally, but paying attention to slightly lengthening the vowel sounds, see how it sounds. Get some feedback from a friend or family member.

Exercise: Connect with the audience

Your role as a communicator is to be present with others. It is very helpful to think of communication as 'not about you', but what is between you and others.

- Pick a typical social event you would like to work on.
- Notice what people are doing and saying, e.g. around the family meal table, in a meeting or in the audience to whom you are speaking.
- Comment on what you notice; let people know that you see and hear them.
- Make it a dialogue, e.g. 'I have heard what you believe, now let me share what I think.'
- Connect with people by communicating through your voice and your body so that it is easy to be in your presence.

Exercise: Tell stories

- People love stories far more than lists of facts, so take them on a journey they can imagine being on with you. You'll find they will be much more willing to join in.
- Stories have key *characters, a challenging situation, a critical moment* and *a change or transformation*. People are engaged by descriptions of situations to which they can relate, imagery that helps them visualise the story as if they were there. A good way to structure a story is *SEES*:
  - Situation – where are we? Describe the scene.
  - Event – what happens?
  - Emotion – how do you and others feel? How does this evolve or change?
  - Significance – why are you telling us this? What's the message for us?

There are many types of stories: personal, metaphoric, stories about people realising their potential, cautionary tales and jokes, to name a few. They are an ancient form of information exchange, the way cultures learn and values develop. Humans are the only species able to learn through story; all other animals have to actually *have* the experience in order to learn from it. So use that natural ability and experiment with telling stories.

Physical presence

The body must be part of the storytelling, otherwise your voice will be flat and the audience won't believe you. Make sure you warm your body up to prepare for interaction, using the flexibility movements from Chapter 8 (pp. 151–61). Allow your natural instincts to take over as you express your words with your body as well as your voice. Gestures are the visual equivalent of language and, together with words, help give your message integrity. They also help the speaker's voice come to life, supporting vocal variation (moving the pitch of the voice higher or lower). They are a visual representation of the concepts and emotions being communicated. For example, emphatic gestures, such as both palms down, will help the speaker end a statement confidently, increasing gravitas and authority. That physical movement also helps the speaker avoid an upward inflection that brings uncertainty to the voice.

What kind of vocal and physical presence do you typically bring to situations? When tidying up the kitchen, do you bang things around, frequently breaking glasses, or are you precise, placed and careful? Do you enter a room and take centre stage, your thoughts bubbling over to communicate, or do you slide in and move to the side, quietly greet people and hope not to be noticed?

In 2002, I worked as movement director on a production of Shakespeare's *As You Like It* with Sue Parrish at Sphynx Theatre Company. Every male role was to be played by a female actor and vice versa. One of the research exercises I assigned the actors was to journey home exploring the walk of the opposite gender, imagining that in every way you were built like them, appendages and all! A female actress came back the next day and I asked her to share her experience. 'It was odd,' she said, 'people got out of my way, and I got home ten minutes faster than usual.'

> **LIFE HACK:** Bear in mind the typical physical compo-
> nents of your behaviour style and, on your journey to
> work, try using an opposite type of physical energy. If
> you always seem to be moving fast, driving forwards, then
> try moving a little more slowly, accommodating others
> as you go. If you are very measured and regimented and
> cross the road in the same place every day, mix it up, lift
> your eyes, look around you, swing your arms and break
> your routine.

Exercise: Extend your 'bubble' and 'cast your net'

- As you walk into a room, be inclusive. Imagine you have a bubble inflated all around you, and that it keeps inflating until everyone in the room is in your bubble. This helps you calibrate the physical energy levels you need to engage.
- Imagine you breathe right to the edges of your bubble. Martin Luther King needed a huge 'bubble' to connect with 250,000 people on the steps of the Lincoln Memorial during his 'I Have a Dream' speech. How many speakers have you seen with a 'deflated bubble' – too little energy for the audience?
- As you start to speak, cast your eyes over everyone in the audience, like a fisherman casting a net for his daily catch.

For every situation, the vocal and physical presence that you choose dictates whether you radiate or drain energy, stimulate or stifle thoughts, generate positive or negative emotional states.

Make the most of every moment of connection and communication you have and value your incredible expressive body and voice – they are the only vehicle you have for making your unique impact in the world.

Engaging presence and communication styles are very important to stimulate the collaboration needed for creativity. Next, let's now explore how our bodies and voices give rise to flexible thinking and how we can be at our most innovative and creative.

12

CREATIVITY AND INNOVATION

How to generate insight and influence the future

> Think left and think right and think low and
> think high. Oh, the thinks you can think up if
> only you try!
>
> —DR SEUSS

Human beings are innately creative and innovative. Our survival has depended on it. If water is 5 miles away, we'll engineer a pipe and transport it. Parenting requires creativity to adapt to children's ever-changing needs, as does surviving on a tight budget. When harsh realities such as redundancy hit, our ability to reimagine ourselves is essential.

At the same time, we are creatures of habit and engage in traditional practices that run counter to creativity and innovation. For example, meetings often start with a round of updates that go on for too long and sap energy. A lack of creativity results in no one asking, 'Why are we doing it like this? Is there another way?'

As innovative as we are innately, and as innovative as many organisations are becoming, why are there still areas in our work and in our lives where creativity is lacking? One theory is that education has a knack of drumming the creativity out of many of us. In Sir Ken Robinson's famous 2006 TED talk 'Do Schools Kill Creativity?' (a must-see), he tells the story of choreographer Gillian Lynne, who was failing at school until a doctor identified that her difficulty sitting still was not because she was 'educationally subnormal', as some educators had labelled her, but because she was a dancer. Gillian Lynne went on to choreograph *Cats* and *Phantom of the Opera* on Broadway.

Another theory is that society rewards us most for *convergent*, rather than *divergent* thinking, and we have developed the habit of making decisions before creatively exploring all options.

Creativity depends on divergent thinking, analysing broadly and deeply, experimenting and making new connections. Innovation is a longer process in which creativity plays a part and divergent thinking as well as convergent thinking are needed. When you innovate, you invent something, or find a new way of doing things that gets adopted by society, culture and industry and changes the way people behave. The first stage of a typical innovation cycle is *immersion*; the second is *inspiration*, and both of those rely on divergent thinking. The third and fourth stages are *implementation* and *influence*, which require switching between convergent and divergent thinking. If you have an idea for an innovation, allow plenty of time for the divergent stages at the beginning, and work hard on achieving enough influence or backing to ensure success in the final stages.

Creating dance pieces for my company in the 1990s and early 2000s followed the cycle of innovation exactly. I spent a year immersing myself in the theme; reading, collecting imagery, watching films, researching related history or science, current affairs, absorbing other artists' work. The inspiration or vision came late in that year, as I would begin to see snatches of the piece in my mind's eye, inspired by the dancers and other collaborators. Planning and executing the rehearsal period, premiere and tour formed the implementation stage, and influence came through the reviews and dialogue with the public and stakeholders about the impact of the work, its contribution to the art form and culture as a whole, and the opportunities that arose from it. Over the years I learned that the deep thought and connections made in the immersion period combined with the power of the dialogue with collaborators and dancers was what led to successful pieces. I wonder whether in other walks of life, in governments and corporations, thinking deeply and divergently before implementing change could create better outcomes.

So, what can we do to improve our capacity for creative, divergent thinking? This is particularly important today because across most major corporations there is a focus on innovation. At some, it is central to their culture. For example, Pat worked closely with Facebook for several years and learned that 'hacking' ideas presented by others internally and externally is expected and encouraged. Facebook refers to it as 'The Hacker Way', an approach that involves continuous improvement and iteration. Hackers believe that something can always be better, and that nothing is ever complete. It is the methodology behind the company's success: build, ship, iterate, never settle, improve constantly, disrupt everything. There are entire days carved out entirely for hacking and spaces dedicated to playing games – all designed to foster creativity and innovation.

Today's 'gig culture' is driving and motivating many professionals to create innovative revenue streams from multiple sources. In a recent training session at WeWork, Pat was working with a large group of millennials (all full-time employees happy in their roles), many of whom talked about their 'side hustle' – something other than their main job that brought in additional income. We're also seeing an increase in entrepreneurship. Many people are choosing to develop and launch their own innovative products and companies, and there are critical humanitarian, health and ecological issues that the world faces where innovation is necessary for our survival and development.

CAMILLA ROSS JOINS THE GIG CULTURE AND FUELS HER CREATIVITY...

Despite graduating with a degree in theatre, Camilla spent many years working as an accountant. After enduring what she describes as the 'endless stress of long hours, unprepared clients and working by someone else's rules', she finally acknowledged to herself that she was unhappy and gave up the security of that role to fulfil a long-term dream to establish a theatre company. While building the theatre company had its own challenges, it created a different type of stress that was far more manageable for Camilla because she knew she was doing what she was meant to do – and yet something was missing. Camilla found she missed accounting. She now teaches accounting alongside her theatre work and genuinely enjoys it – even when teaching an 8am class after a late-night rehearsal. She discovered that tapping into a variety of talents and interests has generated more energy, creativity and satisfaction than pursuing either interest on its own. As Camilla said, 'The key is that they are each things I genuinely enjoy doing. Each enables me to recharge. I have the best of both worlds.' Pursuing disparate interests and loving what you do enables us to enhance a positive mood and foster creativity.

Trust, novelty, vitality and positive mood all increase the chances of having creative ideas. Just before a creative connection is made, the visual cortex of the brain relaxes and we enter a momentary calm alpha wave brain state. To increase the chances of having an insight, it helps to close the eyes, relax and clear the mind. When people are wary of each other, their eyes have a sharper focus, inhibiting visual cortex relaxation and reducing creativity. Research from the University of Florida in 2003 showed that high levels of the threat chemicals cortisol and adrenalin reduce co-activation across brain networks, so people are less creative if they are over-aroused, feeling socially uneasy or threatened. When one person in a group is experiencing a low mood, it can be contagious and the serotonin of the entire group can drop. Conversely, if you smile at people as they enter a room to take a creativity test, their serotonin levels rise and their scores improve.

> **LIFE HACK:** To stimulate creativity and relax the visual cortex of the brain, take a walk, change your viewpoint or look at beautiful things in art or nature.

Dopamine is the most important chemical for creativity. It enables connections across multiple areas of the brain – including vision and imagination – and is released when things are novel, fun and when you look at them from different perspectives. It is also released when you see stimulating or inspiring scenery (art, for example), and is critical in our desire to reach our goals. A quiet mind and an internal focus help so that ideas can be captured rather than drowned out by too much external data. Don't try *too* hard, though, because making an effort to be creative impedes ideas. We need to relax, let go, and let them come naturally. As you'll read later, it is also important to detoxify the brain through sleep. Have you ever woken up in the morning with the solution to a problem in your mind, clear as day? According to research in 2004 from the University of Lubeck, Germany, sleep inspires insights; in another study, REM sleep has been shown to specifically enable problem-solving. Pat and I both keep a notepad and pen by our beds because our work requires constant creativity and we often wake in the early hours with a solution suddenly front of mind.

Innovation involves risk and determination and a clear head to structure the work, which means DHEA, testosterone and acetylcholine are other important ingredients in the innovation cocktail. It can be frightening, exhilarating and hard work, and we need energy and vitality to sustain us through the highs and lows of innovation projects.

JOHN CREATES A CULTURE THAT FOSTERS CREATIVITY...

Pat's husband, John, is a former financial services executive. Earlier in his career, he was leading a regional sales team. They needed a new strategy, and John thought he knew the best approach. People trusted each other, so with plenty of *oxytocin* in the team, they felt comfortable telling John he was wrong. He was receptive, unthreatened and curious, showing high *DHEA*, and asked the team for ideas, releasing *dopamine*. Three new ideas emerged in addition to John's, one of which met with a lot of resistance and was considered 'crazy' by all but a few staunch advocates. They couldn't reach agreement on which approach to adopt, so John took a risk and suggested they divide into four teams, with each team using one of the four proposed approaches for an entire quarter. This solution gave everyone status and restored balance, releasing *serotonin*. They all agreed that the approach that generated the best results by the end of the quarter would be the winning strategy and would be adopted by the entire team. In the end, the 'crazy' idea was the most successful and later was implemented company-wide, significantly improving performance. Both the approach taken by John and the idea adopted are excellent examples of innovation in action.

Our habits and patterns of movement and behaviour affect our convergent and divergent thinking, and we can use this to our advantage. One study from Stanford University in 2014 showed that when seated, 50 per cent of people tested had high-quality new ideas. In comparison, while walking, 95 per cent of people tested had high-quality new ideas – meaning we are 45 per cent more likely to have a good idea when we are walking. It didn't matter if they walked on a treadmill or outdoors, it was the simple act of walking that made them more creative.

Dr Peter Lovatt, also known as 'Dr Dance', at the University of Hertfordshire, UK, published research in 2013 that shows how structured, repetitive movement improves convergent thinking, and that flexible, spontaneous movement improves divergent thinking. The types of sport we choose or the type of dance or fitness class we attend, the type of yoga we practise or the type of holidays we take all have an impact on our thinking. The more freestyle choices help us to think creatively and the more repetitive choices help us think in a more structured way.

For naturally divergent thinkers who may struggle to focus on implementation, archery, ballet, fencing, climbing, oil painting and tidying up their desk at the end of every day will help. Creating order, organising your body and environment, punctuates divergent thinking and enables you to capture the essence of what you have explored and begin again the next day with a clear head. Naturally convergent thinkers who want to increase their ability to be creative will benefit from activities like aikido, salsa dancing, cliff diving, joining the society of abstract expressionist painters and practising walking away from a less than perfectly organised desk, ready to pick up again in the morning. Creating a little chaos and moving in ways that are flexible provokes connections between multiple brain areas – memory, emotion, experience – rather than only the pre-frontal cortex where decisions are finalised.

Writers, actors, dancers, musicians and choreographers consider carefully the conditions they need to be creative. To write, I personally need absolute quiet, and I favour mornings to do this, especially the first two hours of the day, when my brain is at full power. Then I run with the dog, do some yoga, and practise either paced breathing or free breathing depending on whether I need stability or release. I always read snippets of different kinds of books in the evenings to stimulate my mind in different ways. I also escape into an historical novel or a TV drama to leave my problem-solving mind alone for a while. Bouncing ideas around in conversation and asking questions is really important for me. My eighteen-year-old son, Angus, often has valuable, fresh insights to share with me on any topic.

Choreographer Wayne McGregor uses a few different approaches to maintain his creativity. First is variety: he likes to have a diverse portfolio of projects he calls 'feeders'. Rather than jamming his schedule full for the next ten years, he protects time in his diary so that he is free to take on interesting opportunities. For example, when we spoke with him, he was working on the film *Fantastic Beasts and Where to Find Them*, had just completed a drone/dance installation piece, and was about to begin a new dance work for his own company. Second, he stimulates the senses. For his first meeting with sculptor and collaborator Edmund de Waal (who uses smooth porcelain, which, unfired, is like fine playdough), Wayne visited Edmund at his studio. They talked about their collaboration while manipulating the raw porcelain in their hands. It was like playing with solid milk or silk. The smoothness of touch and the moulding movement was pleasurable, so more dopamine was released, boosting their creativity. Because of this, and because such tactile activity forms a distraction for the decision-making parts of the brain, allowing a deeper connection to occur between parts of the brain associated with creativity, they had a completely different – more creative and divergent – conversation than they would have had if they'd met in an office somewhere. Third, Wayne creates an environment where others can be more creative, which requires mixing things up a bit. For dance rehearsals, he primes the rehearsal room with music before the dancers arrive, varies the dancers' orientation in the room, and asks lots of questions.

We use a similar approach, incorporating music and variety into our own training design and coaching. Many coachees start by saying they literally have no thinking space in their diaries. One of Pat's clients recently observed that the top performers on the sales team were those who religiously set time aside for creative thinking as part of their strategy to increase their sales opportunities. It is very important to take charge of your time and environment. Changing things around, doing things differently, is important for us all. As a general rule, sitting still for too long inhibits creative thinking. Consider having standing or walking meetings. Working with people, collaborating and, as we have already learned, moving the body regularly stimulates creativity and dopamine release. Variety, such as using music, changing the layout of a room or setting for a meeting are aspects of flexibility that benefit us all.

LIFE HACK: Blocked? Bored? Change your space, start something new. Bring an object to a meeting to spark discussion or ask some new questions.

COMPANIES IN MOTION HELPS A UK LEISURE ORGANISATION TRANSFORM ITS FORTUNES...

A government-funded local authority leisure department responsible for swimming pools, council health facilities and youth and community projects in the South West of England needed to respond quickly to funding cuts and a restructure in order to become a financially viable enterprise in a matter of months. Mindsets had to shift to think in an innovative and enterprising way. Yet, the large team of managers was despondent and disheartened.

With Physical Intelligence, we helped them explore how they would need to behave in order to achieve the task, giving each behaviour a movement and a thought process. By embodying each behaviour, their energy for the challenge ahead come flooding back – an important first step.

We also helped them represent and find solutions to some of the real dilemmas they faced using human tableaus. This helped to draw out key themes from emotional scenarios and they were able to decide how to approach the future. The head of HR told us, 'A week after the programme, twenty business improvements were logged and there was an unprecedented level of enthusiasm and focus. Three months on, with vivid pictorial memories to remind them, every manager present has created a plan for improvements in their area of responsibility and submitted it to the CEO. We are really tackling the need for a changed culture and structure now. The positive attitude is contagious.' The CEO wrote to us saying that our methods were 'some of the most stimulating and innovative approaches to embedding leadership skills that I have ever seen'. We were delighted to be able to help.

LIFE HACK: To stimulate creativity, download the app created by Edrease Peshtaz called Oblique Strategies. Consult it every day and you will receive a word or phrase that encourages you to think tangentially. It's fun.

Deadlines can both help and hinder creativity and innovation. Some people say they feel very creative leading up to a deadline. Raised adrenalin and cortisol levels bring urgency to accelerate us to the finish line. If there has been enough time for immersion and inspiration earlier in the process, then this acceleration will be enjoyable and exciting. If not, cortisol levels will be uncomfortably high as people sense vulnerability in the project and just wish they had more time. Sometimes, a great idea can come too late or we lack the courage to throw something out at the last minute and replace it with something better. Planning a creative or innovative process is important, allowing time for each part, while maintaining flexibility at critical points.

LIFE HACK: Think of something now in your life that is not working for you. Stand up, move your body – twist, swing, shake – and come up with as many possibilities as you can for approaching it differently.

If a project is on a very tight timeline, you will benefit from moving fluidly and quickly between types of thinking. To make the transitions efficient, change your body state and your environment and give yourself clear time allocations for each. That will increase the odds that you will have a flash of inspiration – a creative idea. In addition to her home office, Pat has a few other 'work stations' around the house and finds she uses those other locations most when working to a deadline or on a particularly challenging task. Just shifting to that new environment gives her a boost of energy and creativity.

LIFE HACK: If you need to switch from convergent to divergent mode between meetings, reset your body, breathe freely, stride out, swing your arms while taking a circuitous, scenic route to the meeting where you'll need divergence.

Understanding all this increases creativity and innovation, so let's get into training.

Let's train: Creativity and innovation

Try making your body tense and muscle-bound, then say out loud, 'I feel creative and adaptable.' Do you? Can you feel the discord between thought, feeling and the body? What physical state makes you feel most creative? Physical tension and a fixed focus are unhelpful, whereas a relaxed, alert state is more conducive.

Exercise: Creativity and innovation checklist (you alone)

Your physical, mental and emotional state is equivalent to the soil in which a seed will germinate and grow. To encourage new ideas and insights to come to you:

- Release muscular tension – be flexible in your body;
- Practise free breathing (pp. 144–5);
- Create social ease – remove sources of conflict;
- Smile;
- Try a change of scene – a new vista or look at art;
- Stimulate new thinking by reading and learning widely;
- Quieten your mind and use an internal focus;
- Don't try too hard;
- Sleep;
- Walk; and
- Decide on the other conditions you need.

Exercise: Creativity and innovation checklist (you and others)

Very often we collaborate on projects, building on each other's ideas. A conducive environment will ensure that innovative ideas are fully realised. We need:

- *Trust* – To create trust in groups, give opportunities to socialise and for each person to disclose their personal story.
- *Novelty* – Vary your environment and do things differently. Create novelty/fun, e.g. play a game, tell a story, bring in some playdough, watch an inspiring scene from a film, engage with an expert from a different discipline – bring them to talk to you.
- *Senses* – Do something with your hands. It stimulates the senses and occupies the pre-frontal cortex, so other parts of your brain can make creative connections.
- *Vitality* – Bring energy and confidence and use open and bold language.
- *Divergent Thinking* – Use free-form versus organised movements and environment to promote improvisation. Remove desks and upright chairs, have discussions while standing, walking, stretching, loosening the limbs, lounging on sofas or beanbags.
- *Positive Mood* – Remind people of their value and how they stand to benefit.
- *Risk-taking* – Be disruptive – free constraints – don't play it safe and do things the way you did last time. Purposely disrupt your/others' thinking and feeling even if it is uncomfortable. Approach deadlines boldly – don't converge or try to perfect too soon. Be brave about changes even at the last minute.
- *Immersion* – Read, experience, research, talk to others. Ask group members to bring material: books, pictures,

articles that relate to your project to share. Map the territory, encourage diversity of approach – no idea is a stupid idea.

- *Inspiration* – Look at issues through different lenses to increase idea generation. Use Creat-if (see below) and Open Space technology to see how ideas cluster. (Open Space is a way of engaging people in making collective decisions by creating time and space for people to engage deeply and creatively around issues of concern to them. The agenda is set by people with the power and desire to see it through rather than being pre-determined – giving full ownership to the group. Find out more at www. openspace.dk).
- *Implementation* – Create project plans, test prototypes, focus on step-by-step processes, exercise patience. Be ready to switch to divergent thinking when needed. Be open to surprises.
- *Influence* – Generate external support for what you are doing. Be inspirational, realistic and logical about your project. Invest time in creating materials and rehearsing how to tell your story so that others want to back it.

Exercise: 'Creat-if'

'Creat-if' is a term coined by Companies in Motion. It is a technique that enables you to ask, 'What if?' in relation to a situation that needs creative thinking. It stretches you to look at things from different perspectives, through different 'lenses', testing out how they feel for you and discovering what kind of solutions they offer. It is a great exercise to use when something seems difficult or blocked, as it will put you in an exploratory mindset, enabling you to generate multiple ideas in relation to a question or problem. You can use it individually or in groups – whichever is most appropriate for your situation.

First, decide on a question. You can apply the 'Creat-if' technique to any type of individual or group question, such as:

- How will we put on the school concert this year using limited resources?
- How can I find a new job?
- How shall I best revise for my exams?
- I want to do *x*. What are my options?
- Profits are down. What shall we do?

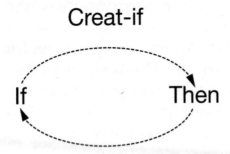

The principle of the exercise is to address your question by starting with an 'if' statement and completing it with a 'then' statement. You can start straight away, noting all the 'ifs' that come immediately to mind. Then you can use prompts such as the examples below to stimulate different types of thinking, responses and solutions.

Make notes on the 'ifs' that you use on the left side of the graphic, and the new thinking that those options provoke – the 'thens' – on the right side.

- If you were five years old facing this question, what would you say/do?
- If you were ninety-five years old facing this question, what would you say/do?
- If you changed nothing, what might happen?
- If you were radical and took the most risk, what would it be?

- If you chose the safest option, what would that be? What would happen?
- If you didn't care what anyone thought, what would you do?
- If you turned the question on its head, what would that look like?
- If you chose a piece of music that would help, what would it be?
- If you were an astronaut/a teacher/a clown, what solutions might you suggest?
- If you asked for help, who or what would that look like?

'Creat-if' can be used to explore your approach to pretty much any problem or question. Here is an example: I'm thirty-five and unhappy with my job. I want to build my own business, but I have a family to feed.

Using 'Creat-if', responses might be:

- If I was five years old, then I would say, 'Get out there – you can do it!'
- If I was ninety-five years old, then I would say, 'Life's too short. Take the first step towards doing what you love.'
- If I changed nothing, then I would stay where I am and try to count my blessings, but I would die a little every day.
- If I took a risk, then I would hand my notice in tomorrow and start building my business (a stressful option).
- If I took the safest option, then I would give myself a year to do market research on the start-up while holding down the job.
- If I didn't care what anyone thought, then I would reveal my dream to my family, boss and colleagues and discuss options.

- If I turn the question on its head, then it becomes: 'I'm going to be someone with at least two careers. It's just a matter of time and having a solid plan.'
- If I chose a piece of music that would help, then it would be 'Start Me Up' by the Rolling Stones.
- If I was an astronaut, then I would build a solid business plan – one that enables me to look at the world with wonder – and ensure I have health and safety checks built in.
- If I was a teacher, then I would say read about how others have done it and ask myself what I'm learning from this.
- If I was a clown, then I would learn how to juggle (as a symbol for the next stage in life) and make sure I know how to laugh at myself.
- If I can ask for help, then whenever I get stuck I'll reach out to my personal group of advisors/mentors.

Having used the 'Creat-if' exercise, I now have options. I know how I want to approach this. I feel liberated and realise that I can achieve both things. It is such a useful technique to help find creative solutions.

We have more choices and are more creative than we think we are. No situation need ever feel static. We can always change our approach, either through changing our attitude to it or through changing the external parameters. There are many practical ideas in this chapter, and the final 'Creat-if' exercise can be used in a vast range of situations. You need never feel stuck again.

Agile, creative thinking and all aspects of our flexibility go hand in hand with light meals and exercise. Let's explore the fundamentals of nutrition and fitness for flexibility and discover how carrots and apples may have given Steve Jobs an innovative edge . . .

13

NUTRITION AND FITNESS FOR FLEXIBILITY

How to support creativity and flow through food and fitness

> Notice that the stiffest tree is most easily cracked, while the bamboo or willow survives by bending with the wind.
>
> —BRUCE LEE

We have already experienced how physical, mental and emotional flexibility supports our potential to be adaptable, creative and positive. Underlying that, what we eat and how we approach our fitness play a crucial part. Overloading with carbohydrates weighs us down in every sense, whereas eating lighter meals keeps us nimble and helps us attain a greater range of movement. Here, with the help of nutritionist Justine and personal trainer Rob, I will share some guiding principles for achieving and maintaining flexibility through food and fitness.

Nutrition

- Eating together is a common and wonderful event that most societies and cultures use to promote social bonding.

Sharing food and drink itself releases oxytocin that binds people together.

- Food is one of life's pleasures. When we prepare or buy healthy food that has fantastic flavour, we generally love eating it, rather than being ensnared by the chemicals in that oh-so-tasty bag of crisps or takeaway burger. Every time we taste something delicious and flavoursome, we get a release of dopamine.

- Eating lighter, easily digestible foods keeps us feeling more mobile. For example, to feel less heavy/sleepy after lunch, choose rice (preferably wholegrain) as opposed to always grabbing that sandwich. Gluten in wheat can make even those who are gluten tolerant feel sluggish.

- Fresh fruit and vegetables are a good source of fibre, which keeps the gut healthy and your digestive system moving.

- A Mediterranean diet is great for flexibility because sunny climates provide fresh vegetables in plentiful supply, tomatoes that are full of antioxidants to help us detox and often fish or white meat rather than red meat. Olive oil is a 'good' fat that promotes a healthy heart and low cholesterol.

- Oily fish (e.g. salmon, mackerel, herring, lake trout, tuna, sardines) gives you the joint-easing and brain-pleasing omegas.

- Sushi lovers will have good flexibility. Apart from the benefits of raw oily fish and rice mentioned above, iodine in seaweed is important for brain development and is critical for thyroid function.

- Minerals such as potassium and magnesium are vital for many biochemical reactions in the body, including conducting electricity via neurotransmitters, nerve impulse, muscle action and cardiovascular health. They are found in soya products, nuts, grains and many fruits and vegetables, such as leafy greens, spinach, asparagus, chard, kale, tomatoes, white and sweet potatoes (with skin), bananas and citrus fruits.

- Bananas are known as a creativity food because they contain serotonin – responsible for happiness. Independent neurons in the gut release more serotonin in response to bananas. Although it was thought that blood/gut serotonin and brain serotonin were separate and gut serotonin could not influence brain serotonin levels, studies (for example, from the University of Ulster in 2004) show that blood serotonin levels also correlate with positive mood, which, as we have already established, contributes to our creativity.

- Good-quality dark chocolate (at least 70 per cent cocoa content) contains the amino acid tryptophan that also causes the release of serotonin by gut neurons, enhancing mood and creativity. Good chocolate also releases neurotransmitters phenylethylamine and dopamine, associated with heightened mood and pleasure, and research from the University of California in 2004 shows that because dark chocolate is high in flavonoids (powerful antioxidants and immune system nutrients found in nearly all plant foods), it promotes better blood flow through the arteries, thereby improving cardiovascular function. Enjoy!

- As we have learned, dopamine is a critical reward and pleasure chemical and is important for creativity. Addiction to the quick dopamine fix that you get from sugar, alcohol or junk food is surmountable by finding other delicious foods that are good for you that are high in the amino acid tyrosine (and cousin phenylalanine). Tyrosine releases dopamine and is found in plentiful supply in many food groups – dairy, eggs, fish, fruits, organic meats, nuts, vegetables – and, combined with spices, herbs and chillies that release endorphins (natural feel-good chemicals), will satisfy your pleasure and reward chemistry completely. *Tom Kerridge's Dopamine*

Diet is a breakthrough book on this topic. Recipes take a long time to prepare, but you will experience delicious and exotic spices and ingredients that may be unfamiliar to you. It's an education and your taste buds will thank you.

- I have heard people say that Steve Jobs favoured apples and carrots in his diet, foods high in the amino acid tyrosine, a precursor of dopamine. Research from Leiden University in the Netherlands in 2014 shows that tyrosine significantly improves the deep thinking of the kind that is vital to innovation. Additional rich sources of tyrosine are Parmesan cheese, edamame beans, lean beef, lamb, pork, chicken, salmon, seeds and nuts.

Fitness

- Stretching our bodies in order to stretch our minds is important for all-round flexibility. There is a growing body of research that shows how yoga and Pilates classes help develop mental agility, and the flexibility stretches in Chapter 8 (pp. 162–5) will achieve this too.
- Stretching in the swimming pool, using the buoyancy of water to support the joints, helps dense muscle bulk to stretch better by encouraging tense muscle fibre to release, and creating space in the muscle fibres and joints.

LIFE HACK: Begin a physical stretch of your choice now. As you stretch, practise psychological flexibility. Notice your thoughts and feelings. Remind yourself that some things hurt, some things don't – that doesn't make them good or bad, right or wrong. Rather than judge your body and how your body feels, observe and accept it. Feel how much more agile that makes you overall.

- Swimming goes hand in hand with the theme of flexibility. Water soothes, refreshes, detoxes and makes us feel, move and behave with greater flow.
- We covered hydration under nutrition in the strength section, and I want to reiterate the importance of hydration for fitness and flexibility. Muscles need water in order to maintain their elasticity. The flexibility movement sequence in Chapter 8 (pp. 155–61) enables the body's fluids to move, flush and refresh the body and brain. This is more effective when the body is well-hydrated.
- Walking is perfectly acceptable as your main form of exercise or as an activity on days when you are not strength training. If current trends continue, it is estimated that by 2020 the average British citizen will become so sedentary they will expend only 25 per cent more energy per day than if they spent the whole day sleeping. Being inactive can take three to five years off your life. The minimum activity level for adults aged between nineteen and sixty-four should be 2.5 hours of moderate activity, such as walking, per week, in bouts of ten minutes or more. Here's how to use walking to develop fitness and flexibility:
  - Walk for thirty minutes a day.
  - Walking at a good stride, just above your comfortable pace, walk for fifteen minutes in one direction.
  - Note how far you get on day one (note a house number or landmark).
  - Walk back for fifteen minutes (aiming to get back by the end of the thirty minutes).
  - On days two and three, repeat this target.
  - On day four, get a couple of houses further or reach a new landmark by the fifteen-minute mark.

– Repeat on days five and six.

– Go farther on day seven etc.

Walking is also linked to creativity. As we already learned from the experiment at Stanford University, researchers found that after the action of walking, subjects were 45 per cent more likely to have a high-quality creative idea.

- As mentioned earlier, golf is the perfect flexibility sport because of the liberating aspects of the golf swing action, which boosts serotonin, oxytocin and dopamine.

- Dance more! When that favourite song comes on, dance in your kitchen to release pent-up tension.

- Racket sports, especially squash and badminton, are fantastic for flexibility because they require you to move swiftly around the court and be highly responsive and adaptive. They also include the 'swing' action.

- Fitness classes such as aerobics, Zumba, yoga, Pilates, step and spinning are social and enjoyable; book yourself in for one per week to boost your oxytocin while raising your fitness level. Make sure it is a class that is at your level, otherwise your dopamine will drop, motivation will evaporate and you won't want to go again.

- Having a dog is great for the owners' fitness levels since they have to be walked, raising dopamine levels by being regularly out in nature. I am a converted dog owner and most of the top performers we talked to are, too.

- Different kinds of exercise have different impacts on mental and emotional performance:

  – For complex thinking, problem-solving and multitasking: try weight lifting.

  – For memory improvement: try aerobic exercise, especially high-intensity interval training (HIIT).

- To integrate thoughts and emotions and deal with fear and anxiety: try whole-body stretches such as downward and upward dog or forward bends.
- Attention, visual processing and switching between tasks: try circuit training.
- Control over cravings and appetite regulation: try HIIT (see pp. 303–4); ghrelin, the hunger hormone, is reduced by aerobic exercise.

A note on getting enough daylight and flexibility

Take off your shades and get light into your eyes when the sun shines. In Scandinavia, which has long hours of darkness, light cafés have been pioneered and these have now come to the UK. Light releases serotonin, the well-being chemical that makes us *feel* lighter and more flexible. After growing up in Philadelphia and attending school in Boston, Pat lived in Brussels for four winter months in her early twenties. She had never lived in a place so consistently overcast and instinctively, on the rare day when the sun would shine, she would literally run to the windows, throw them open and soak it up. The loss of sunlight can be a shock to the system, can reduce the desire to move, and can increase feelings of heaviness and the desire to sleep. (See the Research and Resources chapter (p. 450) for a useful daylight gadget that you can use on the move in winter months.)

There is a lot to enjoy when you build in new food and fitness habits. Though remember that spontaneity is important, too. If you are unhappy about your eating, drinking or exercising, then question why using the 'Bemotion' technique from Chapter 9 (pp. 170–1). See if you can transform the way you feel about eating and moving to enable you to take pleasure in them, making sure that the all-important flexibility chemical, dopamine, is in plentiful supply.

Now, let's make some decisions about how to rehearse and perform our new flexibility habits effectively by taking a selection of them forwards into our daily practice.

REHEARSE AND PERFORM: FLEXIBILITY

It is time for action. We'd like you to spend a week experimenting with the techniques covered so far, then you'll be ready to perform with flexibility every day.

Here's how to go about rehearsing and performing your flexibility alongside your strength techniques.

- Retain the five key strength techniques that are becoming habitual.
- Choose five of the flexibility techniques that you particularly like.
- Rehearse them for one week to explore the best way to integrate them into your daily life and discover what the right triggers are. (Take a look at our habit-stacking ideas and suggestions for triggers below.)
- Then perform them daily for the rest of the month until they become second nature.

(You can come back at any time to choose more techniques to rehearse; then perform those too.)

Here is a reminder of all of the techniques we learned in the flexibility section. Remember this is a menu, so just select those you feel like applying first. Read down the list and mark the ones you think will be most beneficial to you, then you'll put them into a programme.

☐ FREE BREATHING – To release tension, after an effort, breathe freely in and sigh the breath out (with relief).

☐ MOT (Map of Tension) – Remember the body scan to find your tension hotspots and the personal movements you created to address them? What was/is your body telling you?

☐ FLEXIBILITY AT YOUR DESK – 'Shoulder Stretch and Drop', 'Torso Twist'.

☐ FLEXIBILITY AWAY FROM YOUR DESK – 'Golf Swing' to release tension, 'Shake Out' to release build-up of negative emotion or to unblock thinking.

☐ FLEXIBILITY MOVEMENT SEQUENCE – Pre-workout, 'Free Twist', 'Butterfly', 'Figure of Eight', 'Flow', 'Freeing the Hips', 'Freeing the Neck'.

☐ FLEXIBILITY STRETCHES – Post-workout, 'Lunge/Hip Flexor Stretch', 'Forward Bend', 'Kerb/Step Stretch', 'Torso Twist', 'Shoulder Stretch and Drop', 'Neck/Head Rolls and Side Stretches'.

☐ DANCE LIKE NO ONE IS WATCHING – When that song you love comes on, use the moment to move, let go and be spontaneous.

☐ BEMOTION – Deal with circular thinking and consciously monitor emotions, thoughts and actions. At moments of heightened emotion, slow things down and choose your response.

☐ RELATIONSHIFT – Think of someone who is very different from you. Notice the impasse when cortisol rises; reverse and 'shift alongside' them. Make time to consider what it is like to be in their shoes.

☐ TRUST-BUILDING BEHAVIOURS – Remember the table of behaviours? Both non-verbal and verbal behaviours build trust. Consider which of the trust-building behaviours you already do and which you want to work on – for example, maintaining good eye contact, using people's names etc.

- [ ] FLEXING PREFERRED BEHAVIOURS – Make a plan to be flexible in your interactions with others, adapting your style to that of others.
- [ ] FLEXIBLE VOICE
  - [ ] VOCAL DRILLS – Vary your pitch range (vocal interest). Lengthen your vowels (emotion and trust). Bring your words to life – connect with their meaning.
  - [ ] CONNECT WITH AUDIENCE – By what you say, let people know that you see and hear them – ask questions, invite dialogue.
  - [ ] TELL STORIES – Include a situation, an event, the emotions you and others were feeling, and the significance to the listener (*SEES*).
- [ ] FLEXING PHYSICAL PRESENCE – Use your 'bubble'. Remember to expand it to calibrate your energy levels to reach everyone in the room. 'Cast your net', including everyone with your eye contact and physical presence.
- [ ] CREATIVITY AND INNOVATION CHECKLIST
  - [ ] YOU ALONE – Create the conditions you need in order to be open-minded, including releasing muscular tension, breathing freely and stimulating the mind and the senses.
  - [ ] YOU AND OTHERS – Pay attention to the environment for creativity by creating trust and novelty while encouraging risk-taking and disruptive divergent thinking. Maintain a positive mood by valuing people's contributions so that they continue to get deeply immersed in thinking together. Use Open Space and encourage people to make clear plans for implementation of ideas.

☐ CREAT-IF – Remove blocks and change your approach by creating 'if, then' options.

☐ NUTRITION – Eat to promote flexibility. Fresh is best, choose rice (not always bread), eat oily fish, 70 per cent cocoa dark chocolate and bananas for creativity. Experiment with exotic flavours and recipes to release more dopamine.

☐ FITNESS – Walking is excellent for fitness. Vary your training programme and remember the importance of stretching before and after your workouts.

Now, let's habit stack:

ON WAKING

- Monitor tension. Consciously scan through your body and do an MOT (Map of Tension) movement (pp. 145–9) of your choice.
  Trigger: Swinging your legs out of bed; feet touching the floor.

- Check for any circular thinking you may have experienced during the night; use 'Bemotion' (pp. 170–1) if you need it.
  Trigger: Completing your MOT.

IN THE SHOWER

- Warm up your voice by doing vocal drills, pitch slides and speaking the days of the week with vocal variation.
  Trigger: Turning the water on.

ON LEAVING THE HOUSE

- Walk to work or part of the way there – use this for your fitness. (Buy a rucksack so that your body is balanced as you walk.) Time yourself and walk briskly.
  Trigger: Closing the front door; pressing 'go' on the timer. (You may also use closing the front door as a trigger to set up posture technique (pp. 43–8) for the day. If so, just add the two triggers together in a sequence that works for you.)

ON THE JOURNEY TO WORK

- Use 'Relationshift' (pp. 175–6) to prepare your interactions for the day. Ask yourself whose perspective you need to understand. What might they be thinking and feeling? Determine which of these require you to flex your behaviour style. Look at or think through your schedule for today; imagine people's faces – when/with whom is cortisol likely to rise?
  Trigger: Reaching a particular landmark/point in your journey.

AT WORK

- Prior to sitting down at your desk, practise a flexibility movement.
  Trigger: Putting your bag down by your chair.

- Immediately after you sit down at your desk, do a 'Torso Twist' (p. 152) on each side.
  Trigger: Sitting on the seat.

- In meetings, use your flexible voice and presence.
  Trigger: Your hand touching the meeting-room door.

- Widen your 'bubble' (p. 197) to include the whole room and 'cast your net' (p. 197) by making eye contact with everyone as you enter and sit down.
  Trigger: Opening the door or entering a meeting.

- Check your hotspots from your MOT throughout the day and use the movements you chose as remedies. Move every hour.
  Trigger: The pre-set reminder on your phone, watch or activity tracker goes off.

- For presentations, connect with your audience. Practise the first few things you will say in private, lengthening the vowels and connecting with your words emotionally. Include stories to boost oxytocin and dopamine and make your presentation compelling.
  Trigger: An alarm set for thirty minutes before your start time.

AT LUNCHTIME

- Practise 'Free Breathing' (pp. 144–5) as you finish up before taking a break. 'Sigh' the breath out and create a feeling of relief.
  Trigger: Logging off your computer.

- If you take care of your fitness at lunchtime, use pre-workout flexibility movements (pp. 155–61) and post-workout stretches (pp. 162–4).
  Trigger: Putting trainers on and standing up/finishing workout, before taking trainers off.

- Choose a rice-based lunch instead of always grabbing a sandwich. Finish with a serotonin-boosting banana.
  Trigger: Queuing to buy lunch or preparing food at home.

IN THE AFTERNOON

- Apply 'Creat-if' (pp. 212–15) to a situation where divergent thinking is needed to create a range of options and ideas. Use this technique to for solve one of the afternoon's problems.
  Trigger: Going to an informal area for five minutes, before sitting back down at your desk after lunch.

- For meetings, ask yourself what you can do differently. Use your creativity and innovation checklist (p. 210). Consider how you can set up the conditions for creativity.
  Trigger: Reviewing your diary and planning for the week ahead.

- Practise 'Relationshift' (pp. 175–6). Identify someone you need to understand better today. Send them a message of support or a request for a conversation.
  Trigger: Logging back in after lunch.

- Flex away from your desk (helpful in mid-afternoon) – 'Golf Swing' (p. 153), 'Shake Out' (p. 154), 'Free Twist' (pp. 155–6), 'Butterfly' (p. 157), 'Figure of Eight' (p. 158), 'Flow' (p. 159), 'Freeing the Hips' (p. 160), 'Freeing the Neck' (pp. 160–1).
  Trigger: An alarm set for 3pm – or whenever your energy is usually lowest – goes off.

OUT AND ABOUT

- Think about a number of routes that you regularly walk (even if it is just to the break room), and plan to walk with freedom, swinging your arms freely, expanding and releasing tension. Where possible, take calls standing and walk as you speak. Walk whenever you can because it helps with problem-solving and creative thinking.
Trigger: Standing up.

- Use twists and 'Shoulder Stretch and Drop' (p. 151) on the tube or in a taxi or between meetings.
Trigger: Getting in a bus, taxi, or on a tube – as the door closes.

ON THE JOURNEY HOME

- Practise free breathing (pp. 144–5) to let go of the day's tensions.
Trigger: Walking out of the building door or sitting down on the train/bus.

- Review trust-building behaviours, e.g. using names, managing expectations you applied that day. Consider which relationships need more of that tomorrow.
Trigger: Sitting on the train/bus, after ten free breaths.

- Use 'Bemotion' (pp. 170–1) to process emotion from the day, gain understanding and mentally rehearse new behaviour.
Trigger: Completing your review of relationships.

IN THE EVENING

- If you do your regular fitness programme in the evening or you walk the dog, add a flexibility movement sequence

(pp. 155–61) prior to or while in the park and flexibility stretches (pp. 162–4) afterwards.
Trigger: Entering the park/walking the dog; completing your workout/walk.

AT HOME

- Mark the transition from work to home by changing out of work clothes and do a 'Shake Out' (p. 154) to discharge emotion from the day.
Trigger: Closing the wardrobe.

- Enjoy dopamine-releasing foods such as eggs, fish, fruits, organic meats, nuts, vegetables, combined with spices, herbs and chillies that also release endorphins. Imagine how good it tastes and prioritise fresh food for the week.
Trigger: Buying food/deciding what to eat.

WHILE COOKING AND EATING

- 'Dance Like No One is Watching' (p. 165) – play some music, move to it spontaneously, enjoy the rhythm and feel the boost in your serotonin and dopamine.
Trigger: Closing the oven door/throwing the chopped veg into the pan etc.

- Use 'Relationshift' (pp. 175–6) to give and receive support from family and friends – talk about their day and yours.
Trigger: Sitting down to eat.

- Treat yourself to a few squares of 70 per cent cocoa dark chocolate after your meal to boost serotonin.
Trigger: Sitting down on the sofa after dinner.

Extras:

- Use 'Relationshift' (pp. 175–6) in challenging conversations whenever you notice defensiveness or defeat – switch on your mirror neurons and seek to understand them.
  Trigger: Feeling the cortisol rise and the charge of emotion.

- Practise 'Free Breathing' (pp. 144–5) – the sigh of relief before or as you transition to the next task.
  Trigger: Noticing times of intense focus and rigidity.

- Use stories to inspire others. Use your personality and creativity to be compelling.
  Trigger: Seeing people glazing over, for example, on the fifth PowerPoint slide.

- Let go of minor details that are not important by using your MOT as you change your thoughts.
  Trigger: Noticing tension gathering in your body.

Choose the five flexibility techniques you think are most important for you. You will not be able to integrate all the techniques at once. Do include free breathing (pp. 144–5) technique and MOT/flexibility movements (pp. 145–9/155–61), though, as they are fundamental.

Once you've decided upon your five techniques, you must find crystal-clear triggers – moments in your day to which you can attach these habits, just as we did in the previous section. Remember, they need to be simple and easy to implement.

Make a note of your own flexibility programme and triggers here:

Technique	Trigger

Rehearse: Seven days

Take the first week to experiment with what works for you. Remember that making small changes in a number of areas adds up to greater change overall. At the end of seven days, you will have a good working knowledge of the techniques and will have explored ways of integrating them into your life. Adapt the routine to suit you at the weekends.

Perform: Flexibility

Having practised and settled on what works best for you, the rest of the month will fall easily into place. You have a fail-safe plan to embed new flexibility habits. The techniques you've chosen should sit easily alongside the strength techniques that you are using. Enjoy integrating them into your life in order to be able to release tension and move more, process emotions constructively, and utilise your voice, physical presence and self-awareness to build superb relationships, while being creative and innovative in the process. You are becoming more physically intelligent every day.

Now it is time to turn to resilience. In this next section we will discover how we can develop a more robust physical, mental and emotional approach to life that enables us to bounce back quickly from setbacks and learn and grow in the process. You can marry resilience techniques with strength and flexibility techniques at the end of the next section or you can skip to endurance if that is more of a priority for you. See you there.

PART 3
RESILIENCE

Introducing Resilience

Do the one thing you cannot do. Fail at it.
Try again. Then do better a second time.
The only people who never tumble are
those who never mount the high wire. This
is your moment. Own it.

—OPRAH WINFREY

In 2013, Companies in Motion conducted a survey of 100 professionals from all walks of life to find out how they used their Physical Intelligence to be more resilient. Seventy-seven per cent of people said they had no resources for dealing with additional pressure at home or at work. In other words, they lacked resilience. Resilience is our ability to bounce back quickly from adversity – physically, mentally, and emotionally – to adapt to change and to grow and learn while doing so.

PHYSICAL INTELLIGENCE HELPS A TECHNOLOGY PROVIDER TO BOUNCE BACK...

Not only individuals, but entire organisations can suffer from low resilience, especially after a period of underperformance. An accountancy division of a major technology provider was hitting a low. New competition in a climate of accelerated technological development meant they needed to take greater risks, embrace individual responsibility, let go of old ways and adopt new ones quickly, but people's mood was very low. Individuals needed to step up and take responsibility, and the organisation had to break down their silos, and find support for a new set of behaviours across all departments. They used Physical Intelligence to help them build a climate of unity, trust and optimism, showing how positive momentum can be created in teams and organisations.

Against all odds, the division achieved double-digit growth and became the highest-performing part of the company. Physical Intelligence helped people connect with their plans at a personal level and take personal accountability. Since applying the Physical Intelligence techniques, they are ahead of delivery against key initiatives and are starting to improve their business performance yearly in terms of revenue and profit, and their people engagement and customer satisfaction scores have improved. As the managing director shared afterwards, 'Thanks to Physical Intelligence, we're on track for a very successful year in a challenging market.'

Lowered resilience is caused by being under threat, literally, or feeling threatened over an extended period of time, often triggered by change, loss, grief, trauma, or disappointment, or months of high risk and high challenge without enough support or recovery time.

With Physical Intelligence, we can take charge of our response to pressure and start to thrive. Periods of high challenge and stress make us more resilient in the long run if we learn from them. In this section, there are resources and techniques to help you relax, generate optimism, let go of the past and give and receive support.

Genetic factors are at play here. As we know, serotonin has a big impact on mood and behaviour. Multiple studies on serotonin transporter genes show that they come in paired strands of varying length, short or long. If you have two short serotonin strands, you are highly likely to suffer anxiety and low confidence. If you have one long and one short strand, you will do better, but have a propensity for vulnerability. If you have two long serotonin transporter gene strands, you are more likely to thrive despite the environment in which you are nurtured. Stephen Suomi at the National Institute of Health in Maryland, USA, has led this research and correlated it with behaviour in rhesus monkeys who share the same serotonin gene (SLC6A4) as humans.

However, the expression of these genes is by no means fixed. Two researchers, Bruce Ellis and Thomas Boyce from the universities of Arizona and British Columbia, established the Dandelion/Orchid effect in children in 2008, which has now been linked to which serotonin gene combination you have *and* to how you are nurtured. 'Dandelion' children with two long serotonin genes thrive anywhere and adapt to change easily. Those with a short serotonin gene are the 'Orchids'. If ignored or maltreated, they are more likely to suffer from depression, become drug addicts or spend time in prison – but, if they receive proper attention and support, they can grow up to be society's happiest, most successful and creative individuals. A small piece of encouragement or feedback to an Orchid child will be ingeniously applied and they become brilliant in ways that Dandelion children will not. There is growing confidence in such plasticity in adulthood, too. People who apply resilience techniques and overcome low mood often end up with greater resilience and success than people who haven't had to work so hard for it.

When we lack resilience, our adrenal glands (that sit on top of our kidneys and decide how much energy needs to be released in order to meet our changing circumstances) struggle to cope with the pressure we are under. They are required to keep us going at pace, but without enough recovery time and with too few resources and with toxins building up in our brains and bodies. If you drive a car hard, foot flat down on the accelerator, the engine will race and flood. If you slam on the brakes then accelerate again quickly, the car will break down sooner than if you accelerate smoothly, apply sustained rather than sudden force on the brakes and service the car regularly. The same theory applies to our adrenal glands.

For highest resilience, we need cortisol levels to be optimal; not too much, or too little. When the pressure to perform is on, we want the adrenal glands to be able to produce more cortisol so that we can rise to the occasion without worry or anxiety, and then we want them to be able to recover quickly through relaxation. The danger of high cortisol over extended periods is adrenal fatigue or burnout – when our adrenals begin to fail to produce enough cortisol or adrenalin to keep us alive, until we reach a point when we cannot get out of bed. At its most serious, this is a life-threatening condition and needs immediate medical attention. Thankfully, although the term 'burnout' is used to describe the exhaustion after intense effort, most of us only ever experience mild burnout. Given the current pace of life, however, mild adrenal fatigue is more common than you might think. If you have any doubts about your adrenal function and frequently experience low energy levels, please do seek medical advice.

To avoid mild burnout, recognising 'overdrive' is very important. Overdrive is when you just can't take your foot off the accelerator. It can feel exciting, even exhilarating, to work and work and hardly ever stop, but when you feel the need to be achieving and busy all the time, your physiology will soon tell you 'no'. Your heart may race, your skin may start to look grey, your digestion may suffer, you may get frequent colds and notice you are making minor mistakes. For me, diary errors are the first sign that I need to step back and work *smarter*, not harder.

Others experience overdrive as frequent low-level anxiety. High baseline cortisol puts the body in a heightened state of vigilance where adrenalin frequently floods your system.

ALESSANDRA OVERCOMES PERFORMANCE ANXIETY...

Alessandra Ferri is a mesmerising dancer who appears completely in control on stage. Yet she told me about a time earlier in her career when she was often extremely nervous and suffered from stage fright. She would have terrible trouble sleeping one or two nights before a performance. Adrenalin was coursing through her body when she wanted to be resting; her heart was beating hard, jumping out of her chest, and she felt really anxious. Then, one day, a friend in New York asked if she had ever tried just telling the anxious voice to shut up. She hadn't. One night, heart beating fast, she tried it. 'No,' she said. 'SHUT UP. What you are saying is not true.' She said she sounded really convincing, ordering that voice to stop, because she really had had enough of feeling like that. From that moment on, instead of being at the mercy of her chemistry, she was in the driving seat.

'By saying no to this anxiety and doubt,' she said, 'I also accepted the fact that I am not perfect, but what I have is a gift, which is giving to other human beings through dance. That is really what I am doing, and giving is a beautiful thing, through giving my heart and soul. People give their heart and soul in many ways but mine happens to be through dance.'

Ever since then, Alessandra's performance nerves dissipated, she suffered much less anxiety and found a new kind of presence in performance.

Serotonin, oxytocin, DHEA, testosterone, dopamine and acetylcholine all play a part in our resilience. In different ways they each interact with cortisol and adrenalin and play a part in balancing them.

Serotonin is one of the most important chemicals for resilience. You can think of it as a cushion that regains its shape after absorbing shocks so that they have less impact on our core well-being. When serotonin is high, our bodies tend to be more expansive because we feel more sure of our place in the world and are able to bounce back quickly. When cortisol rises, serotonin drops – taking with it our well-being and sense of status; we retreat or recoil because our system is under threat. Serotonin and melatonin (the chemical necessary for sleep) are close cousins, which is why a high cortisol/low serotonin combination can lead to tense or fitful sleep.

Oxytocin levels change as we assess the quality of our social bonds. When cortisol rises, we tend to feel isolated because all we can do is focus on our problems. We either lean too heavily on people or cease to ask them for help. High cortisol can also make us communicate with others from a threatened state, often aggravating relationships by snapping at people when our resilience is low. Reaching out, being honest and engaging in constructive communication are vital to raising oxytocin levels, and being well-bonded drives cortisol down again.

As we know, DHEA is fundamental to our long-range emotional and mental stability. When baseline cortisol levels are too high over an extended period of time, gradually the levels of DHEA decline. When DHEA is high, baseline cortisol becomes optimal and the adrenals function well. Remember, paced breathing practice boosts DHEA, making it vital for resilience, as well as strength, as are all of the breathing techniques we have been learning.

Testosterone is power. For those of us who tend towards hyperarousal, testosterone nudges up when cortisol rises. When our resilience is low, we may start to throw our weight around and be rather bossy or dictatorial. On the other hand, for those of us who tend towards hypoarousal, as cortisol rises, testosterone drops and we silently shut down, collapsing inside, at the same time desperately wanting relief from our problems.

Dopamine delivers the relief that we seek. We want a feeling of reward, rather than punishment. We sometimes say we have a 'punishing schedule'; resilience is being able to turn this into a rewarding schedule by changing our mindset and emotions. When dopamine drops and we feel unrewarded by a situation, cortisol rises, making us feel unhappy with the outcome. Unless we want to spend a life avoiding things, in order to be resilient we need to confront things that we don't like in order to learn from them.

Acetylcholine is critical for recovery and relaxation. Recovery breathing (coming up in Chapter 14), massage, hugs and stroking pets, or simply closing the eyes and being quiet for a moment, all instantly stimulate this vital recovery chemical. Earmarking time for recovery is an important aspect of building resilience. For dancers, athletes, nurses, pilots, school students preparing for exams and many others, balancing effort and recovery is critical for ongoing high performance. It is a basic human need to engage in restorative activities: time alone, time in nature, seeing friends, taking holidays, playing sport. They are also part of the overall health of the parasympathetic nervous system that delivers acetylcholine into our bloodstream.

What actions are you currently taking to support your resilience? For a period of several years, Pat was in a role that required constant global travel – home for one week, gone for three, home for two, gone for four etc. In the early days, if she wasn't working on the plane she felt unproductive, even guilty. Eventually, however, she realised that with so little time to herself on the ground – home or away – she needed to reserve the time in the air for herself – to read a book, listen to beautiful music or watch a film. She had become used to feeling depleted but, having made this change, she started to have more energy and more capacity.

During two months of intensive writing, every Sunday I explored a new country walk somewhere in South West England. It was very important to leave my desk for a day, even though sometimes with a deadline looming I had to tear myself away. I wasn't so wise earlier on in my career. While I was choreographing dances between 1987 and 1998, every moment was spent immersed in work. I only spent time with dancers, artists and producers, and went from the studio to preparation for the next day with very little break. It took becoming a mother to change this pattern. I loved the strict work schedule at the time, but it needed to change. It made me a very intense person to be around.

We also build resilience by applying a positive mindset to challenging events at work, home and play. Having hope and confidence in the future is important, and in this section we will discover how to rebuild optimism, learn from disappointments and setbacks and then let them go, able to move into the future with renewed energy.

Our resilience relies on us being socially connected with other people, on giving and receiving support. Feelings of isolation or loneliness take a particular toll on resilience. People with strong networks and societies and organisations that seek to share information widely fare much better in times of challenge than those who don't.

Practising resilience techniques in times of less pressure is important, so that we have resources available when pressure increases. These resources for resilience are drawn from three types of fitness:

Emotional fitness

Emotions alert you to situations where action is needed, but unease, worry and doubt drain energy, whereas self-awareness, naming emotions, asking for advice and taking charge give you energy. If we are emotionally fit, we can produce enough cortisol to rise to challenges, but not so much that we go into overdrive when the levels of the other resilience chemicals, especially serotonin, suffer. Letting go of disappointments and learning from your mistakes is important, as well as developing supportive and giving relationships that nourish you.

Mental fitness

If our mind is filled with chatter and noise, like a constant whirring in the background, then we are using up energy on unproductive types of thinking. You heard about Alessandra's stage fright and how she overcame it. The constant stream of data from the world around us can lead to distractions and overload, and we need to be able to focus. The brain is a high consumer of energy and needs a good oxygen supply, which means that effective breathing practice leads to a fit and healthy mind. Meditation and mindfulness, which we will look at later in this section, also help with mental fitness.

Physical fitness

Exercise is a significant performance-enhancer, supporting mental and emotional fitness. The same system we use to recover from physical exertion – the parasympathetic nervous system – is used to recover from mental and emotional pressure. If this recovery system is sluggish, then life's setbacks hit us much harder. Regular exercise is key to building resilience, rebalancing cortisol, boosting serotonin and releasing mood-enhancing endorphins. To build resilience, we need to get the heart rate up and down through physical activity at least three times a day, forcing the recovery system into action. We'll discover how to do that in the nutrition and fitness chapter and through small changes – such as by climbing stairs to your office, power walking to the station, running with the dog – you can maintain resilience even at busy times.

PHILIP APPLIES RESILIENCE STRATEGIES TO OVERCOME STRESS...

As the department head for a financial services company, Philip was used to being busy. His department was heavily involved in the increased regulatory requirements associated with a financial crisis. As one of the most experienced senior managers, he had to take on additional responsibility both within his own team and to support other areas. It was very demanding of his time, attention and intellectual energy, leading to more stress than usual. Despite being reasonably self-aware, he found it enormously beneficial to work on his Physical Intelligence.

He said, 'Claire helped me understand specific breathing exercises to further reduce stress. She also gave me other techniques to manage my stress levels and mindset – recording, stretching and relaxing, as well as monitoring my heart rate and bringing it down. Physical Intelligence brought structure and awareness to some of the things I had been doing and took those to the next level. Claire also suggested useful and practical techniques to set myself up for the day. I have a routine for leaving the house – shoulders back, head up, organising my thoughts and focusing on my mindset as I walk out the door.'

Part of being resilient means working out what your vulnerabilities are. My sister Gillian was born with spina bifida, a condition where part of the spinal cord is exposed through a gap in the backbone, often causing paralysis of the lower limbs and sometimes a learning disability. Luckily, Gillian was cognitively unaffected, but during her young life she went through countless surgical interventions to improve her life expectancy and her mobility, sometimes laid up in plaster all the way up to her chest for stretches of six weeks after operations on her spine.

We were a really happy family, but there was also a great deal of worry. Young children form irrational beliefs, and somehow I got it into my five-year-old head that Gillian's disability was my fault and that I should be able to fix her. Because I was so drawn to dancing, I developed a form of survivor's guilt. Part of my journey to resilience in early adulthood was to let go of that anxiety and grow and learn from it.

We all have our personal histories and they impact our resilience. The more we understand and the better our processing techniques, the more resilient we become and the more we can live well and happily and bring our best to the things we invest in and care about.

First, let's discover more about how relaxation and recovery support our resilience, and learn techniques that can transform the way we live our busy lives.

14

RELAXATION AND RECOVERY

How to relax and renew in a fast-paced, demanding world

The time to relax is when you don't have time for it.

—SYDNEY J. HARRIS

Although crucial for resilience, many people find it hard to fully rest and relax given our fast-paced lifestyles. Often, when we finally do get a holiday, we either immediately get a cold or find it takes the entire holiday to wind down properly. Disengaging with our technology becomes increasingly challenging in our world of 24/7 communication. To combat this, we need to weave more restorative and relaxing activities into our day-to-day lives.

Relaxation blocks the harmful effects of stress chemicals adrenalin and cortisol by stimulating the parasympathetic nervous system function and the production of acetylcholine. As we discovered in the chapter on breath, we need a robust parasympathetic nervous system and good vagus nerve function to ensure a ready supply of acetylcholine. This is important in order to bring us back to balance quickly (homeostasis) and improve learning, memory and the ability to keep a cool head under pressure. We enable this by creating regular micro-moments of relaxation – the time it takes to let go on one breath, a Saturday afternoon nap or a hot bath.

Relaxation shouldn't only happen during a holiday. It should occur daily, through the smart use of our time and energy and an effective wind-down routine at home. Effective breathing is important, as is a period of renewal between high-pressured situations (such as meetings at work) – even just a moment to pause for breath is beneficial, as otherwise the adrenals keep pumping out adrenalin without enough acetylcholine to balance it out.

The journey home from work is also an important and useful time. Too often we are in a negative state of mind, particularly on packed trains without a seat or stuck in traffic. Changing your mindset about this moment of your day from pain to pleasure is the way forwards. By having something effortless and enjoyable to read, watch or listen to, we reboot dopamine levels. It could be a soap opera, TED talks or a documentary series – whatever you really like.

One of the biggest mistakes low-resilience people make is that they don't diarise rest and recovery. Look at their calendar – there are no days that say REST, there are no holidays booked in. When you look at the calendars of high-resilience people, however, you'll find they diarise their downtime and have their restorative activities planned in: a massage every week, a date with an old friend, a few dinner parties or social events. Don't be that martyr with the sob story about never taking holiday, completely exhausted, and driving their team into the ground. Be the person who recognises overdrive, can pull back from it, and manages expectations. Be the person who understands how to rest.

In my twenties, before I started using Physical Intelligence techniques in a structured way in my life, I used to throw all my energy at my work, worry about getting everything per-fectly right, then end up exhausted, with lowered resilience. Now, having developed Physical Intelligence and applied it, I have enormous reserves of energy, and can work in a way that doesn't deplete me, by building in short recovery times.

I think about work and life as all part of the same system. Whatever work I am doing, I take pride in it and do it to the best of my ability so that my attitude supports my resilience. I take holidays, but I never feel desperate for them now because I apply Physical Intelligence resilience techniques and relax and recover on the job as much as I can. I also find that a change of scene or specific type of activity is sometimes as good as a rest. When we invest time in that kind of ongoing rest, everyday things like walking the dog retain their restor-ative power.

> **LIFE HACK:** When you know your schedule is very demanding, look through your diary for short windows of respite and write 'REST' in those blocks. Then approach those windows in an extra-restful way bearing in mind the need to *REST* – **R**etreat, **E**at, **S**leep and **T**reat yourself. It is also a reminder not to put anything else in the diary during those days or windows.

When we are in the midst of a busy week in a fast-paced, demanding environment, evenings can feel very short, particu-larly if you are working across time zones and emails continue to come in morning and night. The quick wind-down of a glass of wine or a beer is tempting because there is immediate effect. However, recovery breathing and sequential relaxation (techniques we will learn shortly) are just as effective and it is really worth cultivating your ability to relax and recover at will using your Physical Intelligence.

Parents need to be especially careful to get enough rest. Full-on weekends spent with the children, always with partners, caring for parents, helping out other family members or socialising are unlikely to allow you enough time to recuperate. Even the most social among us needs time alone. Review your support system and arrange for someone else to take the reins while you recuperate. Do the same for someone else in return. We recommend two hours per weekend alone, just for you – walking, having a massage, taking an afternoon nap, meditating, reading quietly with a large 'Out of Office' or 'Do Not Disturb' sign on your door. This takes some organising, but is vital for resilience.

Ryan, a coaching client, was getting very little relaxation and recovery. His weeks were absolutely without respite, and he was supporting family members at weekends. After much discussion, he committed to the same monthly ritual – a Turkish barber haircut with a head and shoulder massage and hot towels. He says, 'I've added it to my routine and find the peace and quiet of that experience very relaxing.'

Building resilience over time so that we can rely on our 'bounceback' mechanism is important if we are to consistently be at our best. One way to gain energy and positivity is to work on the clarity of our mind.

How to gain clarity of mind

In 1975, Herbert Benson MD published a book called *The Relaxation Response*. It was one of the first in the West to give credence to the medical benefits of meditation. Now, with the explosion in the use of meditation by individuals and in corporations in recent years, people are more receptive to his suggestions. Mindfulness training has helped the US Marine Corps make better decisions in extremely stressful circumstances, and soldiers have used Transcendental Meditation to help recover from PTSD. The Bank of England offers mindfulness sessions, and Google has created the 'Search Inside Yourself' project using mindfulness meditation as well.

Meditation provides a simple technique for recovery and superb bounceback from stress. At Companies in Motion, we have built this into our resilience practice.

Boosting the immune system

The impact of all types of meditation on our immune system is significant. Research from the universities of Tokyo and Okayama in 2015 shows that it has a positive effect on the amount of SIgA (Secretory Immunoglobin Antibody) found in mucus on the inner surface of the nose, mouth, trachea, lungs and gut. SIgA thickens the mucus, making it more difficult for cold, flu and digestive system viruses to penetrate into the cells and the bloodstream. A sample group of those who meditated developed a thicker mucus and higher levels of SIgA than those who didn't, indicating a more robust immune system. To learn more about the science and potential regarding different types of meditation, read Herbert Benson's book *The Relaxation Response*, and Stephanie Shanti's book *Prisoners of Our Own Mind*. And try MUSE, a brain-sensing headband and app that helps you meditate with biofeedback.

In addition to meditation, we need time for reflection so that we can make conscious decisions going forwards. When Pat talked to American football player Jarrod Barnes about this, she was impressed by how strategic he is about his relaxation and recovery. The time for reflection is something he *schedules in*, believing it is the greatest way to gain perspective. He says, 'You need time to think about what you are doing, what you did this past day or week, how you utilised your time and how certain things made you feel, even how certain foods made you feel. But also how all of that impacted you mentally, emotionally and spiritually. Our society moves so fast and focuses so much on instant gratification and trying to do more and more and be bigger and better, that time for reflection as the norm has been lost.'

Let's train: Relaxation and recovery

Exercise: Sequential relaxation

Even when we think we are relaxed, there is often residual muscle tension and shallow breathing. The 'progressive' or 'sequential relaxation' technique was developed by an American physician called Edmund Jacobson in the 1930s. He was the first to prove that the technique was effective against insomnia and high blood pressure. Tensing and releasing muscle groups provides a great release, and this kind of exercise can easily be done on a train journey or before going to sleep at night.

Working sequentially through the different muscle groups of the body, use your out-breath to tense and your in-breath to release. Most people like to breathe out and tense over a count of five, hold for a few moments, then breathe in and release over another count of five.

Work through your body as follows:

- Toes, feet, heels and ankles
- Calves, knees and thighs
- Bottom, lower back and lower abdominal muscles
- Middle back and middle abdominal muscles
- Upper back, chest and shoulders
- Arms, hands and fingers
- Head, neck, face and jaw
- Whole body

- At the end, sit, stand or lie still and imagine your muscles are full of fine sand that pours out through tiny pores in your skin, draining away tension.

The relaxation response

Meditative practice changes the type of brain waves that are most prevalent. We don't want beta waves – they are chaotic. We *do* want alpha, theta, and delta waves, however, because they bring clarity, calm and deep relaxation. According to Herbert Benson MD and many other researchers working to understand the physiological changes as a result of meditating, this is easily detectable in brain scans of both novice and experienced meditators.

Exercise: The relaxation response (as devised by Herbert Benson)

- Relax, especially the eye muscles and jaw.
- Select a word, e.g. 'one' or 'flow'.
- Breathe in and, silently, in your mind, speak the word repeatedly on the out-breath.

You can use this technique in the moment you are becoming overstressed, or you can set a timer for you to take ten minutes aside at an allotted time. The idea is that you are able to gradually live *in* the relaxation response. It becomes a part of you.

Exercise: Alternative meditative breathing practice

Count each breath in and out up to ten.

- Breathe in and mentally count one.
- Breathe out and mentally count two.

- Breathe in and mentally count three, and so on up to ten.
- Then, begin again at one. (Continue this pattern for ten minutes.)

Recovery breathing

Despite your best efforts, there may still be times of high pressure. If you are feeling overwhelmed because things are going wrong or if your heart rate is racing and you feel exhausted or in overdrive, then you need to use recovery breathing *immediately and regularly*. Otherwise, you will not be able to make your best decisions.

This technique is used by many physicians, including Harley Street psychiatrists, as part of programmes to help stressed businessmen and women, negotiators and CEOs who are suffering from burnout get back to work. After recovery from burnout, individuals come back far stronger and more resourceful than they were before, often reporting up to 10 per cent improvement in the quality of the outcomes they achieve as they continue their careers. The long out-breath enables heavy, toxic carbon dioxide to be expelled properly from the lungs and allows lighter oxygen to enter. The counting enables you to regain control.

Exercise: Recovery breathing

- Put two fingers on your pulse point in your wrist or neck. Count the pulse for a minute. Record the number. Write it down.
- Find somewhere to recline or lie down. Rest your hands face down on your thighs.
- Breathe out all the way.
- Breathe in deeply.

- Pause for a moment.
- Breathe out while counting to ten (press your fingers one by one onto your thigh as you count).
- Expel all remaining air.
- Repeat ten times.
- Retake your pulse. You should experience a drop in pulse rate – through breathing practice you can change your physiology and instruct your body to regain a calm focus.

It bears repeating here that real burnout is a serious, life-threatening condition. It is advisable to see a doctor and receive medical support in addition to adopting a full pro-gramme of Physical Intelligence practice under supervision. Signals of burnout are: frequent panic attacks, regularly feeling overwhelmed, feeling isolated, anxious, joyless and just about coping, having your heart rate regularly racing out of control, crying, feeling extreme fatigue, and breaking out into sweats.

REST

R – Retreat
E – Eat
S – Sleep
T – Treat

Retreat: We all need short retreats away from the hustle and bustle of life. Holidays and weekends are vitally important because they provide time for the adrenal glands to fully recharge. Make time for the following activities in your sched-ule. Select those that most appeal to you and schedule them into your calendar before you finish this chapter:

- Nap
- Walk in nature
- Practise recovery breathing
- Swim
- Do yoga
- Stretch
- Go to a relaxation class
- Soak up some sunshine
- Spend time with family and friends

Eat: Salads and sunshine go hand in hand. Whether on holiday or a staycation – or on any day of the week for that matter – challenge yourself to do the following:

- Take time to prepare fresh food, meat, fish and vegetables, experimenting with new and healthy recipes. This brings sensory pleasure and boosts the feel-good chemical dopamine, as well as helping the liver to recover from all those times when we grabbed a quick sandwich, reached for the sugary snack or had that extra glass of wine.
- Drink lots of water.
- Eat beetroot, which helps to cleanse the liver.
- Explore restorative non-alcoholic drinks that stimulate the parasympathetic nervous system with your nutritionist. Magnesium and camomile combinations are excellent.

Sleep: Many people know that seven to nine hours' sleep is optimal for human beings, yet many people get far less.

- Waking to an early alarm day after day is demanding on the adrenals, so allow yourself to wake naturally a couple of days a week. This may add only thirty minutes or an hour onto your sleep cycle, but it is still beneficial. This is because when we wake naturally, cortisol (which wakes us up in the morning) and melatonin (the sleep chemical, a sister of serotonin – the balance, happiness and well-being chemical) rebalance and the clearing and healing process that happens in our brains while we sleep can be completed rather than interrupted. If you sleep uninterrupted and allow yourself to wake naturally for an extended period of time, the brain and body is cleansed, inflammation is reduced and healing occurs.

- Plan a holiday where there are no activities that require an alarm clock.

Treat: There are two types of 'treats': those that are nice to start with but to which we are mildly addicted (sugar and alcohol being the main contenders), and those that are truly restorative. Keep the addictive treats to a minimum and develop a habit of indulging in the latter. Good treats boost dopamine (the pleasure and reward chemical) and serotonin (the happiness chemical). The next time you are tempted to reach for the addictive treats, do one of the following instead:

- Immerse yourself in a good novel
- Consume healthy food and drink
- Have a massage
- Have a good, supportive conversation
- Appreciate a hot shower or bath
- Attend the theatre
- Visit an art gallery
- Go out dancing
- Play a game of sport

It can be a real challenge to switch into *REST* and enjoy it. The foot remains rigid on the accelerator and it takes time and skill to touch the brake without derailing the vehicle. However, you now have plenty of resources to *REST*, to be used both in the moment and as part of your strategic planning.

Having overhauled our relaxation and recovery habits, let's move on to consider our attitude to resilience in more depth. How can we develop a realistic yet optimistic mindset and understand how to process the negative impact events can have on us quickly and robustly? Let's find out.

15

THE CHEMISTRY OF OPTIMISM

How to generate a robust mindset

*[Having searched for a poignant quote
about optimism and drawn a blank, I
asked my son Angus what it means to
him. He said:]*

Optimism shouldn't be an excuse to avoid
your problems, but a tool to help you solve
them and say, 'I can do this.'

—ANGUS DALE

Let's dig deeper now into some demanding but rewarding techniques that enable us to regain optimism in the face of challenges. Optimism is easy when things are going well, but can be the first thing to go when setbacks happen. Sometimes the world appears to be out of our control and we need techniques to get our hands back on the wheel.

In moments of doubt or pessimism, our protective, defensive mind says, 'Why bother? . . . nice try, but it'll never really work out for you . . . stay under the duvet . . . who are you to expect great things of yourself? . . . don't expose yourself . . . it's not worth it . . . is this where I mess up once and for all?'

And then there's the classic 'imposter syndrome', which may add: 'Will I be found out as a fraud?' Such thoughts arise when our sense of personal status drops. It is a different story when the reviews are great. We feel expansive and proud, like someone with a purpose who has a right to be here.

Serotonin, oxytocin and dopamine are the critical ingredients for optimism. When a setback happens, our self-esteem drops, our bubble bursts and we fear our social status will drop with it. In this frame of mind, it is far more difficult to take the actions necessary to move forwards. People fear they will be passed over for promotion, won't be accepted into that university course, won't make their parents proud; an actor fears the phone will stop ringing; sports professionals fear losing form and being beaten by younger athletes. In the strength section, we explored how accurate analysis and learning from failures is critical to competitive success and the chemistry of confidence. For the chemistry of optimism, we need heightened awareness of our emotions and the courage to face up to the negative ones, enhanced body awareness and a shift in mindset.

A learning mindset

Psychologist Dr Carol S. Dweck's research on growth versus fixed mindsets has changed the way we think about optimism. A growth mindset interprets any setback or mistake as an area for growth rather than a failure leading to loss of confidence. Feedback is therefore welcomed, as it provides useful direction towards areas to work on, rather than providing a commentary on personal traits, good or bad.

LIFE HACK: Think of a setback or mistake you have made. With an imaginary camera, zoom in and see a 'close-up' of yourself. Remember the intensity of the feelings at the moment of impact. Now zoom out and hover in wide angle over a view of the whole scene, including events past and present. See all the elements that are contributing. Know that you are not alone and that others have experienced, or are at this very moment experiencing, similar situations. Decide to be curious and to learn.

Cultivating a learning mindset is addressed in a technique we call 'Bounce Positive'. This involves being able to frame all events as learning opportunities and to develop a robust, realistic optimism. Being optimistic is, as philosopher Leibniz puts it, the mindset of the 'best possible world'.

In this chapter we will explore how to reboot serotonin, oxytocin and dopamine levels by using our bodies, processing negative events efficiently and applying a learning mindset to everything we do.

How we interpret events affects our outlook. We can learn to generate realistic optimism, a proactive state that creates optimal mental and emotional health. Research indicates that optimists have higher-paid jobs and will persevere for longer on tasks than pessimists; they also have stronger immune systems. Beware though – extreme optimists are also more likely to smoke and are less likely to prepare adequately for important events or save funds for the future.

Our history has a strong bearing on how we interpret events. The amygdala, the emotional centre of the brain, is the quickest but least accurate to respond. Close to our memory banks in the hippocampus, it checks every current event against the past, looking first for threats to survival. We have to be able to identify, recognise and refute irrational threatened responses and choose responses that generate realistic optimism.

Our priming – what people tell us is true prior to something – is also important. Neuroscientist Sara Bengtsson's research in 2011 showed that when students were primed as 'stupid' in relation to a task, they were less likely to reflect on errors and learn from mistakes. If they were primed as 'clever', they reflected for longer and their performance improved. For our overall resilience and for our optimism, we need to take charge of that priming.

Our inner voices, formed in our past, prime us in certain ways by telling us stories in our minds that create inner conflict. We need to know who these voices are, where they come from, which we should listen to and how we can integrate them so that we can live peacefully with ourselves.

Alessandra commented on this, saying, 'Isn't it true that we feel at peace if we integrate all the aspects of who we are? I mean, you can't get rid of your shadow or your insecurity, or your ego. We have all those things and it's part of being human; you can't suddenly be a saint. We are at peace when we embrace them all – even the dark side. If one side is not balanced then we go into a tunnel of darkness, which we all do from time to time.'

She continued: 'This is quite a new discovery for me in the past year or two: this real vision of these inner voices that tell me things, and some of it is your inner voice that wants to sabotage you. We all have these in different proportion, but I have decided that I don't want that side of me to take over, so when I see it happening I try to say, "Sorry, NO." This is how I use my willpower. If you have a strong will it doesn't mean you don't have the side of you that wants to give up – we all do. Sometimes I let it have a little rope, just to give it a little satisfaction. Then after a day or two I say, "That's it – done." Every human being needs to find their most positive self.'

With that inspiration, let's train our mindset to be optimistic.

Let's train: The chemistry of optimism

You will learn five techniques to promote optimism – 'Jump', 'Bounce Positive', 'I Won't/I Will', 'Curiosity Generator' and 'The Falling Leaf', which uses the power of visualisation to quell the inflammation that occurs when your system is in a severe threat response.

Exercise: Jump

The act of jumping changes how we feel. If we jump for joy, then we can also *generate* feelings of joy through jumping. Everything about the act of jumping defies defeat: it is all about rebounding, pushing up, reaching higher, bouncing back. You can do this exercise on a carpeted or wooden floor or grass (avoid concrete flooring as it is too hard); some people even like to use a trampoline. The older we get, the less we feel we should or can jump. It is important to defy this notion. Do this exercise daily, building up the amount of time you spend jumping. (If you have past injuries or medical conditions, please check with your medical practitioner prior to trying this and do not execute this exercise if in any doubt of its safety.)

- Find a place with a 'giving' or cushioned floor.
- Ground yourself.
- Bend your knees – directing them over your toes.
- Push away from the floor and … jump!
- Land in the same position you started from – bending your knees.
- Continue jumping for ten seconds on days one to three, then rest a day. On days four to six, jump for fifteen seconds, then rest a day, and so on, until you build up to one minute. Use the kerb/step stretch for your calves afterwards.
- Notice how jumping makes you feel more optimistic.

Exercise: 'Bounce Positive'

I used this technique frequently in 1993, the year when my dance company reached critical acclaim. Without it I do not believe we would have achieved what came next. I was creating a new work entitled 'Grace Not Grace' to be performed in the season of dance called Spring Loaded at the Place Theatre in London. This represented the achievement of a five-year goal, so the stakes were high. As much as I was excited, I also felt scared. My mind would often interfere with my creativity, particularly on the journey to and from rehearsal. So, every morning and every night, I did a 'Bounce Positive' process to regain my self-esteem and my belief in the project. Following the London performances, we were chosen to represent Britain in a series of prestigious European festivals. Because I had maintained my optimism along the way, I was able to fully celebrate our success. We deserved it, and I could look towards the future with pleasure and excitement, not fear. I still use it regularly to this day.

- *Situation.* Think of a situation recently that has made you feel less than optimistic about the future. Identify the specific moment when you felt your chemistry drop and relive the moment in your mind and body. Describe the physical sensations you felt and name the emotions. Place your hand on the area of your body where you felt the impact of the emotions.
- *Self-talk.* Write down the negative statements, accusations and assumptions running through your mind, e.g. I will never be able to cope with this quantity of work, I have no resources, I am not good enough to do this, I am incompetent, I will be found out, I should toughen up, my boss thinks I am failing, I am a bad parent, so-and-so is a fool, things always go wrong in the end etc. Notice how harsh

and accusatory such assumptions, absolutes, judgements and criticisms can be. (This part of the exercise is not very pleasant, and you may experience some powerful emotions, but it is necessary.)

- *Overcome negativity.* Now, move your focus from your amygdala-driven background mind to your pre-frontal cortex – the front of your mind. Consider each statement above in a more objective way. Take deep breaths and keep processing your emotions as they arise.

- Use robust logic to *verify, deny* or *question* each statement. For example, if your self-talk is, 'I will never be able to cope with this quantity of work', then examine the use of the word 'never'. The statement claims to know what will happen in the future. A more helpful statement might be: 'There is a lot to do and it is important that I take stock and manage expectations – I will set aside time to consider my options.' This exercise is not about glossing over issues; rather about facing them head-on, and looking at them with objective reality and positive self-regard.

- You may verify a statement such as – 'The budget has been cut', or 'I find *x* difficult to manage.' These are accurate statements about the reality.

- A deniable statement might be – 'I am just no good.' First of all, it is too absolute. Is there really no good in you? Second, it is too broad. What are you 'no good' at exactly? Notice how inaccurate absolute language is and how it blocks our self-respect.

- A questionable statement might be: 'My boss regrets appointing me.' This statement is an assumption and it is important to acknowledge that it also is a loaded, absolute statement. 'Dan is frustrated with me' is also questionable. He may well be frustrated but perhaps it is about something else entirely. 'This won't turn out well' and 'I am going to mess this up' are questionable and deniable statements. Apart from their inherent pessimism, they are framed in the future tense, so how can you know?

- *Acknowledge reality.* Once you have a series of statements that you have verified, denied or questioned, accurately describe what the reality of the situation is and what is really true about you. Too often, we quickly jump to irrational conclusions that whirr in the background like a rogue programme running in the background of your computer, reducing current processing power. Notice resistance but continue to take your own side. Be fair and balanced in your view of the situation. So, it might be: 'Dan shouted at me. I don't fully understand what is going on, so I will be sure to ask him. Meanwhile, I know that I am competent; I am doing my best in a challenging environment.'

- *Choose actions.* From this realistic perspective, consider what choices you are making, what actions you want to take, and how you can be creative with your situation. For example: 1) Talk to Dan when the time is right; 2) Put an hour aside to look at priorities with a cool head; 3) Call a mentor for advice on how to manage expectations and push back on timelines. As you do this, you may notice a sense of weight lifting from you – serotonin and oxytocin levels are rising and you should feel a resurgence of optimism.

- *Capture learning.* Finally, ask yourself, 'What did I learn from this experience and how can I embed this learning? What historical "rabbit hole" is the source of my interpretation of this event? What specifically can I watch out for in future situations to pre-empt this reaction?'

Thought patterns change over time and create a different set of emotions and long-term attitudes. We can 'hack into' interpretations in order that we can make different choices. With practice, you will be able to 'Bounce Positive' quickly, taking thirty seconds to a minute to verify, deny or question thoughts. Sometimes, where new situations arise and emotions run high, it is important to give this exercise ten to twenty minutes in order to understand your reactions more deeply.

Exercise: 'I Won't/I Will'

When life throws something at us that we did not choose – for example, an illness, death of a loved one, a redundancy, or trouble with one of our children – it is natural to resist. Cortisol rises rapidly and our entire system becomes inflamed. Depending on whether we tend towards hyper- or hypoarousal, we feel anger and resentment or hopelessness and resignation. So what can we do? Somehow, we have to live through the situation in hand, be willing to accept it, become stronger and learn through it. We must try, hard though it may be, to find peace, opportunity and motivation for positive action.

PAT COMES TO TERMS WITH LOSING HER MUM...

Many of us relate to losing a loved one and how hard that can be to accept. Pat's mum was eighty-two when she was diagnosed with late-stage cancer of the gallbladder and given only months to live. All of the doctors were saying that there was no treatment they could offer other than palliative care.

Initially, Pat, a natural problem-solver, wouldn't accept it. She railed against it, writing to contacts around the country, ready to move heaven and earth to find a solution. In private, she railed forcefully against the limitations of medical research, her deceased father and death itself, a process that enabled her to express the 'I won't' – the denial – fully and forcefully.

The physical act of 'railing' – shaking her raised fists in the air, screaming to the heavens, verbally expressing the emotions in private – allowed Pat to process and move through the various emotions, which ultimately enabled her to relinquish the desire to control her mother's treatment, release the resistance and accept the inevitable. When she did that, a sense of peace descended, allowing Pat's primary focus to be on what she *could* control – creating a peaceful, comfortable environment in her home where her mother spent her final days. While it was still a devastating time, it was a blessing for Pat to be able to care for her through her illness. The 'I will' created a sense of peace.

'I Won't/I Will' is a powerful private exercise that discharges the chemistry of extreme negative emotion and replaces it with the chemistry of optimism.

- Prepare by securing a private environment where you can speak out loud.
- Place your hand on the area of your body where your emotions are having the most impact.
- Breathe and feel the full force of your resistance.
- Use this force to say out loud, or in your mind, 'I won't have this, I don't want this.' Repeat these phrases – or versions of them – again and again, expressing the full force of the resistance, until you run out of energy. Some people like to push against a wall or make fists and punch the air. Some people cry during this part.
- Once you feel your energy is sapped, pause, and breathe.

- When you are ready, try saying the words 'I will take this on' or 'I will handle this'. You are not saying you submit to what others want, or something that will be harmful to you: you are saying you will accept what is happening – you will apply your energy and commitment to dealing with it and take clear-headed, positively motivated action. Some people like to stand still, open the chest, open the palms of the hands and look up.
- Now, if you have committed fully to executing the steps above, you will have literally changed the negative charge of the emotions you were feeling and be able to decide what you will do now. What action do you choose to take?

The choices that occur to you after you discharge the chemistry of shock and resistance are often surprising. We unearth resources that we did not know we had.

Exercise: 'Curiosity Generator'
Once you know how to become more optimistic with regard to individual circumstances, it is worth practising this next technique which fosters curiosity as an essential feature of learned optimism and a growth mindset. Curiosity is a strong desire to learn or know something, and the spirit of enquiry is a great alternative to snap judgements and presumptions. Broadening the mind enables us to understand multiple perspectives and be more resilient in situations of conflict. Curiosity is vital in conversations that may need to cover difficult ground, or where there are strong feelings, because it enables you to discover and respect others' perspectives as the starting point for finding resolution.

- Choose a situation that you find difficult to understand.
- Note down three statements, assumptions or judgements about this situation.

1. ....
2. ....
3. ....

- Notice how your body feels – note it down.

....

- Notice which emotions you are experiencing – note them down.

....

- 'Zoom out' – see the whole situation in wide angle.
- Breathe freely and put your body and mind into an open and receptive state – i.e. release tension, sit/stand tall and center yourself.
- 'Release your inner five-year-old'. Ask yourself and others, 'why, how, where, what, tell me more ...'
- Start your sentences with 'I am curious, tell me ...'
- Note down your insights.

....
....
....

- Be patient – the answers may not come immediately.
- Note down the ideas this process gives you for moving forwards in the situation.

....
....
....

Exercise: 'Falling Leaf'

Here is an exercise that will allow you to manage acute negative emotions, dissipating them enough so that you can continue your day. As we know, stimulating the visual cortex of the brain releases dopamine; through the 'Falling Leaf' visualisation, we can temporarily turn negative emotional states into more manageable optimistic ones.

- Do three 'recovery' breaths (use a long out-breath over a count of ten, counting on your fingers – see recovery breathing technique, pp. 258–9).
- Locate the physical centre of the negative emotion in your body.
- Ask yourself: What does it feel like? What is it saying?
- Imagine a leaf gently floating down to rest on that area.
- As it settles in your imagination, let it spread a balm that dissolves the negative emotional charge.
- Allocate time at a later date to look at the root cause of this emotional state using the 'Bounce Positive' technique (pp. 268–71).

JANETTE USES THE 'FALLING LEAF' VISUALISATION TO CALM AN EXTREME THREAT RESPONSE...

I used this technique just yesterday on the telephone while speed coaching Janette, a nurse working in the health service. There were rumours of job cuts at work and she was afraid of losing her job in the huge restructuring of health care happening in the NHS in the UK. Upset and in tears with her body shaking, she was in the grip of an extreme threat response, believing that her options were being reduced. Her instincts told her that she was being pushed out and she described a horrible dark feeling in the pit of her stomach.

We did not have time to do a 'Bounce Positive' (pp. 268–71) or 'I Won't/I Will' (pp. 271–3) exercise as she was due back in surgery, so I asked her what the dark pit in her stomach was saying. She answered, 'It wants this to be settled; it wants to feel secure.' I then asked her to visualise a leaf, falling and settling lightly on the dark area in her stomach, spreading a balm. As the leaf settled, within five seconds she said, 'I can feel that working already.' Imagining a simple natural process – a leaf falling – created a fast and powerful diversion from the threat she was feeling and enabled her to bounce back in this difficult moment. She repeated the falling leaf visualisation twice more and was able to get back onto her shift feeling calmer and better resourced until our next session, when we could work through her challenge in more detail.

Some people like to manage their expectations using cynicism or pessimism so that they can never be disappointed. Habitual thinking of this nature holds us down and reduces our overall resilience. What happens to us in life may not always be what we most want, but it is how we respond to it that makes us resilient. You now have a number of resources to take charge of your own optimism. Go forwards and use the techniques in this chapter to bounce back quickly from anything life throws at you with a realistic optimism that is of your own making.

Letting go is the next piece of the resilience puzzle. Some memories and experiences are worth remembering because they are constructive – they bolster us and drive us forwards; others need to be let go because they hold us back, using up vital energy resources as they go around and around in our minds, emotions and bodies. Letting go is not easy, but is an art we can all learn.

16

LETTING GO

How to put negative experiences behind us

> It's hard to be clear about who you are
> when you are carrying around a bunch of
> baggage from the past. I've learned to let go
> and move more quickly into the next place.
> —ANGELINA JOLIE

Simon, a parent of two teenage daughters and a senior executive in a major corporation, loved his family and his job. He had been widowed two years earlier and had fought hard to find balance as breadwinner and father. One Wednesday, he received a voicemail from his daughters' school. The eldest was truanting and had shared with a teacher that they shouldn't bother calling her dad at work because he was always in meetings and wouldn't be home until late evening anyway.

A feeling of abject failure seeped through him. He suddenly felt overwhelmingly tired, casting an eye over the endless to-do list for next week's board meeting. He had to get home and stay there until things were straight. Ostensibly resilient and resourceful, Simon had been living in a fragile balance for a while – taking on too much, not getting enough support and hoping for the best. Putting others at risk was not his intention.

Simon was offered coaching with us and we were able to help him let go of the past and move forwards into the future.

This was obviously a serious problem, and Simon felt responsible. We are not saying it is easy, but in the turmoil of things not going to plan, it is useful to have a process to follow to ensure that the future is not tainted by the past.

Sometimes people dwell on problems, which drains energy and can lead to high cortisol levels. Even when all efforts are being made to move forwards, thoughts and feelings about the past can hold us back. There is often a residue left by intense physical, mental and emotional experience, especially when we are on a learning curve and things around us are changing. Consciously thinking through events in our minds can help to process our learning, but going over and over them, letting them interrupt sleep patterns and waking thought processes, is unhelpful and unnecessary. How good are you at letting go?

JARROD BARNES LETS GO...

Jarrod can still vividly recall giving up a touchdown during a nationally televised Ohio State football game with 20 million people watching. He was so disappointed in himself that he felt like quitting football altogether, but this was mid-season – he had to keep going. As a perfectionist, it was especially difficult for him. He felt he had let himself and, more importantly, the team down. Replaying the moment over and over in his mind, he wished he could turn back the clock. It was months before he felt mentally and emotionally like himself again.

He said, 'It almost broke me because I had put so much of my identity into my performance. I had to realise that football is what I do, not who I am.' Jarrod spent a lot of time on self-reflection and focused hard on self-advocacy. He spoke to mentors outside of football, too – a critical move. Athletes put on a brave face, so being able to let that drop and be vulnerable was important. Jarrod now looks back on that experience as a gift because it has enabled him to help others.

LIFE HACK: Thoughts that go around and around in your head are not self-reflection, they are rumination. Reach out and talk to someone.

Events are remembered in the body as well as in the mind. An injured dancer remembers the moment of injury acutely. A doctor alone in the emergency room who cannot get a respirator inserted in time to save a patient's life remembers acutely how it felt. This is the chemical imprint of a moment in time marking an emotional and mental state as physical sensation, what neuroscientist Antonio Damasio calls a 'somatic marker'. For both the dancer and the doctor the moment was painful and unrewarding, so the *human being* shies away from such a situation, while the *dancer* and the *doctor* have to regain confidence in it. They cannot forget it or be naïve and risk it happening again, but have to face up to it, integrate it and let it make them stronger.

The 'Letting Go' technique enables us to move forwards positively. This may mean letting go of minor irritations from the recent past, letting go of major events or disappointments, letting go of significant periods of unhappiness in relationships, or relinquishing old ways and exploring new ways of doing things. We need to work with different timeframes as we let go, for example:

- You miss out on getting tickets for the concert that your favourite band is playing at; your internet was down at the critical moment and it is now sold out.
  Turnaround time for 'Letting Go': maximum one minute.

- A negotiation, deal or project has ground to a halt after months of hard work. You have an important meeting later today for another deal or project that is also at a critical stage. The pressure on that meeting to deliver a successful result is now increased. How can you effectively move forwards and leave the first experience behind you? You want a clear head and a relaxed approach but that's the last thing you are feeling right now.
  Turnaround time for 'Letting Go': maximum one hour.

- You took extended leave to look after a seriously ill family member and as a result have missed out on a high-profile opportunity that should have been yours. A competitor or colleague was awarded the work and the opportunity has grown significantly over a ten-year period. It represents enough additional income to put the kids through university, pay off the mortgage and stoke up the pension and unless you can put it behind you, you will be reminded of this loss every week and every month, draining your energy. This could linger for years, but you don't want this to eat away at you.
  Turnaround time for 'Letting Go': for a serious event like this, between one week and a month if you work hard at it.

Sometimes the way we tell and retell bad things that happen, or the way we harbour resentment towards others, can indicate that we haven't fully let go or accepted events in the past. We need to be careful not to keep rekindling the fire, but to express, digest and put things behind us.

What do you currently do to let go of negative events? A silent scream as you come out of a meeting that bombed? Do you put your hands on your hips, shake your head and take a long out-breath? Do you talk through an event over and over with a spouse or partner until you run out of steam? Or withdraw from people until the unease subsides? As you may have guessed or already know, none of is are fully effective.

> **LIFE HACK:** Tony Robbins promotes the ninety-second rule – vent for ninety seconds about a situation you don't like, then move on.

Resilient individuals have developed a resilient mindset: a way of thinking that enables them to adapt to pressure and change; not only bouncing back, but growing and learning. Having more awareness of a constructive process for letting go will enable you to become more skilled at it, reducing the amount of energy drain and promoting your resilience.

Exercise: 'Letting Go'

- Recovery breathing: Do three recovery breaths to start the process. As always, breathing is a great place to start, reducing levels of toxic carbon dioxide and boosting oxygen intake and acetylcholine, while reducing cortisol levels. (See pp. 258–9 for full exercise.)
- Retreat: Find some respite. A tennis player sits between games and puts a towel over his or her head to have a private moment away from the public eye. Go to a private place and find your equivalent. For example, fold your arms and rest your head forwards on your arms. Close your eyes, breathe and stay for a while.
- Notice how and where the event is impacting on your body.

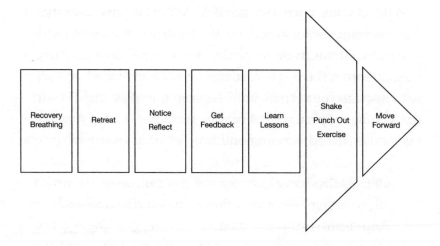

- Reflect: From this position of retreat, rest and think for as long as you need to, then slowly open your body out into a full winner pose. You have to face up to the event, which requires a boost in your testosterone. You can also use the 'Bounce Positive' technique (pp. 268–71) as a tool for reflection.
- Get feedback: Ask, 'Can we talk?', 'What would you have done in my position?', 'What ideas do you have for what I could do now?' These are great questions to ask a trusted friend, advisor or mentor, and one great reason for having a social network of support. When you reach out to others, oxytocin rises, which drives cortisol down and may give you immediate relief. A study conducted by Dr Thomas Gilovich, a professor of psychology at Cornell University, USA, showed that if people have an experience they say negatively impacted them, once they have the chance to talk about it, their assessment of the value of that experience goes up. A stressful or scary event in the past can then be looked back on as an invaluable character-building experience.
- Learn lessons: As soon as we apply a learning mindset

to situations, we regain self-worth and a sense of status; therefore, serotonin rises. We rebuild our own sense of social status from the inside. 'What might you be learning from this?' is a great question to ask others when they come to you with their challenges (after they let off steam in their ninety-second venting session).

- I imagine each event that I want to let go of as a letter in an envelope: On a stage set in my mind's eye, I look inside the envelope and take out the piece of paper on which my learning is written. I throw the envelope into a chute leading to a furnace, symbolising letting go of the negative story of the event, and I watch it burn. Then I read the letter with my learning written on it, and peg the paper with my learning on it up on a clothes line at the back of the stage, alongside other learning letters. You can create your own version of this.

- Shake/punch it out or exercise: Disperse residual chemicals of emotion and recharge your parasympathetic nervous system by using the flexibility shake-out, punch it out, or go for a run, play a squash match or do something that requires vigorous physical activity. Don't sit and dwell; get up and move.

- Moving forwards: Dopamine rises when we see the future in a more positive light, renew purpose and form new goals.

- Imagine the past like a coat that you have been wearing for a while: As you move forwards, visualise taking the coat off and leaving it on the floor behind you, stepping away from it. In your imagination, turn around and see it there behind you and feel happy as you turn again and walk away from it.

- Sometimes we need to let go of people who keep jumping into our thoughts long after we have completed our interaction with them, or people who are no longer part of our lives: Create a picture in your mind's eye of an environment where you can place together all the people that you have worked with that day/week. I picture a stage area with a large red sofa facing away from me. I see them walk in, sit together on the sofa and talk to one another. In the visualisation, they process their experiences without the need for anything more from me – I let them go. The next day I bring the next group onto the sofa, and the first group leaves. I make this a habit as part of my journey home. I am creating spaces within the architecture of my mind that enable me to let go quickly.

- Sometimes we need to have a conversation with someone to put the past to bed and explore the future: There may be new boundaries to find, new agreements to make. Having arranged to speak, here are some guidelines for handling those conversations:
  - Ask for their perspective on the past and how to move forwards.
  - Explain your perspective, requests and desires.
  - Respect their point of view, even if it differs greatly from your own.
  - Agree what you will both do, how you will go forwards now.

In practice, you may loop back and forth between these elements as you work on your 'Letting Go' process. It is rarely linear or perfect. Remember, for minor things you may only need to visit a few of the elements briefly. For major life events, a loss that causes grief, a relationship break-up or major change at work, things can take longer.

Simon's truanting daughter provided a wake-up call for them all. As Simon worked with our help on letting go, the family created a new start. They downsized and moved into a funky apartment closer to the vibrant city centre where Simon's company was based. Drama and dance had always been favourites of the girls and there were theatres and cafés for them all to visit. The girls started a new city school and are thriving. Simon has just met someone whom the girls love, but they are in no hurry to join forces. Letting go allowed them to design their life to suit them.

Now it's over to you. Think of a live situation that you would like to work on and begin your process of letting go.

Remember: we cannot do this alone. Our relationships and networks are an important part of our resilience, as we will discover in the next chapter.

17

FINDING YOUR SUPPORT

How to thrive through receiving and giving

> We don't have to do it all alone, we were
> never meant to.
>
> —BRENÉ BROWN

We cannot live without each other. Social contact is a vital human need, like food and water. Young babies cannot survive without physical and verbal contact, children cannot learn, adults cannot thrive. The experience of losing someone close to us is experienced as physical pain and the joy of working alongside people who we trust and who lend us support gives us physical pleasure.

Finding these vital social connections is crucial for our resilience so that when we are experiencing adversity we can rely on their support. There is compelling research linking positive social relationships with health and longevity. Matthew Lieberman, in his book *Social: Why Our Brains Are Wired to Connect,* and other social cognitive neuroscientists have shown us that it is not our ability for abstract reasoning that has put humans at the top of the food chain, but our ability to live and work together in groups.

Does money make the world go round? No; the incredible

chemical oxytocin does. As we already know, oxytocin is the neurotransmitter responsible for social bonding and trust. It orchestrates our social behaviour, enabling us to find our support and to want to give it to others. The foundations for creating positive social connections in later life are laid down early through body and eye contact with our parents. At that point in our lives, if we are lucky, oxytocin levels are as high as they will ever be. In the absence of oxytocin, however, and where there is stress, conflict or a parent or guardian leaves, cortisol levels rise and our young selves unconsciously feel the threat of isolation, instinctively knowing that we need our 'group' or 'family' for survival.

If, as children, we do not have the experience of having our needs met by adults, or the social aspects around us are not explained to us by members of our group, we find it harder to find our support in later life. We are less likely to give and receive support, ask for help and seek to resolve conflict, and more likely to go it alone, fall out with people and feel unrewarded by social situations. We all have our social quirks, and learning about ourselves as social beings is part of growing up. When people upset us or we don't like working with them, if we can 'lean into' the difficulty and work to resolve conflict, rather than isolating ourselves, we stand to create some of the strongest supportive bonds we will ever have.

In times of stress or during extended periods of working long hours, we are also less likely to reach out, and more likely to become isolated. We need people in our social group who care about us and watch out for us to help us get through those difficult times. A simple, everyday example is if Pat and I are working long hours in our home offices, both of our husbands will call out, text or email us from wherever they are in the house inviting us to join them in the kitchen for lunch, triggering us to take those important breaks. Such social relationships are built on giving *and* receiving support, being reliable and maintaining connection. Each person's support group is unique. We have to take responsibility for figuring out the support we need and piece our own personal support team together.

CAMILLA ROSS NEGOTIATES THE SUPPORT SHE NEEDS...

Camilla was diagnosed with breast cancer nine years into building her theatre company. A private, self-sufficient person by nature, Camilla initially thought she could handle things on her own. She said, 'I didn't want everyone to know. I knew that I needed to heal quietly v. fielding calls and emails from well-meaning people.'

However, she soon realised she needed people around her and strategically created her support team. In addition to telling close family and addressing teaching and theatre commitments, she chose people carefully, including a dear friend and breast cancer survivor who lived far away but could provide critical first-hand advice, and another friend who lived nearby and could provide local support and sit with Camilla's husband, Jack, while she was undergoing surgery.

She thought she had it all sorted out, but Jack needed more. He processes things differently and needed to share the news with more people. They negotiated a compromise that gave them both the support they needed: Jack could tell whomever he wanted, provided that he explained what Camilla needed – that no one reach out to her directly. The experience elevated oxytocin levels, bringing Camilla and Jack even closer together.

Oxytocin is like social 'dark matter': when it is present, it is an invisible force binding us to each other and we feel supported and connected. When it is absent, it is the cause of great disconnection and loneliness. It draws people together in the face of challenges and disasters, temporarily obliterating social and cultural divides, driving our ability to empathise and ensuring the survival of all humanity. The absence of it drives people to war, taking them so far apart that they can no longer feel for each other.

In the microcosm of our own lives, knowing this enables us to be more physically intelligent. We can influence how we interact socially by noticing and managing the rises and falls in our oxytocin levels. By increasing them at critical moments, we can improve our contribution to our families, groups, societies and cultures while finding the support for ourselves that is crucial for our resilience.

Your personal support team

Everyone striving to do their best in any walk of life needs a personal support team; family, friends, colleagues, mentors, advocates, people who will help you because they care and want to support you. Many without close family will tell you that cultivating close friendships has been important for their resilience.

When I was starting up Companies in Motion, I had a young baby, was living on a really tight monthly budget, and had very little business experience. Two key areas of support came through exchanges. I organised a childcare swap with a friend, which gave me a day of free child care, and I set up a mentoring partnership with another local mum who had business experience and was setting up a garden design business. We coached and supported each other, listening, advising and boosting confidence when it waned. Inviting exchanges with people is a fantastic and economic way to find our support.

LIFE HACK: What do you need and what can you offer others? Is there a reciprocal arrangement that you can suggest that enables you to give and receive support?

In addition, depending on your needs and income, physical support for your body and mind from experienced professionals such as physiotherapists, osteopaths, masseurs, doctors and other kinds of physical therapies that involve human touch is recommended as regular maintenance, not only when you are feeling unwell. Emotional and mental support from people who are trained to listen and advise us, such as psychologists and coaches, is highly recommended and in some cases in the UK can be accessed through the National Health Service.

MEGAN MITCHELL FINDS HER SUPPORT...

Working on the morning show means Megan has to be awake by 2am in order to be at the studio by 3.30am and on air by 5am. An extrovert who is energised by being around others, Megan found that the 5–6am hour was the most challenging because she was still feeling tired. To increase her energy and warm up her voice before she goes on air, the first member of her support team is the security guard at the front desk in her building. She makes a point of speaking with him as she leaves each morning. Then, at 3am, while en route to the station, she calls her closest friend, a night owl who lives in a time zone three hours behind her. A thirty-minute conversation with him energises her. Megan often hears from her mother after the show; she lives in a different part of the country but live-streams Megan's show and calls her with feedback, tips (even commentary on lipstick choice!) and encouragement. The station also provides professional support by way of trainers who will watch Megan's videos and provide more detailed analysis. In addition, every few weeks Megan calls a mentor who is passionate about storytelling to update him and receive constructive and positive feedback, and participates in a group workout session on Monday and Tuesday mornings. This system of support is carefully constructed to ensure that Megan can do her job really well. It keeps her cortisol down and her oxytocin up.

When we ask someone for help, it indicates our respect for them and elevates their social status. Not only do they get an oxytocin boost, they get a dopamine and serotonin boost too, so we are doing people a service when we ask them for help. As adults, asking for advice from peers and mentors reduces anxiety and helps keep us healthy and happy. For example, when others in Camilla's personal circle eventually learned about her illness, a few expressed anger that she had not told them earlier about what she was going through or asked them for support. Their status was lowered because they weren't asked for help – a sign that they were not part of 'the tribe' – and they experienced a drop in oxytocin and dopamine and a rise in cortisol, a chemical shift that often manifests itself as anger.

> **LIFE HACK:** In times of stress at work, when you feel there is little time to connect with people outside of the essential work conversations, take a moment to think about your support team. See their faces in your mind's eye encouraging you. Notice the 'feel-good' oxytocin boost as you think about them.

The power of networks

For professionals in any field, networks are considered vital for developing our careers as a source of support, advice and recommendation. Some people whom I have connected have helped each other find new jobs, move into new roles and become lifelong friends with each other, which gives me incredible satisfaction. I know they would go the extra mile for me too. Pat can trace the entire trajectory of her professional and personal life as an adult back to one networking conversation at the age of twenty-one during her junior year in college.

Because we share knowledge and experience across networks, problems can be shared and solved more quickly. Ideas grow and develop in a collaborative way, improving the quality of collective thinking. Giving and receiving support through networks in this way builds intelligent, agile and resilient cultures, societies and organisations.

> **LIFE HACK:** Be proactive and creative in connecting people in your network. Decide on something cultural you would like to do – e.g. go to the theatre or see a film or art exhibition – and invite people who you believe will get along and whom you would like to get to know better. The dynamic of giving and receiving drives social networks.

Neuroeconomist Paul Zak's extensive research, published in *Harvard Business Review* and in his book, *The Trust Factor*, reports that in organisations that share information broadly and intentionally build relationships, and where leaders ask for support, there is 76 per cent more engagement, people have 106 per cent more energy, they are 50 per cent more productive, 29 per cent more satisfied with their lives, have 13 per cent fewer days sick and 40 per cent fewer cases of burnout. He has tested oxytocin levels in the bloodstream of thousands of employees across many industries and cultures and has shown that trust and purpose reinforce each other, creating a mechanism for high oxytocin levels over a longer period. Robust networks and finding support, therefore, are part of our happiness and a cornerstone of our resilience.

Giving back

Finally, a crucial part of you finding your support comes as a result of giving back. A Harvard Business School study equated the well-being gained from donating to charity with a doubling of household income. Another showed that if you volunteer regularly, the well-being improvements equate to a salary increase of $55,000. When students were told to spend a small amount of money on someone else, they were happier than if they were told to spend it on themselves.

Pat used to chair an organisation called Philly (Philadelphia) Volunteers, which held its major annual event during the Christmas season. Young volunteers were paired with disadvantaged children who were given a gift certificate they could use to shop for gifts for their loved ones. Together, they went shopping. Materially, these children had very little – for many, it was the first time they were able to purchase a gift for their family. They were extremely excited and grateful to be able to do so. In the six years that Pat was involved with the organisation, not once did a child ask if he or she could spend the money on him or herself. Those children truly felt that it was better to give than to receive.

Research from the University of North Carolina and UCLA found that people who gained their happiness from service to others carried low levels of biological markers leading to serious illnesses. Those whose happiness came mostly from self-gratification, however, showed higher levels of these markers. Giving back very clearly has a positive impact on resilience.

We'll use the pages below to make an inventory of your support. As you do it, monitor oxytocin and cortisol levels. Notice when you feel tentative or uncertain; this denotes cortisol rising. Notice when you feel happy and supported; oxytocin is rising. Monitoring those chemicals in your body will enable you to spot where you need to create new connections or improve important existing relationships.

We'll start by identifying your personal support team, then look for improvements in your professional and personal networks, and finally you can generate some ideas for giving back.

Exercise: 'Finding Your Support'

Using the table below, list the people who currently support you and what kind of support they provide. Reflect for a while. What support is missing? What can you outsource that would enable you to focus more on your high performance? On the right, create a list of new support you would like to seek.

Support you have	Support you would like

What ideas do you have for finding that support?

Exercise: Developing your network

In the space provided, map out your personal and/or professional network as it is now using a series of circles with names

and lines joining them to you and each other. These can be individuals or groups. Use big circles to represent significant groups or people and small circles for satellite groups or more peripheral individuals. Use thick lines to represent strong oxytocin bonds, thin lines to represent weak bonds.

Now add to the map any new people or elements that could be part of your support network going forwards. Use dotted lines to represent new bonds that you would like to create but that have yet to be formed. Think about:

- Cultivating trusted advisors/mentors
- Socialising
- Asking for help
- Offering support

Exercise: Your 'giving back' list
On the left of the page opposite, write down what you already do to give back. On the right of the page, write down some new ideas. Use the following to generate some ideas:

- Offer support to a family member or friend
- Volunteer for a favourite non-profit organisation
- Get involved in corporate social responsibility projects at work
- Sign up for a charity walk or run etc.
- Donate support to others
- Help others in your street or block
- Offer to mentor someone you think you can help
- Get involved at your children's school

Your 'Giving Back' List	
Current activities	Potential new activities

Make a plan. Put in your diary when you are going to reach out to new contacts, exploring possibilities and making appointments.

Being connected in the way suggested in this chapter gives you greater resilience than you can achieve by yourself. You will have back-up and support when you need it most and plans in place to ensure that you maintain levels of support and connection going forwards. Support is a cornerstone for how humans achieve the most resilience and encompasses how we as individuals contribute to the bigger picture, creating resilient cultures and societies. Having explored and developed new ideas for finding your support, let's move on to look at how nutrition and fitness can also support your resilience.

18

NUTRITION AND FITNESS FOR RESILIENCE

How to support our immune system and bounce back

> Let food be thy medicine and medicine
> be thy food.
>
> —HIPPOCRATES

Resilience relies on the internal environment we create in our bodies and how we maintain it. We need to cleanse our bodies, boost our immune systems, take care of joints and muscles, and believe that our minds have a powerful effect on our health and resilience. Certain types of exercise make us far more emotionally and mentally resilient. By understanding a few basics, you can select new habits to stack into your Physical Intelligence programme.

Nutrition

Antioxidants

Antioxidants are found in what is termed the 'rainbow diet'; brightly coloured, particularly red, orange, purple and yellow fruit and vegetables, such as pomegranates, red and yellow peppers, blueberries, goji berries, raspberries, cherries, carrots and sweet potatoes. They are believed to play a role in preventing the development of chronic diseases such as cancer, heart disease, stroke, Alzheimer's, rheumatoid arthritis and cataracts.

Antioxidants remove toxins from the body, counteracting the damaging effects of the physiological process of oxidation in every tissue in the body. Oxidative stress occurs when the production of harmful molecules, called free radicals, is too high for the body's defence system. Free radicals are chemically active atoms or molecular fragments that have a charge due to an excess or deficient number of electrons. Because they have unpaired electrons, they are highly unstable. They scavenge your body to grab or donate electrons, thereby damaging other cells, proteins and DNA. Free radicals are created by eating low-quality processed foods with additives and can also form from environmental factors such as pollution, over-exposure to sunlight, strenuous exercise, X-rays, smoking and alcohol.

Essential amino acids
Protein in our diet is also important for resilience, because there are essential amino acids we need that we can't synthesise in the body. We must therefore get them through food. They are beneficial for:

- *Mood.* Tryptophan – the precursor of serotonin and the least plentiful of the twenty-two amino acids in food – regulates appetite, sleep, mood and pain, and is found in green tea, dairy products, meat, brown rice, fish, soybeans and, as we learned in the flexibility section, good-quality dark chocolate.
- *Detox and immune system.* Isoleucine is responsible for wound healing, detoxification, immune function and the regulation of blood sugar and is found in meat, fish, cheese, eggs and most seeds and nuts.

- *Protection against viruses.* Lysine plays a role in protecting us against viruses and is found in high levels in red meat, cheeses (especially cottage cheese, Parmesan, Cheddar and mozzarella), fish, soy, shellfish, quinoa, lentils, black beans and pistachios.

Joint and muscle recovery

Turmeric contains curcumin. There is scientific evidence to support the effects of curcumin as an anti-inflammatory agent, and populations with a high turmeric intake such as India, Sri Lanka, Bangladesh and Thailand have lower rates of arthritis and joint damage. In 2017, two British doctors in their twenties, Ted Welman and Jack Faulkner, both with joint and muscle damage from previous injuries, rowed across the Indian Ocean for the charity Médecins Sans Frontières. They had researched the benefits of turmeric and took a supplement every day to enable their muscles and joints to recover quickly from the damage caused by continuous rowing.

Warding off colds and flu

Echinacea has been my tried-and-tested cold remedy for years. If you can catch the first sniffle, it will certainly ward off cold and flu for an entire winter. Our nutritionist Justine Evans also recommends Coenzyme Q10 (CoQ10) as an alternative that acts both as an antioxidant and as immune system support. It works with enzymes in the body to speed up chemical reactions for energy release and the activity of protective responses.

Gut health

When we are stressed, cells in the gut wall can become too porous, allowing undigested food molecules and germs to pass from inside the gut into the bloodstream. This causes inflammation. Collagen helps rebuild a weak or 'leaky' gut and can be found in chicken soup (or other soups in which the bones have been used to make a broth; bone is made of collagen for flexibility and calcium phosphate that adds strength). For all gut issues, allergy testing is a sensible first step, as is investigation of yeast levels and good and bad gut bacteria. Probiotic supplements and live yoghurt cultures support gut health.

If you suffer from reflux, ginger, oatmeal, celery and salad (minus the tomatoes and onions) help, but avoid citrus and exotic fruits (e.g. oranges, lemons, pineapple and mangoes), high-fat dressings and cheese.

Ibuprofen irritates the gut lining, so if you use it regularly and experience digestive discomfort, then consider switching painkillers to allow the gut lining to recover. (Do consult your doctor before making changes.)

Alcohol

Alcohol can be responsible for many irritations in the whole digestive tract, including mouth and stomach cancer and ulcers. I love good wine, but have extended periods when I don't drink alcohol or do so in very reduced amounts. Pat has also reduced her intake to one glass of wine on Friday and one on Saturday, unless there is a special occasion, and she feels better for it. Vitamin C, 1000mg a day, is a wise move after Christmases and birthdays if you drink more than usual, because it supports the liver, which has the job of metabolising alcohol.

Alcohol lowers levels of the neurotransmitter glutamate, which maintains normal brain reaction and energy levels, and it increases the calming brain chemical GABA (gamma aminobutyric acid). The combination of these two effects makes alcohol a depressant. It also temporarily increases dopamine levels, giving you pleasure, but making you need more and more of it to get the same dopamine release, which is what gives alcohol its addictive properties.

Fitness

The most important aspect of fitness for resilience is aerobic exercise, getting the heart rate up and down regularly. This makes our physical recovery and renewal system robust and enables us to recover quickly from mental and emotional pressure (the same system, the parasympathetic nervous system, is used for all three). Extensive research supports the view that exercise is a cure for depression and responsible for improved cognitive function and health. Studies from Japan in 2014, for example, show that thirty minutes of mild daily exercise significantly improves executive function, decision-making and focus.

Top tips:

- Get your heart rate up and down three times every day.
- Get your bicycle out – for local trips, leave the car behind. A quick bike ride is a fantastic opportunity for a short burst of exercise.
- Use your journey to work to walk briskly, jog or cycle and enjoy open spaces.
- Intense interval training for fitness is the best, quickest and most effective way to build resilience.
- Gardening, cleaning, carrying the shopping in from the car and all manual jobs are a chance to get your heart rate up – you can apply the HIIT principle to such work if you wish (see below).
- Always stretch after exercising (see flexibility stretches in Chapter 8, pp. 162–5).
- Use massage for recovery to stimulate the parasympathetic nervous system.

Home or gym training programmes

I am a great believer in variety, so keep mixing up your fitness routine and experimenting. Research supports the effectiveness of quick bursts of high aerobic activity or 'high intensity interval training' (HIIT), so do what you enjoy using this principle. If you like spending an hour in the gym on strength training, that's great, but make sure you alternate it with resilience training. An hour-long exercise regime is not necessary or desirable every day, as your body needs recovery time. Our fitness expert Rob Devenport recommends HIIT because it provides a good, quick (twenty to twenty-five minutes), scientifically proven fitness alternative when time is short. Here are some options:

- The HIIT training format I use is: two minutes' high intensity activity, one minute rest, repeated five times. Warm up first with a short jog for two minutes, then you are ready to go to full intensity. Run or star jump for two minutes at 85–100 per cent effort with a one-minute recovery period in between. With two minutes at the end to stretch and warm down, the whole process takes twenty minutes.
- For keen followers of fitness, Tabata training works on even shorter intervals. Discovered by Japanese scientist Dr Izumi Tabata at the National Institute of Fitness and Sports in Tokyo, working out for four minutes and twenty seconds, four days a week, at high intensity had a bigger impact on cardiovascular and muscle power fitness than a control group that worked out for one hour, five days a week, at moderate intensity. Choose your favourite exercises: push-ups, squats, sprints, star jumps etc., push yourself as hard as you can for twenty seconds, then rest for ten seconds and repeat eight times. For example:

- Warm-up (two minutes walking/jogging/flexibility movement sequence)
- Push-ups (four minutes = twenty seconds on, ten seconds rest × 8)
- Squats (four minutes = twenty seconds on, ten seconds rest × 8)
- Sprints (four minutes = twenty seconds on, ten seconds rest × 8)
- Star jumps (four minutes = twenty seconds on, ten seconds rest × 8)
- Rest (one minute between each set)
- Warm-down (two minutes – stretches)
- TOTAL WORKOUT: Twenty-four minutes

A word about sunlight – we talked about the importance of light in the flexibility section in relation to serotonin production. Sunlight absorbed through the skin enables us to make vitamin D, which is important for immune system function and guards against SAD (seasonal affective disorder), which affects some people's resilience during the change of seasons. Quick bursts of sunlight onto the largest possible areas of bare skin enables the maximum vitamin D synthesis. At the first sign of sunshine, dive outside just for a few minutes and soak it up. Vitamin D is found in a limited range of foods, but ever since the industrial revolution, foods such as milk and cereals have been fortified with it. (NB: Vitamin D supplements should be vitamin D3.)

JANE TAKES HER HEALTH INTO HER OWN HANDS...

Jane, our business partner at Companies in Motion, used to get pleurisy or pneumonia every single winter following a cough or cold. There would be the inevitable antibiotics and two weeks off work. Since applying Physical Intelligence resilience techniques, this rarely happens any more.

Enjoy building your resilience and get ready for an increase in capacity over the next months and years. Your strength and flexibility programme will already be supporting your resilience and it is a lifelong project. Just remember: *you* can influence your health and your immune system, so where your health is concerned, think about your vulnerable points and give yourself a goal; e.g. to make it through the next winter without a cold.

Rehearse and Perform: Resilience

Now it's time to put resilience into action. In this section, there are day-to-day techniques to habit stack, as well as exercises that transform underlying patterns of thinking and feeling to be explored and practised at weekends and in free time. Combined, these will enable you to make significant long-term changes in how you approach adversity in order to thrive. Spend a week rehearsing and experimenting with the techniques you decide to prioritise, after which you can perform them every day for a month, building better bounceback and robust physical, mental and emotional health and happiness.

Only with repetition can we embed new habits, so let's put the work in and reap the benefits. Here's how to go about rehearsing and performing your resilience alongside your strength and flexibility techniques.

1. Retain the key strength and flexibility techniques that have become habitual.
2. Choose five of the resilience techniques that you feel will be particularly helpful.
3. Rehearse them for one week to explore what the best way to integrate them into your daily life is and what the right triggers are. (Take a look at our habit-stacking ideas and suggestions for triggers below.)

4. Perform them daily for the rest of the month until they become automatic.

5. Give more time on weekends and breaks to do the in-depth, multi-step processes such as 'Bounce Positive' (pp. 268–71), 'Letting Go' (p. 281–4) and 'Finding Your Support' (p. 294).

6. When you feel ready, you can come back and choose some more techniques to rehearse, then perform those, too.

Here is a reminder of all the techniques we learned in the resilience section. Read down the list, select and mark those that you feel will be most beneficial. Then we'll put them into a programme.

☐ SEQUENTIAL RELAXATION – Tensing, releasing muscle groups to enable you to relax your body and mind. Much used, this is a very reliable wind-down, especially good for getting off to sleep in a strange hotel room or when you find yourself awake at 3am.

☐ RELAXATION RESPONSE – Try this meditation technique as an option instead of paced breathing; use at the weekend for twenty minutes.

☐ RECOVERY BREATHING – Recover quickly from feeling overwhelmed, panicky or anxious.

☐ RELAXATION AND RECOVERY – *REST* – **R**etreat, **E**at, **S**leep and **T**reat yourself. Make sure you diarise your rest and stick to it – it is a 'must-have', not a 'nice-to-have'.

☐ CHEMISTRY OF OPTIMISM

    ☐ JUMP – Jump regularly to improve optimism.

    ☐ BOUNCE POSITIVE – To rebuild your optimism and self-belief, register the moment that took your emotions and thoughts spiralling down, listen to the self-talk, feel the full extent of negative feeling, self-accusation etc. Use logic to verify, deny or question it. Detach from your threat response and decide what is really true for you.

- [ ] I WON'T/I WILL – When you don't like something but it's happening anyway, punch your arms and fists out into the air and say, 'I won't' or 'I won't take this' strongly and powerfully until you exhaust your energy. Then find a subtle, deep change in your attitude which means: 'Okay. Whatever "this" is, *I will* take this on. *I will* learn from it. I accept that it will teach me something.' This process helps with acceptance as well as ensuring a learning mindset.
- [ ] CURIOSITY GENERATOR – Rather than resisting and blaming, become more curious about why things are happening the way they are, how you want to do things, and what you will learn.
- [ ] THE FALLING LEAF – Visualise a light leaf floating down and settling on areas of the body where you experience pain or unpleasant emotions. Imagine it releasing a balm that gives you immediate ease in acute and troubling situations.
- [ ] LETTING GO – For ongoing troublesome thoughts and feelings, work through the following steps: recovery breathing, retreat, reflect, get feedback, learn lessons, move forwards – all while using a learning mindset.
- [ ] FINDING YOUR SUPPORT
  - [ ] PERSONAL SUPPORT TEAM – Refer to your notes on enhancing your support – make a plan to put this in place.
  - [ ] DEVELOPING YOUR NETWORK – Refer to your network diagram. Make a plan to connect with individuals and groups you noted down.
  - [ ] YOUR 'GIVING BACK' LIST – Refer to your 'giving back' notes. Who do you want to give back to:

charities, CSR projects, mentoring others, helping family and neighbours?

☐ NUTRITION – Antioxidants, turmeric, proteins, low alcohol intake, sunlight/vitamin D for well-being and bounceback.

☐ HIIT FOR FITNESS – Use high intensity interval training to get your exercise done in twenty to twenty-five minutes every other day. On days when you are not training, do still get your heart rate up and allow it to recover three times during the day by climbing stairs or power walking to the station etc.

Now, let's habit stack:

DURING THE NIGHT

- If you are restless or ruminating, sit up, take a pad and pen and do a 'Bounce Positive' (pp. 268–71).
  Trigger: Noticing you are tossing and turning.

- Practise sequential relaxation (pp. 256–7) to get you back to sleep.
  Trigger: You are half-awake in the early hours, with thoughts going round in your head.

BEFORE WORK

- Take a few moments to jump (p. 267), generating optimism for the day. Get your heart rate up.
  Trigger: The kettle boiling.

WORKING AT HOME

- Break up the day by walking/jogging/cycling at some point. Use it to renew your energy.
  Trigger: Pre-set reminder in your schedule alerting you to take a break between tasks.

- Use your personal support network to renew energy and make sure you don't become isolated.
  Trigger: Noticing feelings of isolation and low reward.

- Eat plenty of antioxidants – colourful vegetables, peppers, tomatoes, blueberries, blackberries etc.
  Trigger: Entering the kitchen to choose and prepare lunch.

- If/when the sun shines, even in winter and even if you are really busy, dive outside – expose arms, face and other body areas to the sun for five minutes to top up vitamin D.
  Trigger: The sun coming out.

ON THE JOURNEY TO WORK

- Walk, cycle or jog part of the way to get your heart rate up. Prepare your gear the night before so that you're all set for the morning.
  Trigger: Leaving the house.

- Find a way to get your heart rate up during your journey to work, e.g. take the stairs at the tube, train station or office.
  Trigger: Seeing the sign for 'stairs this way'.

ALL DAY

- In times of stress or high pressure, when you know your heart rate is high and things feel critical, use recovery breathing technique (pp. 258–9) regularly throughout the day as you problem-solve.
  Trigger: Sensing your heart rate begin to rise.

AT LUNCHTIME

- Include lots of colourful fruit and vegetables to get those all-important antioxidants. Look for brightly coloured vegetables and fruit on the shelves or menu.
  Trigger: Walking into a grocery store/looking at a restaurant menu.

- Try a turmeric drink – you can buy them pre-prepared from some healthy sandwich bars, or make your own: ½ tsp turmeric, chopped ginger root, ½ lemon and rind, honey, ½ cinnamon stick, black pepper; add hot water and strain.
  Trigger: Cooking dinner in the evening, or walking into the sandwich bar.

- During lunch, take out a pen and paper and do a quick 'Bounce Positive' (pp. 268–71) to process the morning's events and have an optimistic afternoon. This is particularly important if you are prone to worrying or if something adverse happened that morning.
  Trigger: Finishing lunch.

- If you like to train at lunchtime, do a fifteen-minute HIIT (pp. 303–4) workout (two minutes full-on plus one-minute recovery, repeated five times), then eat afterwards.

Trigger: Alert on your phone telling you it is lunchtime and time to train.

IN THE AFTERNOON

- If you notice any concerns or discomfort, use the 'Falling Leaf' visualisation (p. 275) to soothe.
  Trigger: Sitting back down at your desk/logging on to your computer.

- If problems or blocks arise, use the 'Curiosity Generator' (pp. 273–4) to enquire 'Why?' or 'How?' rather than continuing to try to solve problems by repeating the same approach.
  Trigger: Noticing a dopamine drop, feeling unrewarded, worn down and lacking energy for a task.

- If you notice any resistance building up, especially when you have to do something but it feels unrewarding and you simply don't want to do it, practise a quiet (internal) 'I Won't/I Will' process (pp. 271–3). For major things, make an appointment with yourself at the weekend to do the full 'I Won't/I Will' technique, as well as a 'Letting Go' process (pp. 281–284).
  Trigger: Feeling resistance – a sinking feeling, intense frustration or simply no energy for a task.

ON THE JOURNEY HOME

- During times of high pressure, do ten recovery breaths on every journey home from work and use recovery breathing technique (pp. 258–9) immediately after challenging events to bring your heart rate down.

Trigger: Exiting the door of your workplace or noticing elevated heart rate and quickening of emotion.

- Engage with those who support you – your personal support. Organise to email, text or phone someone in your support network to enable you to reflect and receive support in challenging circumstances.
  Trigger: Sitting down on the train, bus/putting your seatbelt on in the car.

IN THE EVENING

- Talk to family and friends. Don't bottle things up and say, 'I'm fine' when you have things on your mind.
  Trigger: A friend or family member asking you how you are.

- Do an extended HIIT training workout. Vigorous exercise relieves stress and pressure, so if anxiety is building, do one each evening for a week. Head to the gym or a fitness class straight after work.
  Trigger: Walking out of the office.

- Meditate – using the relaxation response exercise (p. 257) or a meditation app – for twenty minutes each day.
  Trigger: Changing into nightclothes before bed.

- Use sequential relaxation (pp. 256–7) to get you into good-quality sleep.
  Trigger: Head touching the pillow, lying on your back.

WEEKENDS, EVENINGS AND DOWNTIME

- Schedule a couple of hours with a close friend at the end of the week to work on 'Letting Go' (pp. 281–284) and 'Curiosity Generator' (pp. 273–4). Make it reciprocal so that you give back as well.
  Trigger: Walking out of the train station on a Friday evening.

- Visit a masseur, coach, osteopath, psychologist weekly to get the support you need and trigger the parasympathetic nervous system by having someone take care of you.
  Trigger: Repeated diary entries.

- Schedule time with a trusted advisor/mentor as often as you need to discuss progress. You'll know what you need, so ask for it.
  Trigger: It's in the diary.

- Place a firm boundary around time with family at the weekend for at least one day.
  Trigger: It's in the diary.

- Volunteer for a cause you care about or help someone local once a week – e.g. an elderly neighbour.
  Trigger: Finishing your lie-in or chores on a Saturday morning.

- Place a firm boundary around time alone for reflection. Take an hour to reflect and think about what you need for the week.
  Trigger: During Sunday morning/afternoon prep for the week (find a point in your day where you still have energy – I find late morning is good).

- Diarise *REST* days (pp. 259–62) – even if you need to work, you can still retreat, eat well, sleep for eight hours and treat yourself.
  Trigger: Preparing for the week.

- Do something you really enjoy – socialise with good friends, go to the theatre, an exhibition, a concert, on a long country walk, to a dinner party, or spend time in the garden.
  Trigger: It's in the diary.

- Diarise holidays.
  Trigger: Make it a ritual on 1 January to block holiday weeks out for the year.

Extras:

- Have a good bounce on a trampoline. There is nothing like a real bounce to give you bounceback.

Five is a manageable number of resilience techniques to start with. You will not be able to integrate all the techniques at once, but do include recovery breathing (pp. 258–9) and *REST* principles (pp. 259–62), and at least one of the chemistry of optimism techniques ('Jump', 'Bounce Positive', 'I Won't/I Will', 'Curiosity Generator', 'The Falling Leaf').

Now you have chosen your techniques, you'll need to find your triggers: clear moments in your day when you can purposefully integrate them. Again, remember that the best triggers are ones you can visualise. They need to be simple and easy to remember.

Make a note of your resilience programme and triggers on the table overleaf:

Technique	Trigger

Rehearse: Seven days

Explore different ways of integrating these resilience techniques into your life until you find the small nudges at the right
times for you that feel most beneficial. Remember the principle
of incremental gain? Every little thing you do to support your
resilience adds up. Some of the resilience techniques are great
to practise at the weekends when you may have more time to
allocate to exploring them in depth by yourself or with family
and friends. If you have children, share them – they usually get
it, and it's great to start them young.

Perform: Resilience

Having practised and settled on what works best for you, the
rest of the month will fall easily into place. You now have a fail-
safe plan to embed new resilience habits. The techniques you've
chosen should sit easily alongside the strength and flexibility
techniques that you are using. Enjoy integrating them into your

life so that you can relax and recover quickly and expertly, handle stress and pressure, take charge of your optimism, let go of the past and receive and give that all-important support.

Remember, times of heightened emotion are important because they indicate that a period of learning has arrived and that action is required. With resilience, we can see life as exciting and challenging rather than stressful; we are able to roll with it and become more physically intelligent every day.

Now it's time to turn to endurance and discover how to push forwards into the future – to be determined and focused, especially when the going gets tough. We will learn how to sustain motivation over the long term and survive and thrive through tough or dark times until we emerge, having achieved what we set out to, to celebrate our success.

PART 4
ENDURANCE

Introducing Endurance

Never for me the lowered banner, never
the last endeavour.
                    —SIR ERNEST SHACKLETON

Endurance is about mental toughness, determination, persever-
ance and planning. It's about having a strategy for sustaining
effort during difficult times and maintaining peak performance over the long haul.

When things are physically, emotionally and mentally difficult, and extreme patience is required to keep communications
open – for example, when your children are studying for GCSEs
and spring seems a long time coming, or you are in the really
tough stages of a project and it's hard to remember why this
chosen path seemed like a good idea – you need endurance.

Dopamine and DHEA underpin endurance. Dopamine
makes us determined because we are drawn to a reward that
we perceive in the future, whatever that may be (e.g. job satisfaction, money, a sense of achievement, feeling alive, surviving
adversity), while DHEA gives us lasting energy reserves that
power us steadily forwards, like the engines of a huge ship
progressing through deep water. DHEA is a precursor of

testosterone and we need the muscle strength and confidence that testosterone brings to support our endurance.

Visualisation is a key tool for boosting dopamine. The ability to imagine other realities, visualise goals to empower us and to take our minds off the discomfort of effort, difficulty and pain, is crucial. Many artists and athletes use visualisation; most practise for five to ten minutes a day, even when resting, in order to maintain their focus and their mental game.

Determination, specifically self-determination, is a defining factor in whether we perform well under pressure without succumbing to the choking effect of over-elevated cortisol levels. While some people are born with grit, it can also be learned and more deeply accessed by working on what truly motivates us.

Motivation is improved when we are aligned with our values and core purpose, doing the work that puts us in our element, and using our strengths to the fullest. Becoming more conscious of such deep motivations makes it more likely that we will persevere.

Self-appreciation and the encouragement of those around us also enable us to endure the difficulties of whatever journey we are on. We need to celebrate our own successes and give and receive appreciation in order to fuel dopamine levels that allow us to focus on challenging goals.

When Pat designs coaching programmes for business leaders, she is adamant about including a module on the power of praise because of its transformative effect on individuals and relationships. She believes wholeheartedly in something one of her colleagues once said: 'Plants need to be watered far more often than they need to be pruned. People are the same.'

It is possible to train our emotional, physical and mental endurance. We can improve our energy levels, handle pain and discomfort, and sleep better by integrating endurance training into everyday life, preparing ourselves to weather challenges. If we plan to push ourselves on easier weeks, we develop stamina for those weeks when the diary is bursting with critical work or difficult conversations and tasks and setbacks are draining us.

What we need for endurance is good analysis and a robust, evolving plan. Your stack of new habits from the sections on strength, flexibility and resilience form part of the plan, and in this section we will complete the picture. A report in *Frontiers in Neuroscience* in 2010 brings together research on how physical activity and learning challenges increase the number of neurons in our brains until the day we die, which means we need never stop learning and developing. New habits take time to become structured into our long-term memory – repetition, practice, planning, and re-planning are the values that drive endurance.

ALESSANDRA FERRI MANAGES HER ENDURANCE...

'My body is a machine that is operated by my inner self. I am the pilot, I go and see the mechanics: physios, masseurs, trainers, and they test it, measure it, help me train. I do forty minutes of body work with trainers before class, and thirty to forty minutes after class. Class is one and a half hours. I treat my body like I own a Ferrari.'

Planning and the discipline of daily class sustain Alessandra, even though her inner voice sometimes says, 'I am too tired', 'No, it hurts too much', or, 'Maybe I'll take a day off'. She doesn't listen to that voice. The constant fight takes energy, but she makes plans that work and she sticks to them.

Alessandra is now a 54-year-old dancer and yet people are still asking her to dance certain roles in three years' time, when she will be fifty-seven. 'I say, "Yes, if I can, I will." When I see that age written down on paper it can seem old,' she says. 'BUT! Age is a state of mind.'

At the end of this section you can select the techniques that you want to apply in an endurance rehearsal week. You will experience how muscle-firming (pp. 333–4) can improve your determination to power through big tasks and learn how to create milestones (pp. 338–40) to stay focused, mark progress and reap the rewards for your efforts.

First, however, let's focus on the long term: identifying a dream, creating a vivid visualisation of the future and working towards achieving it.

19

SEEING THE LONG GAME

How to visualise our long-term goals and dreams

> One of the lessons that I grew up with was
> to always stay true to yourself and never let
> what somebody else says distract you from
> your goals.
>
> —MICHELLE OBAMA

Imagine you have just decided to start up your own venture, run a marathon for charity, go for that promotion or you just started saving up to buy something special. Clear focus on that goal is the first step to achieving it. This chapter is about how to visualise goals and make sure your body's chemistry supports the realisation of them.

In 1990, I set a two-year goal for my dance company to appear in the Spring Loaded festival at the Place Theatre in London. With the help of a coach, I created a clear picture of the stage in my mind's eye. I imagined my mum and dad in the audience and the dancers in the wings. Turn the clock forwards to 1992, and I am on that stage, crouched down behind a chest that is part of the set for a piece called 'Ultramarine'. The piece opens with a surprise when I leap onto the chest, and I must stay hidden until the audience have taken their seats. Alongside first-night nerves, I take a second to celebrate the moment. It hasn't been easy, and there have been challenges along the way, but ... Yes! We have done it!

Adam (thirty-one years old), Pat's stepson, is using visualisation to drive his ambition to work in ecotourism. Described by Pat as a cross between Dr Dolittle and the late Steve Irwin, he has always had an innate love for animals and nature. After graduating with a degree in biology/zoology, then working in zoos, national parks and on geological projects, he narrowed his focus and began to visualise a future – his own ecotourism company in Costa Rica. He envisions a ten-acre base camp situated close to a beach, with a dock, a communal ranch area with a barbecue, volleyball court, housing and classrooms/event space – something that would cater to different programmes: student field trips, corporate retreats, ecotours and luxury tours. He also visualises trips to the rainforest, waterfalls and different snorkelling sites, as well as diving, rafting and mountain biking adventures, and can picture guests getting excited about scientific discoveries. All of these images are clear in his mind's eye. While he hasn't found the exact piece of land yet, he knows the right region and is saving money and identifying future partners so that he is ready to move once he establishes the right location, motivated by his visualisations and his long game to generate the income and experiences necessary to realise that long-term goal.

The visual cortex of the brain is very much connected to dopamine function. Dopamine, if you remember, is the pleasure and reward chemical. When we see something we want, we feel a shot of dopamine. When we step towards it, we feel another shot, and when we reach out and grasp it, we get a bigger shot. If it is edible or tactile, we will feel another huge shot of dopamine when we taste, smell or touch it. Because of the link between dopamine and sight, if we imagine clearly what we want to achieve, picture it, and experience the feelings of pleasure and reward, we are more likely to achieve it. If we don't picture our goal, it may not feel as 'real' and, as a consequence, we may be more easily distracted from our tasks and dreams.

TOP TIPS FROM OUR PANEL ON HOW TO ACHIEVE YOUR GOALS...

- 'Make sure your goals are connected to your intrinsic motivation and a measurable output. Visualise "the best you you can be".' – *Claire Taylor*
- 'Set realistic, step-by-step goals but don't forget to take risks and be vulnerable.' – *Dawn Marie Flynn Sirrenberg*
- 'I dreamed about having all the best resources I needed to realise my dream as a dancer.' – *Alessandra Ferri*
- 'Never set a goal that is a "winning" goal; set a goal for what you want to improve on rather than anything else.' – *George Kruis*
- 'Picture your future life vividly. Focus on the fact that something better is on the horizon – the reward of achieving the goal or hitting the milestone. Think, *I know this is hard now, but when it's over my life will be better.*' – *Karl Van Haute*

Let's begin with some preparatory practice in focusing the mind. Creating a mental image of a goal requires a relaxed focus. If you enjoy this focus practice, you can include it as an exercise at moments when you need endurance. Remember, although you want to be motivated towards your goals, you don't want to feel they are a burden – you need to learn to give your goals appropriate focus; not too loose, not obsessive.

Exercise: Focus practice

When we first close our eyes to visualise a goal, it can be confusing. The mind seems to whirr, not knowing where to settle. Where exactly does the visualisation of a goal take place? If we can visualise well, then the goal is more defined and vivid and we are more likely to realise it. Try this:

Shift the focus of the mind to different parts of the brain.

- Move focus to the front of the brain – notice there is a space there.
- Move focus to the back of the brain, the heavy, round cerebellum, the nerve centre – notice how you become more aware of your spinal column and your senses of weight and touch in your body.
- Move focus to the right side of the brain – see how it feels.
- Move focus to the left side of the brain – see how it feels.
- Move focus to any areas of left or right side that feel underused.
- Rest the mind in the centre of the brain.

Shift the focus of the mind to different body areas. As you do so, imagine you switch on a large light bulb there so that the whole area gets bathed in light. Stay in each of the following areas for a slow count of three:

- Feet
- Hips
- Centre (remember from the strength section, the centre is the point just below the navel)
- Solar plexus/stomach (level with the lower ribs, behind the soft central stomach area where the diaphragm connects to the spine)

- Heart/chest
- Neck/throat
- Centre of the brain
- Above the top of the head

Move the focus back to the area in front of the brain. Most people visualise in this space – what we often call the 'mind's eye'.

Now you are ready to visualise your goals effectively . . .

Exercise: 'Seeing the Long Game'

This visualisation, which we call 'Seeing the Long Game', starts with thinking of something you want to achieve and picturing it in vivid detail. There is no magic wand or absolute certainty here. This exercise simply enables you to clarify your desired destination, build belief and create 'towards' chemistry, in which dopamine is high and cortisol is optimal, by imagining something rewarding.

A specific type of focus is important. Two practical experiments from New York University in 2014 showed that if you concentrate your focus on the thing that you want as if it were in a spotlight, your perception of how far away it is is reduced – it appears more attainable. Also, when asked to walk towards a desirable object but look to the side and all around you – it takes you longer to get there than if your eyes focus solely on the goal. In fact, using narrowed attention can get you there 23 per cent faster. This suggests that visualisation of goals might not only ensure success, but create pace as well.

This exercise can be done alone or with a partner, colleague, friend or coach. It can also be done as a team that is working together towards a common goal. If you are new to using visualisation, choose a place where you will not be disturbed;

although, with practice, visualisations can be conjured up just about anywhere.

- Sit/stand quietly, close your eyes and breathe.
- Let your goal come to mind and begin to picture exactly what achieving this goal looks like.
- Let the visualisation develop so that the picture is highly defined, with vivid colours and textures. Where are you? What are you doing? Who are you talking to? What are others doing and saying? Hear the sounds, smells, tastes as if you were really there.
- Having imagined this moment exactly, allow yourself to feel the positive emotions it generates, the sense of achievement, happiness, relief, contentment, euphoria etc.
- Then visualise the other people benefitting. What impact will your achievement have on your family, your community, your team, your organisation, the wider business community, your country, the world?
- Open your eyes.
- Draw yourself a timeline from left to right on a sheet of paper.
- At the right end, note down your goal and describe the visualisation.
- Decide on the timeframe: six months/one year/two years/five years etc.
- Revisit the mental picture regularly, especially when patience and sustained energy is required. This keeps the long game firmly in mind and the visualisation will give you a dopamine boost each time you picture it.
- Find time to describe your visualisation to someone else (e.g. partner or close friend). Verbalising it will also make it feel more real.

Keep your timeline handy, because in the next chapter we will be adding in short-term milestones and exploring how we can use our bodies to increase our determination to achieve our goals.

20

MUSCLE-FIRMING AND MILESTONES

How our bodies help us achieve our goals one step at a time

Stiffen the sinews, summon up the blood,
Disguise fair nature with hard-favour'd rage . . .
. . . Now set the teeth and stretch the nostril wide,
Hold hard the breath and bend up every spirit
To his full height.

—WILLIAM SHAKESPEARE,
HENRY V, ACT III, SCENE 1

The phrase 'grit your teeth' when we talk about determination makes physiological sense (although we don't recommend it long term). If you grit your teeth and firm your jaw, you automatically hold your breath, which creates a firmness in your abdomen enabling you to engage all of the abdominal muscles in an act of immense effort and endurance. We can use a technique of momentary muscle-firming to build up our determination and work towards our dreams step by step.

Muscle-firming gives us willpower and the ability to withstand immediate pain in order to attend to essential priorities – provided that we believe that doing so will produce long-term benefits. In 2011, researchers from the universities of

Singapore and Chicago published a report, entitled 'From Firm Muscles to Firm Willpower', that shows how the body plays a big part in harnessing willpower and the facility to self-regulate towards the attainment of long-term goals. Participants were instructed to tighten their muscles, e.g. hand, finger, calf or biceps, while trying to exhibit self-control in a variety of circumstances – submerging hands in an ice bucket, consuming a bad-tasting but healthy vinegar drink or being offered tempting but unhealthy foods. Muscle-firming helped at the moment of weakening or avoidance.

> **LIFE HACK:** Which muscles can you unobtrusively tighten? Experiment with how this helps you when your willpower usually weakens or you have to do something you don't want to. It's fun!

Exercise: Muscle-firming

Muscle-firming action(s) work when applied at the specific point in time when your willpower and determination are tested. They are muscle or muscle group contractions that are held for about four seconds, often needing to be unobtrusive enough to be done in public – for example, squeezing your thumb against your forefinger, clenching your buttock muscles or pressing your upper arms into the sides of your body. Experiment with what works for you. (I have two: flattening my hand and squeezing my fingers together and another, more obvious one. I make fists with both hands, firm my arm and abdominal muscles and say (out loud if I can), 'Come on, Claire, you can do this.')

To create your own muscle-firming action:

- Stand or sit
- Experiment with one or two muscle-firming actions,

drawing from the examples above, that make you feel more determined
- Put words to them if you like – words of encouragement or a self-rallying call
- Practise them a few times for familiarity
- Start using them whenever your willpower weakens and you feel like giving up

You'll find that this muscle-firming technique enables you to handle the inevitable setbacks that come with each milestone on the road to your desired outcome or goal.

Creating and working with milestones

While visualising our goals clarifies our dreams and draws us powerfully towards them, if we are to succeed we need short-term, achievable milestones created in a practical and realistic manner with a sequence of tangible actions attached to them.

Milestones, as well as ultimate goals, therefore, should be visualised. The trick is to switch from visualising the long-term goal to the short-term milestone whenever either becomes overwhelming or unrewarding. So, if you've hit a wall and the long-term goal gives you a sinking feeling, then completely switch your focus to the next short-term milestone. For example, when in bootcamp or while on deployment, those in the military traditionally count down the days – ninety-eight days left, ninety-seven days left, ninety-six days left etc . . . If you are working through milestones well, but the deadline means you are going to need to push yourself really hard through days, weeks and months without respite, then focus on the long-term goal instead.

MEGAN ACHIEVES HER AMBITION
BY VISUALISING MILESTONES ...

Morning television anchor and reporter Megan Mitchell is a young person with ambition – and a vision. Her love of media and writing led her to study journalism at Emerson College, and she set herself the goal of becoming the morning anchor on the *Today* show, one of the top morning shows in the USA. Having visualised that clear goal, she set a number of interim milestones, which she also visualised. These were:

- Working on the in-house television channel while in school, which she began doing immediately.
- Being the anchor for *Good Morning Emerson*, the school's morning television programme. (A position she was awarded one year before graduating.)
- Finding a morning anchor position post-graduation. (She created a reel and started looking, leveraging her network, and was hired as morning anchor in a smaller market [city] in the USA right after graduation and worked there successfully for two years.)
- Moving to a morning anchor position in one of the top sixty markets in the USA. (Well before she was ready to make that move, Megan found an agent who turned down positions on her behalf that didn't meet this interim milestone until she found the perfect position, the one she is in today.)
- Her next milestone will be an anchor position in a market (city) in the top ten.

Megan said, 'I have the news on all the time and when I am in my element, I even pretend I am a *Today* show anchor, just to keep reminding myself where I want to be.' To support her ongoing visualisation, she also has a photo of herself behind the anchor desk on the *Today* show set – a very tangible reminder indeed.

Military squads sing and chant rhymes in order to endure long-distance training because it takes their minds off the hardship. Singing together boosts oxytocin, which also reduces fear and gives you courage. On assault courses or at the gym, when you are working towards milestones that stretch you to your limits, the quintessential grunting, aggressive vocalising, hard use of the breath and wide stance draw testosterone levels up in order to meet the challenge and face the risk.

Dopamine can also be released by distraction. When something is tough and repetitive and just has to be done, then, having found your rhythm, imagining the delicious cappuccino that awaits you or what you'll do on your next holiday, or what you'll cook for supper that evening, will distract you. You can also try the opposite: imagining how much worse life could be, creating perspective on how painful this is. Remember, dopamine likes novelty, so be creative with what you do with your mindset as you tackle those milestones.

Severe loss of determination can come in the form of extreme low energy and tiredness when you feel overwhelmed. The thought, *Maybe I won't succeed*, or worse, *I am failing*, scares us. The body slams on its brakes and makes us produce *too much* of the calming chemical acetylcholine, so we feel resistance to carrying on. This is a moment to treat the adrenals kindly and refocus on the next milestone, and if that milestone feels overwhelming, then you may need to add an interim milestone that is more manageable. Once you have a clear, workable milestone in mind, then muscle-firming, jumping up and down, vocalising, breathing hard and fast, laughing (literally) in the face of fear all help to kick-start your energy levels again.

LIFE HACK: When the going gets tough or you've had a setback, grit your teeth, clench your fists, jump up and down to get your energy going – whatever it takes physically – and tell yourself, 'Come on. I am not giving up.'

ALESSANDRA SUMMONS UP THE BLOOD...

At age twenty-one, Alessandra was invited by Mikhail Baryshnikov to join the American Ballet Theatre as a principal dancer, and to dance with him at the MET (Metropolitan Opera House). Having grown into the principal dancer role at the Royal Ballet in London surrounded by friends and supporters, she was suddenly on her own, under enormous pressure. 'I had to fight with myself,' she says. 'It was a huge mental struggle. I had to dance on stage at the MET with Baryshnikov and this was not the time to have doubts.' As she speaks, she firms her muscles, her fists clench and her lips squeeze together, remembering the circumstances. She then adds wisely, 'Of course the fight always appears to be with circumstances, but the fight is always actually with yourself.' As we have already established, your level of self-determination dictates whether pressure chokes us or focuses us.

LIFE HACK: When you realise that fear is holding you back, laugh in its face!

People have dreams. They tell me they would love to start a company, write a book, grow vegetables on an allotment, design and build their own house, travel the world, and yet many go on with their lives day to day with those desires unrealised. Visualising the future *and* realistic planning are both important.

TOP TIPS FROM OUR PANEL ON
TACKLING MILESTONES...

- 'Put accountability around your milestones, for example, by sharing them with a coach or teammate.' – *Jarrod Barnes*
- 'Milestones shouldn't be *too* fixed so that you can't adjust them on the way.' – *Claire Taylor*
- 'If you don't quite reach a milestone, go back and re-evaluate, focus on what you can learn, what you can do better next time; never feel a sense of failure.' – *Camilla Ross*
- 'Sometimes life can get in the way of the milestones we set in youth. If you need to take a detour or a new path, remain open, curious and studious. Keep learning. Celebrate new milestones.' – *Dawn Marie Flynn Sirrenberg*
- 'To move through milestones, focus on the long-term goal, lean into it and keep going. Remember that the team is counting on you.' – *Karl Van Haute*

Exercise: Creating milestones

Clarity of thought is vital for creating milestones, so I recommend doing this in a dedicated hour or two, during a day when you have plenty of time for quiet reflection. This thinking creates the groundwork for a detailed project plan. If you are working in a team with others on a project, or you are planning something as a family, then simply follow the steps together and discuss each one. In larger teams, you can split into smaller groups, with each group working on a different part of the timeline, then see how they link and overlap when you come back together.

- Remember the goal you worked on in 'Seeing the Long Game' (pp. 329–31).

- Working backwards from your goal, ask yourself, 'What is the penultimate milestone that I'll need to hit?' Create a visual picture for this milestone. Mark it on the graphic you created in the last chapter. Continue to work backwards until you have three to five milestones visualised and planned out with rough time intervals marked.

- In the intervals, write down what approach, focus, behaviour, resources and training are required for you to be able to achieve the next milestone. Remember the creativity and innovation chapter? Consider where you would benefit more from divergent versus convergent behaviour. Be specific – perhaps you need to raise some financing, get others involved etc.

- Now, this next part is unconventional, but it works. Alone or with a colleague or friend, rehearse this timeline. Stand up, clear enough space so that you can walk through it in a line. Talk as you walk, verbalising what it is going to take. Stop at each milestone, visualise it again. How does that feel? Ask questions. Evaluate if the progression makes sense. Make and remake firm plans.

- Rehearsing the milestones prior to executing them in this way sets up the cortisol and testosterone levels needed to respond to the challenge and the dopamine levels needed to anticipate the reward.

- Pin your timeline up on the wall or put it on your laptop or phone as your screen saver.

- As you execute each part of the plan in real time, celebrate each milestone well. Start by using a winner pose – arms in the air – feel the shot of dopamine and testosterone, then share your success with others.

- Use muscle-firming (pp. 333–4) at the tough, painful points or when you feel tired or discouraged – and as you focus on the next milestone, feel the dopamine boost.

- In reality, at each milestone you will reassess and revise your plan for the next based on what you have learned.

In brief:

- Create and visualise milestones
- Celebrate achievement
- Use muscle-firming
- Re-evaluate tactics

Having looked at how to create success milestone by milestone, now we'll look at how we can train and develop our stamina and get that little bit more from ourselves when sustained effort is required to carry us through those moments when we feel like giving up.

21

THE ENDURANCE TUNNEL

How to focus ourselves to move through adversity

> If you do not see light at the end of the
> tunnel, consider it an opportunity to create
> an opening yourself, wherever you want.
>
> —ASHOK KALLARAKKAL

Many people endure not through choice but through necessity. Sometimes we make things tough for ourselves and other times things just *are* tough. Athletes, dancers and highly driven people in any walk of life, on the other hand, endure through choice. The problem comes when life is tough emotionally, mentally and physically and our overall stamina is too low. So, how can we train for endurance in everyday life? What can we learn from athletes and dancers? How does dopamine enable us to persist on our journey when the going gets really tough?

An 'Endurance Tunnel' is a period of relative difficulty when you are fully aware that you will need to apply enormous effort. As you go through it, you hope that you have the stamina to continue to move towards the light at the end of the tunnel despite the difficulty. The danger, unless we apply endurance strategies, is that at the most challenging times it feels as though the tunnel is narrowing or collapsing. We feel hemmed in and overwhelmed.

One way of keeping the tunnel open is with powerful and rhythmic use of our breath to boost DHEA and keep us well-oxygenated. A martial artist preparing to strike a plank of wood and split it in two will use breath to build up 'ki' or 'chi' (energy and force) in the body to be able to apply an effective blow to the plank. They use their breath actively, drawing it in and driving it out strongly, sometimes for a period of twenty or thirty minutes. US Navy Seals use a gadget called a respiratory muscle trainer that makes them breathe against resistance to develop respiratory stamina. Both of these vocations train you for sustained effort in situations of extremely high levels of pressure, war and conflict. However, we can all develop our approach to endurance training without having to sign up for an Iron Man/Woman competition, spend ten years up a mountain in China or join the armed forces. Instead, we'll learn an endurance breathing technique – called 'Feel the Force' – that you can integrate into your endurance practice.

Deep core strength is an important aspect of endurance, allowing us to take the strain without collapsing. As we have been learning, the ability to physically endure gives us mental and emotional endurance. This is particularly important now, as technology automates many of the more physically demanding tasks, such as chopping wood or carrying buckets of coal, that many of us would have done ourselves fifty years ago. The Pilates or yoga class, gym training or our home fitness programmes now replace this and are therefore essential.

I have experienced first-hand the powerful link between core strength, determination and reaching goals. I had a very weak core as a child, even though I was dancing three times a week. I had a bad kidney infection at age five and peritonitis when I was ten. At eighteen, I was still rather frail, especially for the athletic, contemporary work I liked, plus I was a little lost, and ended up in an unsuitable marriage. With a full gym programme alongside my technical dance practice, as well as some serious soul searching, by age twenty-five I had removed myself from the marriage and started my dance company, fully on track with my life. Gym training changed me in a way dance training could not because I learned to work with resistance. This not only made me determined, but it also helped me realise that my mission in life would be Physical Intelligence.

Since then, I have developed a way of training that doesn't require our clients to go to the gym, that works directly on endurance and which I will share with you shortly. As you develop your Physical Intelligence, everything you do physically can support you emotionally and mentally. While writing this book, as we put in long hours pushing for the deadline, Pat and I have been in a number of Endurance Tunnels. In response, I find I automatically want to increase my daily resistance training, adding repetitions and circuits when running and exercising in the park. It is as if in order to bolster the mental effort, I have to galvanise my physical energy as well.

JOAN AND JEFF SURVIVE THEIR ENDURANCE TUNNEL...

Joan Beal, the studio singer who spoke with us about how to keep our voices flexible, is married to multiple Emmy Award-winning composer Jeff Beal. Eleven years ago, Jeff was diagnosed with multiple sclerosis (a neurodegenerative disease marked by progressive weakening and wasting of the muscles). He was extremely fatigued and spent most of his days sleeping, able to compose for only a couple of hours a day and unable to conduct at all. It was extremely frustrating for him because there was so much he wanted to do. The doctors said that while they could work to slow the progression, medical research at that time indicated that the damage done couldn't be reversed. Joan and Jeff were in the Endurance Tunnel, and it had started to collapse.

Joan has a scientific brain and immediately started researching the disease. She believed that if Jeff could increase blood flow and oxygen to his brain, it would have a healing effect. Understanding the brain–heart connection, Joan also believed that in addition to following the doctor's advice, a heart–healthy life would translate into a brain–healthy life. Together, they began a daily practice of exercise (stimulating the parasympathetic nervous system, which releases acetylcholine, counteracting adrenalin and cortisol), meditation (increasing serotonin and strengthening the immune system), eating whole foods (maintaining blood sugar balance and reducing toxins) and getting adequate sleep (helping the brain to heal, which we will learn about more in Chapter 25). On top of that, sunshine and laughter increased dopamine levels, which bolstered Jeff's creativity. The act of composing itself became part of the healing process because the area of Jeff's brain most damaged is the corpus callosum that connects left and right brain hemispheres, critical for creating music.

It isn't a quick fix – you can't see or feel it day to day – but every two years, Jeff goes in for a new MRI and they can see that healing has occurred – there are no new lesions and those that were there are shrinking. Jeff can now jog, ski, compose and conduct. Instead of the disease sidetracking Jeff, some of his most ground-breaking work has come post-diagnosis.

As Joan shared, it's impossible to know if the healing was facilitated by his new lifestyle or simply luck, and it is important to acknowledge that individual results will vary, but there is now significant research on how exercise, nutrition and lifestyle can change the course of the disease and two medical doctors with multiple sclerosis, Dr Terry Wahls and Dr George Jelinek, who have reversed their disease using similar techniques, have published books and research on their findings.

Jeff's health outcome aside, what we do know for sure is that the daily approach to life that the Beals created kept their Endurance Tunnel open. By applying Physical Intelligence strategies, we can all influence how bright the future looks for us.

(NB: We are not suggesting that Physical Intelligence is a cure for multiple sclerosis. We share this story as one example of how a positive approach to lifestyle clearly benefitted the Beals. Please consult with your doctor before adopting any new strategies and do not stop taking any medication without your doctor's advice.)

LIFE HACK: How do you feel right now about the future? Whatever you feel, imagine that the whole of your body, every cell, is smiling. Like a plant growing towards the light, feel your way to the light at the end of the tunnel.

Working to deadlines is one of the most common examples of an Endurance Tunnel that many of us experience. When Pat is not writing books, she is designing complex consulting and training processes, curriculums and programmes that are always tied to deadlines. She moves from one Endurance Tunnel to the next and she simply cannot miss a deadline. Conference rooms have been booked, facilitators have been scheduled, travel plans have been made for twenty or even hundreds of people. The show must always go on. Largely at the mercy of her clients for information (which often comes late), Pat can see multiple Endurance Tunnels approaching ahead of time. Marking out milestones and earmarking reward points (often a square of good-quality chocolate) gets Pat through long hours of hard slog. Fitness and a steely determination are critical. She says, 'I absolutely must maintain belief in my own ability to get it all done. That positive mindset is essential to my peace of mind and my success.'

Where Endurance Tunnels relate to life choices, it is important to be able to exert your will. Some tunnels teach us about our limits and show us that a different way is needed. If we can't redirect the tunnel and if tunnels are too hard for too long, disillusionment follows and life can be painful. (We will look at handling pain of all kinds in the next chapter.)

Let's train: Getting through the 'Endurance Tunnel'

Exercise: 'Feel the Force'

This breathing technique powers up your energy for effort, energising the body and brain and galvanising the emotions to focus when you would rather do otherwise.

- Close the mouth, breathe in through the nose, but instead of letting the air in easily through the higher part of the nostrils, create resistance as you breathe in by sending the breath directly into the space behind the nose, high in the back of the throat (this takes some practice). If you are doing it correctly, you will make a sound rather like Darth Vader in *Star Wars*: a slight rasping sound as you breathe in and out. You will notice that to draw in a full breath, your diaphragm and breathing muscles have to work harder to pull the breath down into the abdomen, because you have created resistance to the airflow.
- Once you have worked out how to do that, practise strongly holding the breath for a slow count of three at

the top of the in-breath – firm up your abdominals as you hold your breath.

- Now, focus on *how* you fill the body with breath. Fill your lower abdomen first, then the middle of your abdomen, then finally fill the top of the lungs and chest, then hold the breath.
- On the out-breath, reverse the action – emptying the chest, middle and lower abdomen in that order.
- At the end of the out-breath you will most likely notice a small pause once you are used to the exercise. Breathe in again as soon as you want to.

Take five, slow, strong breaths in this way. Then, with practice, when you return to normal breathing you should feel a renewed sense of your power and strength. This is a real workout for the breath and gives you a feeling of control. Resistance breathing prepares you to work against any other kind of resistance; I often use this kind of breathing before tackling a huge task.

(NB: This exercise will not be possible if your nose is blocked for any reason. If this is the case, shape your mouth as if you are drinking through a straw – which also creates a degree of resistance – and continue with the exercise as instructed.)

Exercise: Endurance movements
As you will remember from the previous sections, specific movements create specific mindsets. Here are six types of movements to include in your daily practice and integrate into your endurance training.

1. Core Endurance
Sometimes it takes all of our effort to carry on through an Endurance Tunnel. Your core strength, which we covered in Chapter 7, is a vital aspect of your ability to do this. Fully

integrating powerful movement of the limbs and the core will enable you to feel you can approach resistance or pressure of any kind in an integrated way and gain staying power as a result.

Building on your strength training, let's focus in more detail on how to develop your endurance through increasing the time the muscles are under tension in these exercises and varying them to make them more challenging. As you execute the following exercises, try to use the deepest core muscles you can feel to support the movement. Right before each movement, move the shoulders back and down, which will automatically engage the core, and keep them fixed through the whole sequence. Imagine that your core muscles are doing the lifting or pushing. Remember to use smooth, controlled muscle action – three seconds into action and three seconds to recover is the basic principle. Sometimes there will be a hold in between.

Do these exercises carefully at home following the instructions as explained and illustrated, but always listen to your body and adapt where necessary.

Leg Lift

- Stand with both feet on the ground, applying posture technique from Chapter 2 (pp. 43–8).
- Draw the shoulders back and down.
- Lift the pelvic floor and feel the band of muscle across the lower abdomen engage.
- Transfer your body weight onto your non-dominant leg.
- Allowing the leg to bend naturally at the knee, lift the opposite knee up as far as it will go – without lifting the hip or changing the alignment of the pelvis.
- Pause for a moment to find stability and balance.

- Slowly lower the leg and put the foot down, keeping the shoulders down and pelvic floor raised.
- Transfer your weight onto your dominant leg and follow the same instructions to lift the opposite knee. Take the same amount of time as you did working on your non-dominant leg.
- Explore how many repetitions take you to tiredness and add a couple more as a starting point.

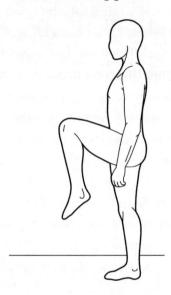

Plank Leg Bend

- Kneel down, place your forearms on the floor in front of you with palms down or hands in fists (rotate the lower arms slightly outwards for greater challenge).
- Now, supporting your body weight on your forearms and elbows, feeling the muscles under the shoulder blades retracting, stretch one leg then the other out behind you, toes tucked under, pelvis off the ground, feet hip-width apart.
- Keep the hips in line with your shoulders – the pelvis should not be too high or too low. (Use a mirror to check this alignment.)

- Visualise dragging your elbows to your hips to add the right level of tension to the plank shape.
- If this feels challenging already, then stay here for a count of five seconds and gradually build up the time a little more every three days up to a maximum of thirty seconds.
- To add challenge, keep the shoulders back and down, engage the core and keep the hips, ribs and spine firmly held in place, then bend your knee on your non-dominant side up in the direction of the elbow on the non-dominant side just as far as you can go. You are unlikely to be able to touch the knee to the elbow, but the knee should move in the direction of the elbow. Take this slowly to start with in order to find out how the movement works.
- Slowly replace that leg next to the other one, and repeat the movement, bringing the dominant knee towards the dominant elbow.
- Repeat five times on each side and add repetitions day by day as you get stronger.
- Focus on quality of engagement and firmness of the core muscles, as if they are moving the leg. Prioritise this quality over quantity, especially as you start learning this exercise.

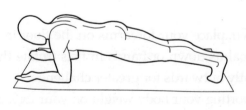

2. Leg and Lower Back Endurance

Endurance Squats

- Stand with the feet slightly wider than hip-width apart. Toes should be pointing forwards or slightly outwards (listen to your body to find what feels most comfortable), arms down by the sides of your body.
- Shoulders back and down, engage core muscles.
- Bring the arms forwards and out in front of you for balance while you bend the knees and move your pelvis back as far as you can, weight on the heels, as if you are going to sit down on a low stool behind you. Only go as far as you can while still keeping the shoulders back and down – aim for thighs parallel with the floor. Knees never go further forwards than the toes and heels remain on the floor.
- Hold, increasing the stretch by moving the pelvis further back and reaching the arms further forwards.
- Keep the core engaged and come back up to the original starting position – legs and arms arriving back at the same time.

- Take three seconds to go down, hold for three seconds, then take three seconds to come up.
- Repeat five times to begin with, and gradually increase repetitions.
- Add pulses – go down to the deep point, up halfway, and down to the deep point again, repeating five times.
- Or try ten squats (down for three seconds, up for three seconds), holding the last one for five seconds.

3. Shoulder, Chest and Upper Back Endurance

Arm Circles

- Stand using posture technique from Chapter 2 (pp. 43–8), arms by your sides.
- Move shoulders back and down.
- Raise both arms slowly to shoulder height, palms down, as if they are being moved by and from your deep core muscles and the muscles under your shoulder blades so that the arm and shoulder muscles themselves are not tense and rigid.
- Slowly circle the arms eight times forwards and eight times backwards, maintaining engagement of the core (imagine you are drawing circles with your fingertips, about the size of a small plate).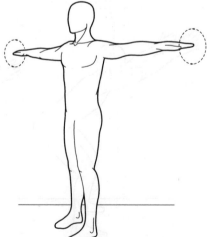
- Lower the arms, maintaining core muscle engagement.
- Repeat five times, then add repetitions as you feel stronger.

4. Ambition Generator

Reach and Harness

- Focus on a point at the edge of the room.
- Reach towards that point with your hand and arm and stretch through the whole body.
- Step or lunge towards the point and reach further.
- When you believe you are stretched to your limit, reach a few millimetres further and make a fist with the hand, as if you are capturing the air molecules at that stretch point.
- Bring the fisted hand into your body to harness the effort.
- Lift the back foot and place it next to the front foot.
- Repeat with the other arm.
- Repeat six times more, alternating arms and reaching in a new direction each time. Breathe while you move.

5. *Equilibrium Generator*

Place and Balance

- Describe two sides of a box with your hands; be precise about the measurement between the two hands.
- Now, change the position of the hands to describe the top and bottom of a box.
- Repeat this action a few times, feeling how steady and placed the movements are. (This is the kind of gesture we might use during a speech if we are talking about how to structure a project.)

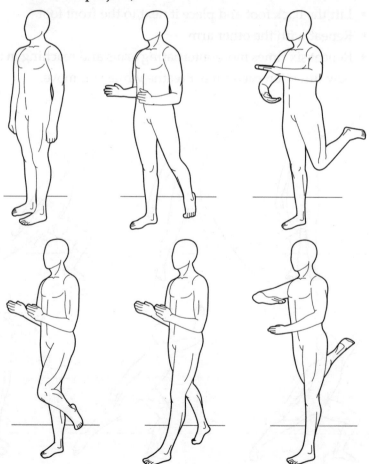

- Now, repeat this arm action, but each time you place the hands on the two sides of the box, step forwards, transferring all your body weight onto one leg.
- While you move your hands onto the top and bottom of the box, take the back foot off the ground and find your balance on the front leg. Try to be completely still while balancing on one leg.

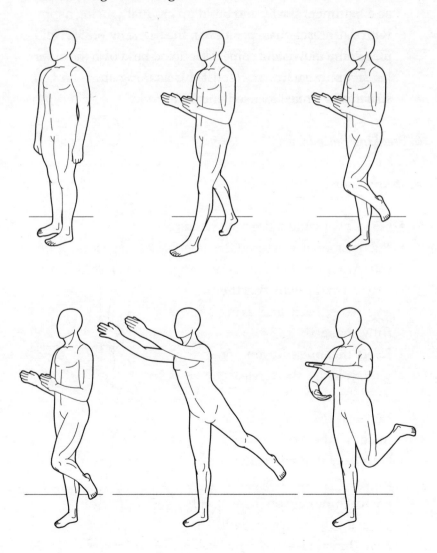

- If you are stable here and would like an extra challenge then reach forwards with your arms and back with your free leg, tipping the body forwards, trying for a horizontal body line: body and leg parallel to the floor, balancing on one leg. (Note: you are unlikely to reach the horizontal unless you are already a dancer, gymnast, yoga practitioner or athlete.) At first, this may feel *very* challenging, so experiment slowly and build up gradually, being happy with the intermediate position in the figure on p. 355. Hold for a count of five and come back up. Repeat with the other leg stepping forwards. Repeat this as many times as you like until you feel focused and balanced.

6. *Breaking Boundaries*

Push and Thrust

- Go to a wall and place both hands on it.
- Put one foot forward and the other back and ground yourself. Arms are bent. All at once, apply as much pressure as you can to the wall. Feel the legs, core, back and arms fully engaged.
- Keep the pressure on for ten seconds, then release and breathe freely.
- Repeat three times. You can imagine the wall to be a boundary that you want to move, or a situation that is encroaching on you. Bench presses at the gym will have the same effect.

Extending ourselves from a strong core, aware of the pressure and demands we are putting on ourselves, but remaining very much in charge, enables us to keep our Endurance Tunnels open enough so that we can move through them towards the light at the end.

By now you are becoming well-equipped to sustain yourself in challenging times, setting goals and milestones and integrating your body and breath towards those goals. Before we do some important work on purpose, motivation and appreciation, let's take a brief look at how to survive adversarial conditions and break through the pain barrier. This next chapter has applications to many significant aspects of life, including emotional pain and grief, handling physical injury and illness and overcoming extended periods of frustration, struggle and strife.

22

BREAKING THE PAIN BARRIER

How to push through extreme discomfort to sustain effort

You can't avoid pain, but you can choose to overcome it.

—PAULO COELHO

Our brains and bodies have a complex neural mechanism called a 'central governor', part of our survival system that keeps us from harm or injury so that when we feel pain or fatigue we instinctively want to stop the activity that is causing it. However, the central governor is very cautious. It kicks in early, well before we need to fear negative consequences. In truth, therefore, our bodies can go beyond what our brains are telling us. This thought alone will help you push yourself on when you need or want to do so – within reason. As we discussed in the resilience section, rest and recovery are important, but we also need to be able to push through the pain barrier; otherwise we wouldn't be able to survive disasters or traumas, climb Mount Everest, smash world records, travel to the moon, endure childbirth or pass exams.

LIFE HACK: Next time you feel at the limit of endurance – the baby wakes up for the fifth time that night, the project you are working on hits yet another barrier, or you are struggling acutely with anything you are doing – think of the overcautious central governor. Know that you can survive this and push yourself to go further than you previously thought possible. Say to yourself, 'I have reserves of energy I haven't used yet.' You will quickly feel less desperate and more positive about your situation.

Building our stamina through a variety of means is important so that we become more confident in our ability to endure hardship. In this chapter, we will learn to create small, powerful nudges to our chemistry to get us through pain and difficulty. We will learn to influence our pituitary gland to release beta-endorphins, the most powerful of the endorphins, our natural morphine-like painkillers, which are secreted into the nervous system to dull pain and make us feel better. They can be released on demand if you instruct the brain to take the heat out of the moment – just like flicking a switch.

Imagine that you are out at Sunday morning football. It is windy and raining, your eight-year-old is playing and having a fantastic time, and you are supporting from the sidelines, enduring the weather conditions. You have a choice: you can either focus on the bad weather, hunch up and complain, or trick the brain into taking the pain away, enabling you to sustain your performance as a parent, supporting your child on the pitch, perhaps even enjoying some camaraderie with other mums and dads.

One surprisingly simple technique for mild pain relief is smiling. When we smile, both serotonin and endorphins are released in ourselves as well as others, which helps us to endure especially challenging times in life.

LIFE HACK: If you are out running and reach a point where your legs start to really hurt or you feel you simply can't go on – try smiling. It'll help!

Prior to a cricket season, with months to prepare, Claire Taylor would deliberately break an aspect of her technique. She would brutally deconstruct it and feel the pain of not being able to do it well, then, by setting goals and milestones, she would reconstruct it again more strongly. She calls it 'bursting the bubble'. She says, 'Sometimes really stressing yourself physically helps your mental endurance. You can absolutely do more than you think you can, so pain is good from that respect. In fact, it is a pre-emptor and enabler of change.' Similarly, many professional golfers regularly rework their swing and have a very similar experience. As the saying goes, 'No pain, no gain.'

Belief changes our pain threshold. You can see this in the placebo effect. Research from Aberystwyth University, Wales, shows that cyclists who believe they have been given a new, legal performance-enhancing pill, which is in fact a placebo, can cycle 2–3 per cent faster. Scientists believe that the placebo effect works in such a way as to trick the hypothalamus/pituitary gland that there are no barriers to enhanced performance. The *belief* in the effectiveness of the pill, the thought process itself, releases beta-endorphins, thereby reducing pain and fatigue.

Similarly, the *expectation* of pain or fatigue can influence how much pain we feel. Just today, I coached a client who had cracked a number of ribs ten years ago. His body was reluctant to execute a flexibility twist because his nervous system was *still* primed for the pain, even though his ribs had healed many years ago. His pain was created in his brain. Research from UWE Bristol has noted that in people with osteoarthritis, the degree of structural damage or inflammation does not tally with the amount of pain they feel. It seems that it is in fact the patients' *perception* of how much danger they are in that influences the severity of pain they experience. For more on the science of pain and fatigue, see *Cure: A Journey into the Science of Mind Over Body* by science writer Jo Marchant.

Dancers live with physical pain every day and come to know which physical pain is normal wear and tear that can be worked through and which pain threatens injury and needs rest. I believe we can all do that more effectively. As we discovered when we did our MOT in the flexibility section (pp. 145–9), our bodies talk to us, and tension and pain are primary alerts. If we know and *believe* that our brains alert us to pain long before we have reached our limits, we can be less afraid of pain and more inquisitive, creative and robust in our response to it.

Most injuries I had as a dancer enabled me to come back stronger. As I rehabilitated, I integrated that part of my body more into the whole, understanding what that part needed, paying attention to how it felt, a little like filling in detail on a map.

When there is very little dopamine or endorphins in the system, no extrinsic or intrinsic reward (because personal resources are at their lowest), no one cheering you on or paying you extra attention, many will give up the fight. Your system screams at you, 'I can't take any more. STOP RIGHT NOW!' At this moment, visualising the pituitary gland providing beta-endorphins can save the day and give you just enough of an edge to get you through the wall. Every time you do this you come back stronger next time.

Exercise: 'Breaking the Pain Barrier'
The people we coach love this exercise. Take a look at the picture overleaf. The pituitary gland, a pea-like structure in

the centre of the brain just behind the eyes, synthesises and stores endorphins, the holy grail of natural pain relief – our own personal morphine. Beta-endorphins are the most potent of all. Visualise the gland and the beta-endorphins as strands of proteins, like beads on a necklace, coiled up and placed in burgeoning sacs, ready to explode into the body.

Under extreme physical duress, the body releases endorphins naturally to enable us to survive. As neuroscientist Candace Pert outlines in her book, *Molecules of Emotion*, and in the experiments by psychotherapist Evelyn Silvers in the 1980s, we can instruct the brain to release these pleasure chemicals to bind to receptors all over the body, limiting pain and discomfort. Such chemicals sustain our peak performance for longer periods under challenging conditions. Here is how to practise this technique:

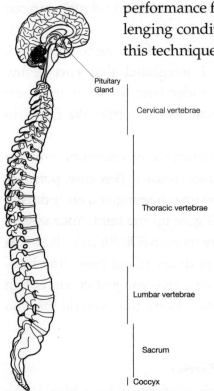

Pituitary Gland

Cervical vertebrae

Thoracic vertebrae

Lumbar vertebrae

Sacrum

Coccyx

- Close your eyes, visualise your pituitary gland in the brain – let the picture form in your mind's eye.
- Say to yourself, 'Easy' or 'More in the tanks', and remember that your brain creates pain well before there is any danger – i.e. you are safe right now.
- Count down from ten, visualising the pituitary gland producing more and more pleasure

chemicals – beta-endorphins. See them build up, held in bulging sacs dangling from the tip of the gland.

- Let this picture develop as you count down.
- When you reach number one, let the sacs burst open and the beta-endorphin molecules charge down into your spinal cord and out into your nervous system to the multiple pleasure receptors.
- Breathe – let the endorphins flood to all of the body parts that need them.
- Immediately feel the switch as pain and discomfort turn to pleasure and greater ease.

This exercise will give you temporary relief from physical pain or emotional discomfort lasting a few minutes – which is sometimes all you need to get through a barrier. If you build up your practice, you will see how it can help you perceive adversarial conditions in a different way – not something that is happening *to* you, but a manageable transformative event.

Even if we are free of acute physical or emotional pain, it's easy to get into the habit of complaining and feeling that we have to endure life's trials. I use this technique to change how I feel about typical mundane tasks, such as doing the accounts or filling in the tax return, and my son Angus uses it during exam revision. Now, let's build on this attitudinal shift and look at the chemistry of motivation and appreciation.

23

The Chemistry of Motivation and Appreciation

How to capitalise on what drives our will to achieve

If you are working on something exciting
that you really care about, you don't have to
be pushed. The vision pulls you.

—STEVE JOBS

'Come on, Steve!' 'You can do it, Diane!' 'Fantastic job, Uzma!'

As you turn the final corner of the marathon route, exhausted and spent, you hear family, friends and the crowd shout encouragement; you hear your name, you hear cheering; you see smiling faces looking at you. It gives you just the uplift you need to make it to the finish line. Even though every part of your body hurts, the pain seems suddenly less, and you receive a much-needed burst of energy. Your chemistry receives a triple boost of the top 'feel-good' chemicals: serotonin (self-esteem), oxytocin (love and social bonding) and dopamine (pleasure and reward), along with a healthy dose of endorphins.

LIFE HACK: Who could you cheer on, and who could you ask to cheer you on? Text them now.

Appreciation is a powerful motivator. It is a myth across sales teams globally that money is the most important thing. While it certainly is valued, feeling appreciated and having a sense of accomplishment generally sit above money on the list of typical motivators.

KARL VAN HAUTE GIVES AND RECEIVES INCREDIBLE MOTIVATION...

As part of his US Marine Corps leadership training, Karl was taking part in a 7-mile 'hump' – a conditioning hike carried out while carrying an 80lb pack and a rifle and wearing a helmet and Kevlar vest. During the hump, participants walk in two columns along a 10–20ft-wide trail, and some assume the different roles they might find themselves in once out in the real world.

On the day of this particular hump, Karl's platoon had been in the field for several days and Karl was in the student platoon sergeant role, responsible for making sure the platoon commander had up-to-date information on the people in the platoon by regularly moving up and down the middle of the two columns to check on everyone's progress. Shortly after the hump started, Karl noticed that several people were falling behind. Self-described as 'not the most physically fit marine', he immediately told himself, 'I cannot fall back.' Every quarter- to half-mile, Karl had to report to the platoon commander at the front of the column and then immediately return to the end of the column, motivating everyone along the way to keep moving forwards. As more people fell back and the column lengthened, in order to monitor progress and report in on time, Karl found himself running the entire length of the hump, covering the length of the column, up and down, over and over again. He physically leaned into the task, propelling himself forwards as he worked to motivate the column, shouting, 'Great job, guys. Come on, keep going, keep the legs moving.' Karl believes that those in the column could see how hard he was working and, despite their own strain and audible grunting and groaning, found the strength to motivate him in return, shouting back, 'Good job, Van Haute!' There was a shared energy that helped keep Karl moving, just as his motivation helped keep them moving.

As we learned earlier, we are social beings. Even the toughest marine after a few weeks on a solo survival drill will *crave* a chat with another human. If you have seen the film *Cast Away*, you will remember how important Tom Hanks's character Chuck Noland's proxy friend, Wilson, becomes to him.

Even for the high-testosterone competitor, the social element has a positive effect. When we scratch the surface, the motivation to win that medal, score that try, hit those targets, innovate that product, heal that patient is also for others – whether it be the family, the team, the organisation, your country or your audience.

Imagine you are stranded on a desert island. All you have left is a faded photograph of your family. You can see the mainland in the distance and you just need to finish building that raft. You are hot, thirsty, about to give up. You take out that photograph and see their faces. This gives you the dopamine boost (the need for them) and the oxytocin urge (the love for them) that fuels your second wind. Moving purposefully through the Endurance Tunnel once again, breaking the pain barrier, you finish the raft and set sail for the mainland. We need each other, and the support and appreciation we give and receive is an important part of being motivated.

For American football player Jarrod Barnes, a large part of his motivation comes from 'stepping away from himself'. He says you need to understand that you are part of something bigger than yourself and that this is somewhat lost in today's society, with social media and all the hype around athletes. He told us, 'Motivation had nothing to do with me; it had more to do with my family. I wanted to be a bright spot for them and provide for my future family.' When facing a challenge, he thinks of the psychologist Carl R. Rogers quote: 'What you are to be, you are now becoming.' He says you have to realise that your actions affect other people. Drive is stronger when you step away from yourself, even if you are just thinking about the teammate next to you. It is always more about what he can do for others that motivates him.

How about you? When you visualised a goal that you want to achieve, do you remember how you felt when I asked you to visualise how others will benefit from your achieving that goal? I'll bet that it enhanced your sense of purpose. This is the chemical surge we need to capitalise on.

When you and others are fatigued from continued adversarial conditions, appreciation is a fantastic way to boost the feel-good chemicals and raise energy levels. Instead of continuing to express concern about difficulties, see where effort is being made and acknowledge it by showing appreciation for it. In particular, appreciate behaviour that will be helpful in moving things forwards. In terms of learning, we are much more likely to repeat behaviour when we have been appreciated for it. For example, 'Thank you for putting your socks in the washing basket, it made doing the washing so much easier' is going to be much more effective than, 'Finally! You never usually put your socks in the washing basket!' Appreciation lifts spirits and boosts dopamine.

LIFE HACK: Use appreciation to motivate others. On the way home, send three quick texts/emails thanking/ appreciating people for something.

Language plays a big part in how motivated people feel. We need to use a language of ownership v. blame in order to make critiquing a team or company performance motivational. Choreographer Wayne McGregor has adopted a process used by the Red Arrows aerobatic team. When they return from a flight, one by one the pilots note (critique) themselves first – sharing what went well, where they made mistakes, and where they could improve. Then they note each other. We've recommended a similar approach for many years to managers when coaching their team members.

This practice develops autonomy and relatedness, two critical factors to motivation identified by Edward Deci and Richard Ryan in their 2016 book *Self-determination Theory: Basic Psychological Needs in Motivation, Development, and Wellness.* Developing a culture where individuals can be autonomous (high dopamine and testosterone) yet strongly bonded (high oxytocin) creates the conditions for endurance.

> **LIFE HACK:** Reach out and give appreciation to someone who is going through hard times at the moment.

Self-appreciation and appreciation of what you have is also a motivator. We are often so busy being hard on ourselves, thinking about what we don't yet have or can't yet do, that we forget to acknowledge what we *do* have and what we *have* achieved. Gratitude manuals, giving praise and acknowledging effort are strategies for building motivation that we all should build into our lives.

Purpose, values and mission

Purpose and values give us determination and the desire to test ourselves against challenging objectives and make enormous sacrifices.

Our most basic purpose is to survive – to find food, water and shelter. We also need to have our social needs met. As we learned in the strength section, the five social domains are status, certainty, autonomy, fairness and relatedness (as researched for David Rock's SCARF model), and we respond to the lack of these as if they were survival threats. With enough of these needs met, however, clarity of purpose prevails, increasing our ability to endure adversity. Many Holocaust survivors said they felt they had to survive to tell others what happened. That was their purpose. Sometimes human beings do incredible things; where you might expect extreme hardship and threat to leave a person quivering in a corner, against all odds that person finds a higher purpose and therefore great strength.

Going on holiday as a family with a disabled child revealed the value my parents put on equality of experience and their purpose that we be a 'normal' family. They believed that my sister Gillian should and could experience the cliffs of Cornwall, which involved my father carrying Gillian, aged ten, up a steep and windy coastal path; my mother, pregnant, carrying the wheelchair; and me, aged nine, and my six-year-old brother carrying the picnic and everything else we needed. My mother and father showed their true grit that day. It began with dogged persistence and became a symbol of a family winning through. Singing at the tops of our voices in the car journey back to our accommodation is memorable because our parents showed us all how to have purpose, values and a mission in life.

Many organisations spend time identifying their mission and values, only for them to be filed away in a business plan. But values have to be lived and behaved. That is why when we work with businesses that are undergoing change, we help people to embody the organisation's values and find a personal connection with them.

Shared values need to be talked about, lived and relived together otherwise they will cease to have the motivational factor on an organisation's performance. England rugby player George Kruis shared how this is encouraged at Saracens Rugby Club. On their most recent 'culture trip' (the holidays they take with families designed to reward effort and embed their cultural values), on the coach they were given a card with ten different questions to be used as conversation prompts, which they were encouraged to use with people informally during the trip. George says, 'It is a reminder to speak to people, especially the new lads, about what it means to be a Saracen – about our values, the way we talk to each other and the way we deal with each other and I guess the way we look after each other.'

We all feel most motivated when our task aligns with our values, but some mundane tasks and processes – things that *have* to be done – appear not to be aligned with any value. Don't underestimate them; try to think about them differently. For example, completing the yearly accounts could be driven by the value of orderliness or taking responsibility. Caring for an ageing parent could be driven by the value of giving back, motivating us through the challenge. Aligning actions with values puts us in a 'towards' state driven by intrinsic reward rather than punishment and boosts dopamine levels and motivation. Apply this mindset to that task you've been procrastinating over and you'll find the motivation to get it done.

Let's train: The chemistry of motivation and appreciation

Using the space provided, make notes as you work through these exercises. It is fun to do this with a friend, partner, coach or colleague. Block out one hour and spend thirty minutes per person to kick this off.

Exercise: Naming your purpose

This exercise will either reinvigorate your purpose for doing what you are currently doing in your life or it may reveal the desire to inject more purpose into your life and do things differently. We all have a core purpose – grand though it may sound. What is it you are good at doing? When are you in your element? For example, your core purpose could be ...

- I ... fix things
- I ... explore
- I ... teach
- I ... invent
- I ... provide
- I ... play
- I ... engineer
- I ... dance
- I ... organise

Use the following questions to explore this for yourself:

- What do you love doing?
- What are you good at doing?
- How does this link with what the world needs currently?
- Why do/would people pay you for it?
- How would you now describe your core purpose?
  I _____ (one word)

Exercise: Naming your values

What are your values? The ones that you live by and really believe are most important in life? Give at least your top three, e.g. honesty, trying your best, risk-taking, kindness, adventuring etc.

....

....

....

Exercise: Naming your mission

Your mission is driven by your core purpose and values. To identify that, ask yourself what carrying out your core purpose delivers to the world, culture, society, your work team, community, or family. Consider the impact you have on other people or organisations by expressing and living your core purpose. Determine what the overarching point is to living out your values. Take a few moments to consider then play around with various options (see my example below to stimulate thought). Notice how your body feels as you think about this – when the words are right you will feel a 'towards' response (dopamine up and cortisol optimal – feeling pleasure, and excitement, not fear, dread or obligation).

I am here to . . .

....

....

....

My core purpose...
I dance (whether I am writing, training, being a wife and mother – more fundamentally, I 'dance').

My three top values are ...

- Creativity/Tenacity – never giving up
- Commitment – keeping my word
- Learning – continuous growth for myself and others

My mission is ...

To reveal the intelligence of the body and elevate it in the hierarchy of priorities in our culture. I believe we have the opportunity to become more evolved as human beings, by living more embodied lives.

Who benefits?

Who benefits from you fulfilling your purpose?

I just had a conversation with my brother. I asked him why he cycles competitively, and he began by saying he did it only for himself. He likes having an objective and a sense of achievement; he likes the intellectual challenge of finding out how to go faster as well as the mental, emotional and physical challenge of going through the pain barrier. I told him how his competitive cycling benefitted me:

- I am inspired by him and motivated by him to do my best too (dopamine boost).
- He is stable, so if I needed back-up, he is in a position to help (testosterone back-up).
- He is doing well, which elevates all our social statuses (great for our serotonin levels).
- His sense of fulfilment means that he is emotionally available (oxytocin all round).
- He can contribute to this book.
- I feel proud of him (my oxytocin levels are up).

- He is emotionally, physically and mentally strong, so I don't need to be concerned for his welfare (my cortisol levels are balanced).
- He is an example of commitment to his daughter and my son as they grow into adults (testosterone and dopamine boost).
- I could go on …

Often, it seems, we are inspiring and benefitting others around us without even realising it.

Exercise: Appreciation of others
This exercise will enable you to explore how appreciation is a huge driver. Plan to find opportunities to:

- Notice achievements and helpful behaviour in others
- Appreciate others by going out of your way to cheer them on and thank them for help
- Give data: when, where, what are/were they doing that you particularly appreciate
- Be specific: what is the impact on you?

Exercise: Appreciation of self
Two minutes of mental appreciation of all the things for which you are grateful and all of the things you have achieved is great endurance practice and creates a positive enduring mindset.

At the end of every day, spend two minutes appreciating what you have achieved that day. Make this a habit and do it the moment your head touches the pillow.

At the start of every day, spend two minutes appreciating what you have – a warm bed, a roof over your head etc. Make the trigger the moment you switch your alarm off.

LIFE HACK: Keep a gratitude journal by your bed to record all the good stuff.

How does it feel to have identified your motivation and to appreciate others and yourself? Notice how you feel in your body and emotions. Do you feel the dopamine – the pleasure – in having oriented your focus in such a way? Having named your purpose, values and mission? Notice how motivated you feel.

Now that we have felt the energy gain from the dopamine boost of motivation and appreciation, let's move on to other strategies to gain, rather than drain, energy for endurance.

24

ENERGY GAIN

How to tap into our energy reserves

It takes as much energy to wish as it does to plan.

—ELEANOR ROOSEVELT

When is the best time to push yourself harder, make difficult decisions and do the difficult work? How can you reduce energy drain and promote energy gain? In this chapter we discuss how to take charge of your body and brain, your schedule, and your life.

Energy is the main currency of life. The feeling of renewed energy is great, whether it is energy for your partner, your children, the dog, a bit of keyboard practice, or catching up on a work task in the evening. The executive function of our brains, carried out by the pre-frontal cortex, is extremely energy-hungry. In fact, brain activity as a whole consumes up to 20 per cent of the body's energy – more than any other single organ. Breathing techniques, exercise, sleep and diet are critical factors in having enough energy.

> **LIFE HACK:** A cold shower (turn it to cold for the last thirty seconds) or splashing ice-cold water on your face improves brain function, which in turn improves energy gain.

Depending on demand, energy is generated second by second in every cell of the body and brain by hundreds of tiny organelles called mitochondria that create and release energy using oxygen and food. You can think of mitochondria like mini rechargeable batteries in our cells. The Swedish School of Sport and Health Sciences in 2011 showed that a combination of endurance and strength training (cycling and leg presses) increases mitochondria biogenesis, enabling muscles to produce more energy. Mitochondria increase in number after short periods of intense effort, building our strength and energy efficiency. However, we also know that after long periods of overdrive, numbers decrease, affecting the functioning of many kinds of cells in the body.

Life is a balancing act of effort and recovery. After pushing ourselves, we should recover stronger and smarter than we were before, with more energy as we apply effort again.

> **LIFE HACK:** Pay heed if you do sometimes feel fatigued. This is our body's way of telling us that at some point soon we need to refuel. A good rhythm for working is: push yourself hard, then refuel and recover, push hard, then refuel and recover.

Early in my dance career, I invited Nigel Charnock, who was then a member of DV8 dance company as well as a solo artist, to direct a solo piece I was creating. I experienced how an extreme effort in the short term increases your ability to endure over the long term. Nigel was one of the most physical performers Europe has ever seen. He (literally) threw himself into every performance, taking risks with his body, and he pushed me to do the same. I knew after the first rehearsal, feeling completely spent, that this was going to make me into a far more powerful artist.

TOP TIPS FROM OUR PANEL ON
ENERGY MANAGEMENT...

- 'If you get too wired and excited about significant events, tire yourself out beforehand, work out, focus on something difficult for an hour to discharge excess energy.' – *Claire Taylor*
- 'Look for people to work with who take what you have done and push you to make it more than you thought you could deliver. This makes you stronger and more enduring.' – *Alessandra Ferri*
- 'Doing nothing – waiting – is the most draining activity there is. Use posture, breathing and movement to maintain your energy and mental faculties ready to respond.' – *Wayne McGregor*
- 'Figure out what you need leading up to performances. It is different for everyone. Don't feel guilty if you want to be silent the day before or like to have a nap and a specific routine on performance days. Pull back, find some quiet, warm up and focus.' – *Dawn Marie Flynn Sirrenberg*
- 'Losing momentum can be devastating – for example, taking a break for too long (set a timer so you know when it's time to go back to work). Do something light with your downtime so you don't completely lose momentum and have to start again from scratch. There's always something new to learn.' – *Karl Van Haute*
- 'For many people, when they get busy or stressed, their "me time" is usually the first thing thrown out the window. They rely on adrenalin and caffeine and see sleep deprivation as a badge of honour. Jeff and I have learned that without this restorative "me time", we have nothing to give to others. True energy comes from a rested and restored body and spirit. There is nothing selfish about self-care.' – *Joan Beal*

While pushing yourself (within reason) may make you stronger, a word of caution for those who drive themselves hard. Carlos, a banker who had just completed his first large-scale deal involving a huge amount of work, long hours and responsibility, came to Companies in Motion reporting that he was struggling to make the quick, deep analytical connections he was accustomed to making. He said he just couldn't think straight. The combination of heavy mental demands, extended periods in threat response and not enough physical exercise and sleep had taken their toll. After a month of lowered stress, proper sleep and exercise, his brain recovered fully. Rather than taking his ability to think for granted, he now has greater respect for his brain function.

As we know, mitochondria need recovery time, and glial cells that tidy up the brain need time to do that housekeeping, which they get when we are doing something easy rather than when the brain is involved in difficult tasks. So, give your brain recovery time when it can wander off without focusing too hard; journeys are good for strategic mind wandering.

Lack of exercise decreases supplies of a protein called brain-derived neurotrophic factor (BDNF), which is responsible for the growth of new neurons, while lack of sleep prevents neurons from reinsulating their outer myelin (fatty) sheaths, weakening the electrical impulses passing between neurons. It is important to keep up with physical exercise because it helps your brain grow and to pay attention to sleep quantity and quality, because it helps the brain recover – and as we will discover, it is essential for full waking brain power.

LIFE HACK: The more tired the brain, the harder it is to inhibit overdrive and be objective. What are your overdrive signals? Are you always last to leave the office, and feel it is unfair? Are you failing to find moments of respite to do something to renew your energy during the day? Recognise them. Say to yourself 'STOP', and use your remaining brain power to re-plan how you are doing things.

Breaking down your day

Even when we are well-rested and have plenty of energy, after two hours of thinking about complex things and making decisions, the neural connections degrade. This is because the myelin sheaths that we learned about above, which insulate the nerves, get worn down and reduce in thickness. Therefore, it makes sense to do the difficult thinking – tackling current issues, making strategic plans, working on important projects, tackling creative challenges – when the brain is fresh. Afterwards you can start to pick up the smaller pieces – answer non-critical emails, schedule calls etc. Many of us do the reverse, taking care of easy admin and answering emails first thing in the morning in an effort to clear the decks. We suggest a different plan:

- Make your morning routine prior to starting work as decision-free as possible. Put out clothes the evening before so that you don't have to decide what to wear in the morning, plan key tasks for the following day so that you know before you wake up what your focus will be.
- If you work with business partners and clients around the world or you have clients who respond to emails in the evenings, you may need to do a quick sweep of your

inbox first thing in the morning to look for any 'fires' that may have cropped up overnight.

- Having put out fires and managed expectations, sigh with relief, switch off distractions and put on your 'Out of Office' or 'Do Not Disturb'.
- Dive into those precious first two hours dedicated to tasks you have prioritised. Tackle the 'tough stuff'. Maximise your brain's energy by making complex decisions during this time.
- Train yourself to not constantly check email.
- One of the advantages of waking early when working from home is that you can complete two hours of work straight away – maybe still in nightwear with a cup of tea in hand.
- Have a running list of any small tasks that come to mind in those first two hours, put them on the list and forget them for now – you can do them later.
- After the first two hours, we focus best in blocks of forty-five minutes, so get up every forty-five to sixty minutes to have a stretch and a drink of water, rest your brain for two minutes then dive back in.
- If you work in an overzealous meeting culture or you or others tend to schedule you back to back, take charge of your diary, block out time and be discerning. Attend meetings only if they contribute to your priorities; if they do not, decline with a supportive comment about the content of the meeting. Simply do not allow your calendar to be filled to the brim with meetings that allow no time for lunch, no time to use the loo, no time to actually do the work you need to do. Take charge!
- If you sometimes work in the evening but crave sweet snacks or can only face that piece of work with a glass of wine by your side, it is likely that your brain batteries

(mitochondria) are running low. Decide if you really have to work. If you do, be efficient, use your breath to release energy instead of sugar or wine, then, after completing your work, reward yourself – for example, have a hot bath or savour that glass of wine.

- Ensure you have a wind-down routine or meditation to get you ready for sleep – your adrenalin and cortisol levels will need to come down in order for you to get to sleep.

LIFE HACK: If you are a parent, teach your children to use energy-saving routines early in their lives by talking to them about their brain, and make preparing things the night before fun.

Some people genuinely do have different cycles and perk up late morning, late afternoon or late evening. Once you identify your optimal two-hour slot, apply the same principles as above to block out time for the tough stuff when *you* are at *your* best. People with teenagers will know how hard it is for some of them to wake up and focus early in the morning, and I am in support of schools and colleges starting later for certain age groups. If you *have* to make an early start but are a night owl, you may need to negotiate flexible working hours, be extra rigorous about your wind-down routine so that you can get an early night when you need it and try to get into the habit of scheduling any strenuous or stimulating activities earlier in the day.

Switching between analytical or creative thinking and social media or other tasks or interruptions is less efficient for your brain. Unfortunately, when you take those kinds of unscheduled breaks, it takes a while to get back to the same quality of thinking when you come back, and you may lose deeper thought connections if you keep switching between tasks. Focus creates pace.

LIFE HACK: Always being interrupted by people needing your attention? You will be using energy wisely and work more quickly if you put boundaries around your availability to others.

Managing your chemical cocktail

When you tackle important tasks, testosterone is elevated in the bloodstream because confronting tasks, rather than postponing them or avoiding them, gives you a sense of moving bravely into new territory. If there is any danger, you'll avoid a task; therefore, use the winner pose to increase testosterone levels before starting. Dopamine is boosted as well because you quickly start to feel the rewards of achievement. A morning with a clear head, when memory is sharp and you are able to quickly absorb information, means that acetylcholine is balancing adrenalin (well done!). This confidence and motivation supports the rest of your day, even if your brain is not quite as sharp as the day goes on. Procrastination and avoidance lower dopamine levels and increase cortisol levels, so they are just not worth it.

What we tell ourselves

The kind of thoughts and feelings that we have about ourselves is important. When we perform new tasks, it is difficult to know when enough is enough because we don't have sufficient experience to judge. In this case, perfectionism can be unhelpful. If we tell ourselves we have to get it right the first time and that it has to be perfect, we may not seek feedback when appropriate from someone who does have experience and can help us learn.

Working from home can be very productive without

interruptions or social distractions. However, it is important to also reach out and balance our social needs. For people who like to work more collaboratively, working remotely with people in different parts of the world can feel less creative and take more time. It is important to find opportunities to work alongside colleagues on Skype or VT or make the effort and travel to get together face to face when possible.

If you like responsibility, taking charge and being in control, or if you are someone who feels they have to always be working to their limits, then you'll be in danger of energy drain and overdrive. It is important to share the responsibility. Rather than thinking, *me, everything, always*, think *delegate, select, prioritise.*

Plan your weeks and months using selection and prioritisation. This will enable you to expend energy efficiently on the right priorities. Use 'Seeing the Long Game' (pp. 329–31) and create milestones (pp. 338–40) when planning any kind of project or endeavour.

> **LIFE HACK:** Use your diary to manage your energy – anticipate your energy needs and make provision for them. Schedule in periods of rest.

Let's train: Energy gain

Here are two breathing techniques to stimulate the brain and body, create energy and wake up our mitochondria. Try this in the morning, when stationary at red traffic lights, or if it is late in the evening and you *have* to finish a task and want to keep yourself awake. (Not ideal, but occasionally necessary.)

Exercise: 'Warm-Up' breathing

- Breathe in fully, then exhale through your mouth in short, sharp bursts – as if you were blowing out candles on a birthday cake – until there is no breath left.
- Hold the end of the out-breath for five seconds.
- Repeat five times.
- Experiment with the best position for your lips and mouth and the sound you make to find a powerful out-breath.

Exercise: 'Wake-Up' breathing

- Clear the nose by blowing it.
- Breathe in and out strongly through the nose, building up speed until you are breathing as quickly as you can for as long as you can up to one minute.
- Make sure you use diaphragmatic breathing – belly goes out on the in-breath and in on the out-breath – otherwise you will feel light-headed and dizzy, i.e. you will over-breathe.
- SMILE while you do the faster breaths – you may as well get a serotonin/endorphin boost at the same time.
- Immediately afterwards, feel what is happening in your body and brain. How awake do you feel now? Enjoy.
- After these exercises, you may feel tingly, even a bit light-headed. You have flooded your body and brain with oxygen, feeding the mitochondria and releasing energy.

Exercise: Energy saving

- Identify key activities that drain your energy in the day/ week/month (this could be types of thinking or types of activity). Where is your energy draining away?

- Where in your body do you feel the impact of each energy drain?
- Label each drain.
- Decide on a course of action for each of them.

For example, if you are regularly distracted by a colleague who wants to chat for fifteen minutes before you've even taken off your coat, acknowledge your reluctance, then find time to have an honest conversation with them, and ask them if you can catch up with them at lunchtime instead.

As you name each drain, feel dopamine, the reward chemical, drop (it doesn't feel good). As you decide on an action, feel dopamine rise (it feels better). Easy drains to unblock will get a quick reward; more difficult drains may bring challenging feelings along with them.

This exercise may prompt you to visualise a certain category of energy-sapping, worried thoughts draining away, or it may be that some of your activities do not align with your values so you visualise stopping doing those.

For example:

- If you think *me, everything, always*, note the situations where that kind of thinking is creating a drain and decide what to do about it.
- If you tend to have a mad rush to get ready or arguments with family members in the mornings, note that down as a drain, and make a decision about how to solve it.
- If a particular meeting always runs over time, decide how you are going to influence the situation.
- If you notice negative thoughts regarding an aspect of your role at work that are triggered by something specific, note that down as a drain, and schedule time to do a 'Bounce Positive' (pp. 268–71) to turn that thinking around.

- Feel the change in your body as you commit to your action. Your body knows when you have picked the right action: you will suddenly feel lighter, relieved – signs of a dopamine boost.
- Communicate your intention to change things to people who need to know in order to manage their expectations and gain support.
- Put time in your diary to review progress on these drains in one week and make additional choices as needed, review weekly. (If it doesn't go in the diary, chances are it may not happen.)

You are in charge of your diary and how you spend your time. You are in charge of your energy levels, too, and how you use your energy in each and every situation. By highlighting your energy drains, you can create energy gains and make clear choices, working to reduce feelings of power*less*ness and promote feelings of power*ful*ness. It is very important to explore options and communicate your intention to change unworkable situations.

Sleep is one of the most vital aspects of energy renewal, cognitive function and emotional stability and there is growing understanding nowadays of just how important it is. With this in mind, let's now explore how to sleep well.

25

SLEEP WELL

How to power performance with a good night's sleep

> Sleep is the single most effective thing
> we can do to reset our brain and body
> health each day.
>
> —PROFESSOR MATTHEW WALKER

Sleep has a bigger impact on brain function than any waking activity; there is no more powerful brain enhancer. When we sleep, we consolidate memories and experiences, detox the brain of waste products and regenerate brain cells. This makes a profound difference to our daily performance, enabling us to think clearly and deeply, focus well and handle multiple challenges with ease.

Have you ever had the experience of practising a specific skill (such as playing a sport or a musical instrument) where you repeated an exercise or passage again and again but the co-ordination of a particular movement just wouldn't come, then, the next day, after a good night's sleep, suddenly the practice paid off and you were able to perform? Have you ever woken up in the morning with an insight or solution right there in the front of your mind? Sleep is responsible for this, too. Research from the University of Lubeck, Germany, in 2004 was the first to show how sleep facilitates insight by helping us connect implicit knowledge and memory with explicit knowledge that we have recently gathered, generating that sudden light-bulb moment.

While we sleep, an army of nervous system support cells (called glial cells) in the brain is working hard to support and repair neurons, enabling us to learn not just motor skills, but absolutely anything that has been of benefit or interest to us during the day. They reinforce neural pathways, clean up toxins, deliver nutrients and transport new neurons from their origin to their destination. As we learned in the last chapter, glial cells also rebuild the myelin (insulating fat) sheaths around the most-used neurons in our brains, better protecting them and minimising signal loss when our neurons fire. With enough good-quality sleep, all these processes are completed, brain fog clears, and we have more cognitive power.

The body also recuperates while we sleep. Our liver catches up on processing sugars and fats and regenerates liver tissue. The parasympathetic nervous system produces acetylcholine (the recovery and renewal chemical) and the adrenal glands replenish their stocks of steroids, such as DHEA and testosterone, in preparation for the next day's activity. Muscle fibres heal at a faster rate than during the day and the lymph system drains toxins out of all the tissues in the body, rejuvenating the skin, muscles, tendons, ligaments, organs and the circulatory and excretory systems. The mind processes thoughts and emotions, matching them against memories and deciding which to store in the long-term memory, which to retain in the short term, and which to discard, sometimes representing such links through our dreams. There is a whole lot of clever regeneration going on behind the scenes while we are asleep.

Many of us are, however, getting less sleep than we need. A study by RAND Europe in 2016 concluded that fatigue-related productivity losses in the UK amount to £40 billion. It also found that if we were to increase sleep time from under six hours to between six and seven hours, we would add £24 billion to annual productivity. In the same study, US losses were estimated to cost $1,967 per employee annually, approximately $400 billion in total. Data from the American Sleep Foundation shows that 40 per cent of Americans receive under seven hours of sleep a night. The RAND report puts a 13 per cent higher mortality risk on those who receive less than six hours sleep, which improves to 7 per cent for those who receive between six and seven hours. Neurologist Dr Itzhak Fried at UCLA is the most recent researcher (among many others) to demonstrate that performing on lack of sleep is equivalent to performing while drunk. His 2017 study reveals how sleep deprivation disrupts brain cells' ability to communicate with each other. Mental lapses increase while reaction times decrease significantly on low levels of sleep. This means that, if driving without sufficient sleep, the very act of *seeing* a pedestrian step in front of the car takes longer: the brain is slower to register what it is perceiving.

So, what is the correct amount of sleep, and how do you know if you are getting it? Advice from the University of Loughborough School of Sport, Exercise and Health Sciences says that 'if the sleep you obtain allows you to awake feeling reasonably refreshed, to function efficiently the next day, and to conduct your affairs without experiencing intrusive episodes of fatigue, then you are probably getting enough'. Good advice, but let's get more specific.

Research by Dr Jessica Payne at the University of Notre Dame indicates that 97.5 per cent of people perform best on seven hours of sleep or more, and those of us between the ages of eighteen and sixty-four should get seven to nine hours of sleep a night. This seven to nine principle is widely accepted and borne out in many other studies across the globe, including the Sleep Council (UK) and the National Sleep Foundation (USA).

How can we get more sleep?

The way forwards is a combination of increased night-time sleep, daytime power naps and proxy sleeps (short, intense periods of body and brain rest) all working together to get us to our magic total of somewhere between seven and nine hours of sleep. If you got 7.5 hours' sleep one night but you know that you actually function best on eight hours, then you can top up your sleep during the day.

Inching up the hours you sleep

If you are a habitual six-hour sleeper, adding just twenty or thirty minutes to your sleep time every night is an effective way to start, gradually building up to that all-important seven-hour threshold. It takes time to reset sleep habits, so don't be disheartened if this takes a month or two. Start by going to bed thirty minutes earlier. Set an alarm on your phone to tell you it is time to start your wind-down routine and begin by turning the lights low, taking a hot bath, and slowing your breathing down, for example. Give yourself plenty of time so that you are not rushing about as you get ready for bed. Experiment with how long you need and create a reliable routine.

The art of power napping

For people with uniquely challenging schedules, being smart with your time and with your naps is one effective way to get the sleep you need. Here's how Jarrod Barnes did it when he was playing football at Ohio State while studying for his doctorate. He told us:

'I was in graduate school as a student athlete, which was

unusual. I finished my Masters' and started my PhD in my last two years playing football, so I had to work out how to get enough sleep and be successful academically and athletically. I would get up at 4.30am to do college work and football prep early in the day, be in class or study all morning, then have a twenty-minute nap at noon, prior to practice and lunch. Practice would run from 1.30pm to 7.30pm, then I would take a short fifteen-minute de-stressing nap at 7.45pm. After that I would eat, do whatever other work needed to be done, and get my head down again as soon as I could by 8.45/9pm.'

He had to find a routine that worked for him, and this way Jarrod totalled around nine hours' sleep.

Pat and I also rely on naps, especially when working towards aggressive deadlines or managing extensive travel. While based in Arizona, Pat often has calls with Europe or the east coast of the USA as early as 6am. (Increasingly, these are video calls, requiring rising very early in order to be camera-ready.) On those same days, Pat may also have calls with Asia in the evening. This can happen day after day. She has to listen very carefully to her body and will fit in a quick two-minute sleep or a longer twenty/thirty-minute nap when her schedule allows. When she is traveling globally, she knows that sleep trumps all and will sacrifice food (and, during the worst Endurance Tunnels, even freshly washed hair!) for sleep, to ensure that she has proper brain function.

Without afternoon naps, this book would not have been written. When I am in a writing phase, I start early in the morning and have already been very productive by 2pm, but I like to write until 6 or 7pm. If I become sleepy, instead of fighting it, I give myself thirty minutes, set a gentle alarm, put earplugs in, lie on the sofa and put a soft cushion over my ears and head to further reduce sound and light. It takes me ten minutes to drop off, but then I have a light, restful sleep for twenty minutes (any longer and I would fall into deep sleep, which would make it more difficult to wake up). When the alarm goes off, I have a few moments of reluctance, but soon my brain feels re-energised and I can write for the rest of the day feeling great. Without that rest, writing becomes a slow, arduous process; I become easily distracted and may even find myself nodding off over the laptop.

Proxy sleeps

Short, intense rests of two to five minutes are beneficial. This is called a 'proxy' sleep. You don't actually fall asleep, but your brain goes into an immediate resting place, increasing helpful theta and delta waves that refresh the brain. This really works between challenging tasks or at the beginning of brain tiredness. This was borne out when I was a choreographer running rehearsals. When dancers were flagging, I would call for a two-minute sleep. We'd all lie down on the studio floor and instantaneously put ourselves in as close to a sleep state as possible. On 'waking', we were recharged. The act of lying down signals to the adrenals to stop pumping out adrenalin and cortisol and take a break. At home you can do this, but at work it may be challenging to find somewhere to lie down.

NEGOTIATION AND COMPROMISE TO GET MORE SLEEP

If you live with someone who has different sleep patterns (like I do), then you will need to experiment and negotiate. My husband is in the film industry, so he is either away working crazy hours or at home with a more leisurely schedule. He is naturally more nocturnal than I am, awake until 1am making things in his shed, then asleep until 10am. I need to be asleep by 10.30–11pm and up by 6–6.30am. The danger with this schedule difference is that when he comes to bed he will wake me up in the middle of deep or REM sleep. Because I am sensitive to light and sound, I now sleep with heavy-duty wax earplugs and have negotiated that he adopt a stealth approach when coming to bed – no light, no sound, minimal movement. He realises how important this is to me because I often need to be at the top of my game speaking at conferences and events or in a training room ready to lead a Physical Intelligence session by 8.30am.

If we end up disturbing each other when I have a week of early starts, then I have no qualms about sleeping in the spare room for a few nights. Prioritising sleep enables us to communicate well and be creative with what is happening so that everything else falls into place.

If you have young children who wake up in the night, my advice is to make sure you consider who in the household has the most critical day ahead, then the other does night duty. If you are caring for children alone, try, every second night, going to bed at the same time as the children to top up your sleep.

Sleep quality matters

It's not only quantity but *quality* of sleep that matters – specifically, the amount of time spent in deep and REM sleep.

Sleep cycles last approximately ninety minutes, and the average adult has five or six of these a night. We phase in and out of light, deep and REM (rapid eye movement) sleep during the night. In a restorative eight-hour sleep approximately 50 per cent (four hours) will be in light sleep, 25 per cent (two hours) will be in REM sleep, and 20 per cent (1.6 hours) will be deep sleep. The remaining 5 per cent will be getting to sleep and waking up. In light sleep we file memories, process emotions and our metabolism regulates. During REM sleep, the brain replenishes neurotransmitters that organise our neural networks, which are essential for remembering, learning, performance and problem-solving, and we synthesise new neurons, dream and detox the brain. In deep sleep the body builds and repairs itself, secreting maximum HGH (human growth hormone) in this phase. We come in and out of REM during our sleep cycles, and the amount of time spent in REM increases with each subsequent sleep cycle. If the final cycles of the night are cut short or missed altogether, you'll be short on REM sleep, which may cause brain fog. Alcohol, sleep medication and antidepressants also interfere with REM sleep, so, where possible, naturally induced sleep is highly preferable.

Circadian rhythms, our internal 24-hour clock that wakes us up with the light and sends us to sleep with the dark, are driven by melatonin, the sister of serotonin. Melatonin levels rise when the light fades and cortisol drops, moving us towards sleep. In the morning, melatonin drops and cortisol rises, waking us up. If we are worried, anxious, unhappy or depressed, serotonin levels will be low and we won't be able to synthesise enough melatonin, making our mental and emotional state a significant factor in sleep disruption.

Some people drop off to sleep easily, while others struggle to get into healthy sleep cycles. Any number of factors can affect sleep patterns: parenthood, lifestyle changes, moving home, physical ailments, hormones, creativity, worrying, heavy workload, snoring partners, shift work, travel, ageing, light evenings and mornings during the summer etc. After periods of sleep disruption, travel or heavy workload, it is normal to have a few longer, catch-up sleeps.

Tracking our sleep with wearable technology and apps gives us useful information about what is happening during our sleep cycle and how much deep and REM sleep we are getting. While we shouldn't be overly concerned about natural fluctuations, we should take action to ensure that the quantity and quality of our sleep is as good as it can be.

So let's now look at improving sleep quality with good sleep hygiene.

Sleep hygiene

George Kruis has absolutely no problem sleeping and gets a solid nine hours regardless of whether or not there is a big game the next day. The only thing that can impact his sleep is if he has to share a room while on tour with one of the huge props who snores. He has now worked out who snores and immediately gets himself moved. The point is: take charge of your own sleep needs.

Here are some helpful tips to improve your sleep hygiene:

- *Check bedroom temperature.* A cool room temperature brings on sleep and reduces sleep disruption. Make sure the room you sleep in is no warmer than 18°C (60–65°F).
- *Change your mattress/bed.* The Sealy/Loughborough University 2016 sleep census found that uncomfortable beds were responsible for reducing sleep time by one hour. Mattress technology has evolved significantly over the last decade. If your bed is eight to ten years old, it is definitely time for a change. Couples tend to sleep better in bigger beds. Consider going up a size if your partner's movement tends to disturb you in the night.
- *Bedtime wind-down.* Set your alarm to start your bedtime routine half an hour before you want to go to sleep. Begin slowing your breathing pace, have a hot bath, drink camomile tea, listen to soothing music, turn the lights down.

- *Avoid technology.* Don't expect to dash off a few emails then quickly slip into a blissful sleep. Engaging with technology right before bedtime will stimulate cortisol production (the chemical that wakes you up) just when you need to be winding down. It is best to leave your technology outside of the bedroom. If you must have technology near you at all times, it is unwise to have devices close to the bed or to use them before going to bed. It is better for the brain to wind down away from screens for one hour before sleep. Also, eliminate any light from screens and technology. Compelling research from Harvard Medical School shows that blue light emitted from tablets, computers and smart phones used in the evening affects melatonin production and disturbs sleep. Most devices now have orange filters. Make sure you have this switched on, especially if you rely on a smart phone as an alarm and need to set it prior to sleep or check the time during the night.

- *Limit light from outside.* Blackout blinds and sleep masks minimise light disturbance. In cities and towns, street lamps tend to create ambient light in bedrooms, which inhibits melatonin production.

- *Stretch before bed.* See below for particular stretches that stimulate the parasympathetic nervous system and relax you.

- *Do exercise during the day.* Exercising during the day primes us for sleep. Activities such as walking, running, yoga, Zumba, gardening, dancing and golf all help reset the balance of the nervous system so that the parasympathetic division is ready to kick in as you head to bed.

- *Don't exercise too late.* Vigorous exercise too late in the evening will make it more difficult to get to sleep because you are stimulating the adrenal glands, which continue to pump out adrenalin for a couple of hours or so post-exercise. If you do exert yourself within two hours of sleep because it is the only time you can fit exercise into your schedule, put a tablespoon of Epsom salts in a hot bath to replace magnesium and stimulate the parasympathetic nervous system to help your muscles relax.

LIFE HACK: Walk more during your day to help you sleep at night. Try to have three meetings walking rather than seated throughout the day. If you don't work in a corporate environment, get up and walk around the block during your lunch break. Get off the bus or the tube one stop earlier and walk the last part of your journey.

- *Don't eat too late or too heavily.* It takes two to three hours to digest a meal. A heavy meal at 8 or 9pm may interfere with your ability to get to sleep at 10 or 11pm. Eating well in the evening is important, but if you are prone to indigestion, heartburn or reflux or have trouble getting to sleep, consider eating greater quantities at lunchtime and a lighter meal in the evening.
- *Avoid/minimise sugar and alcohol.* If you have an excess of sugar or sugar from alcohol in your body as you go to sleep, the adrenals will keep going until it is digested. Then, once digested, the liver sends an alert message to the adrenals saying, 'Quick! Release more energy!' At midnight or in the early hours of the morning, cortisol levels rise to meet this energy demand. We need cortisol to wake us up in the morning, but not at 2am! If you do find that sugar and alcohol tend to disrupt your sleep, find other types of evening treats. Remember that dark chocolate (at least 70 per cent cocoa) is delicious and stimulates serotonin production – perhaps for those of us who have a sweet tooth, a couple squares of good chocolate will suffice.

- *Party wisely.* Even if you sleep flat out after partying and drinking excess alcohol, as mentioned above, you will get less REM sleep, which is one reason why the brain feels groggy the next day. If you are a party animal, plan your partying so that you have recovery time. Most people need a day to recover, more as you age.

- *Beware of caffeine.* Caffeine interferes with the uptake of adenosine, a chemical that quietens the brain to enable sleep. If you're a coffee lover, follow the tips for caffeine consumption from Chapter 7 (pp. 111–12).

- *Sleep naked.* Skin-to-skin contact with a sleep partner releases oxytocin – which, if you remember, lowers cortisol levels – so it is in your best interests to sleep naked.

- *Invest in good earplugs.* Wax earplugs that mould to the shape of your ear are one of the most important items in my sleep kit, especially helpful in hotel rooms and when working on trains and planes.

- *Manage your/your partner's snoring.* We all know that as we get older muscles lose their firmness. The frequency of snoring also seems to increase with age. This is often due to a looser throat, tongue and facial muscles, which make the soft palate at the back of the mouth fall back, especially when we lie on our back. This large fleshy mass creates sound vibrations as the air passes around it. We are also more likely to snore after an excess of alcohol or taking sleeping pills because both loosen all of the muscles in the face, tongue and throat, which has the same effect as ageing. Nostril-widening tape and sleeping on the side rather than the back often help, as does limiting alcohol/sleep medication intake. Try relaxing through natural means as a potential remedy. See the 'Combat Snoring' exercise below for a soft palate lifting exercise.

- *Take charge of your thoughts.* Sleeplessness can be due to interfering thought patterns caused by or causing cortisol levels to rise, which wakes you up. If you wake in the night with your mind whirring, instruct your mind to 'STOP', keep a pen and paper by your bed and practise the 'Bounce Positive' technique (pp. 268–71), or jot down what's on your mind and any actions you plan to take using the Energy Saving exercise (pp. 385–7).
- *Try to resolve difficulties when they arise.* Getting to sleep with problems on your mind or arguments in the air can interfere greatly with quality of sleep. Attempt to resolve as much as you can before sleep; let go of what you can't change so that you can get some good rest.
- *Release tension and track emotion.* If you are lying in bed tightly coiled, with your jaw tense, shoulders pulled in, abdomen squeezed, brow furrowed, your sleep will be of lower quality. Use sequential relaxation (pp. 256–7) and try to let emotions play through you rather than holding them back. Since starting this book, I have met so many people who use sequential relaxation to get them to sleep, including a top civil servant in the UK government and Claire Taylor, who was taught the technique when she was in the England women's cricket team.

   LIFE HACK: If you don't sleep well the night before a big event, don't catastrophise – it happens to us all. If you have been having good sleep in the period prior to the event and have been treating your adrenal glands well by giving them enough rest overall, they will repay you by rising to the challenge. I recently had only three hours' sleep prior to giving a keynote session for 150 global leaders, where I was working with a large team of trainers. I used paced breathing and found twenty minutes to meditate in the taxi from the airport. I then focused on what I was doing, trusted myself and all was well.

- *Use your breath pattern.* Breath pattern and sleep are closely linked. A slower breathing rate imitates sleep and releases acetylcholine; a faster breathing rate imitates wakefulness and releases adrenalin. You will remember that paced breathing covered in the strength section (pp. 60–4) is the bedrock of an improved mental, emotional and physical state, HRV (heart rate variability) and vagal tone. If you are breathing well during the day, restful sleep will come more easily at night. We can use our breath to wind us down to get to sleep or get us back to sleep if we have woken early (see 'Wind-Down' breathing, pp. 405–6).

  LIFE HACK: Do you find yourself tossing and turning, semi- or fully awake for no particular reason? Take action. Try one of the following:

  - *Get out of bed.* Lie on the floor and stretch your body, bending forwards and releasing the neck.

  - Get up and do something that uses your 'awake' brain (provided it doesn't involve technology), such as reading a book or writing some notes.

  - Sit up and meditate deeply. Your brain will thank you.

- *Learn how to do nothing.* This is important for true insomniacs as well as restless sleepers and is one of the core principles explained in *The Sleep Book* by Dr Guy Meadows. He shows you how to accept rest, stop battling sleep and learn to do nothing. Stillness can be a place of great pleasure just for its own sake.

- *Take sleep supplements.* These include 5HTP, which balances GABA (gamma aminobutyric acid). GABA stimulates production of serotonin, dopamine and theanine, which supports health by promoting alpha brain waves, reducing cortisol build-up and giving you a relaxed, clear head during the day.

Let's train: Sleep well

TRAVEL AND SLEEP

Sleeping in economy on long-haul flights is a challenge for most people. The inability to lie down means that our adrenals don't get the break they need and the parasympathetic nervous system struggles to kick in. If only airlines would redesign planes so that everyone could lie down. Russell Foster, professor of circadian neuroscience at the University of Oxford, UK, believes in light treatment for jet lag. If you are travelling east, avoid morning light that will wake you up and seek out afternoon/early-evening light for the first few days after arrival. Flying west? Seek out as much light as you can on landing to reduce drowsiness and as much morning light in the few days after arrival.

Exercise: Stretches before sleep

If you feel physically stiff when going to bed or your thoughts are lingering on certain issues, use the flexibility movements in Chapter 8 (pp. 155–61), or experiment with one or more of the following stretches to flush out your brain, slow down your breathing and stimulate the spinal fluid and nerves in the lower spine. Each of these movements helps to ground and detoxify our bodies and brains.

Forward Bend (flushes out the brain)

- Stand with feet hip-width apart, toes pointing forwards.
- Fold the arms over the head.
- Bend forwards from the waist.
- If this puts strain on your hamstrings, slightly bend the knees. (If you have high blood pressure, forward bends should only be held for five seconds before slowly coming up to standing position.)

Prayer Position (promotes slower, deeper breathing to imitate the sleeping breath)

- Kneel and place hands on the floor just in front of you.
- Walk the hands forwards slowly, folding the chest over the thighs.
- Widen the knees and enjoy the back stretch as you walk the arms forwards.
- If you are supple enough then the head may rest on the floor – if not, use a cushion.
- Let the neck relax and breathe.

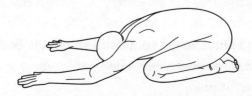

Legs up the Wall (stimulates the spinal fluid and nerves in the lower spine)

- Find a bare wall, ideally in a room where there is carpet.
- Lie down on the floor, on your back with your body perpendicular to the wall.
- Raise your legs so that they are as flat against the wall as possible, with your bottom close to the wall. (You may need to manoeuvre into this position.)
- Enjoy the rest and breathe.

These techniques are also useful if you wake up in the middle of the night and can't get back to sleep.

Exercise: Combat snoring
To keep facial muscles firm and agile in order to avoid a flabby soft palate, do these exercises daily:

- Use exaggerated vowel sounds to shape the back of the throat – *mee, moo, maw, mah, may …*
- Repeat ten times.

- Make an *ng* sound (as at the end of the word 'doing'), then, staying at the same pitch, open the back of the throat up to change the sound into an *ah* sound.
- Repeat ten times.

Also:

- If you are the one who snores:
  - Reduce alcohol and use of sedatives
  - Try nostril-widening tape

- If your partner snores:
  - Train a snoring partner to sleep on their side by repeatedly moving them gently
  - Use heavy-duty wax earplugs
  - Use the spare room

Exercise: 'Wind-Down' breathing
Winding ourselves down requires lowering adrenalin and cortisol and boosting acetylcholine and melatonin. This can be done while going through your wind-down routine or when you are already lying down. Many of our clients, friends and family swear by this technique.

- Breathe in for one, breathe out for one, breathe in for two, breathe out for two ... Keep increasing the length of the breath until you find a repetitive pattern that feels right to settle on.
- Keep breathing in this ratio.
- Can you feel yourself slowing down?
- On each out-breath, let yourself feel heavy, and sink into the comfort of the bed.

Not only will you drift off easily, the quality of your sleep will be enhanced, encouraging theta, delta and gamma brain waves. You can also use this technique if you wake early and want to drop off again.

Exercise: 'Mind Retreat and Sweep'

Imagine a retreat that works for you – a peaceful, soothing place (a mountain top, a beach, a boat gently rocking on a lake). Visualise yourself there. If thoughts interrupt, use a mind sweep technique. Imagine curtains, a snow plough, or someone sweeping thoughts away to reveal the image of your retreat again. Let the chemical tide of serotonin and melatonin usher in a feeling of pleasure and stillness.

Exercise: Sequential relaxation

For locked-in tension, start at the feet – squeeze, then let go; move up to the lower legs – squeeze, then let go; carry on sequentially through the body until you reach the top of the head. (See pp. 256–7 for full exercise.)

Exercise: 'Replay Your Day'

To bring a sense of certainty to the mind and body, think through what you did that day, event by event, simply remembering your actions and mentally replaying them one by one. This reduces cortisol levels. If you had stressful events happen from the minute you woke up, then choose a part of the day that went well or that was stress-free and mentally walk through your actions.

Exercise: 'Count Backwards From 500'

Similar to the above, the brain is occupied in something mundane and some people feel comfort in the simplicity of counting numbers.

Exercise: 'Count Your Blessings'

Think through all the good things there are in your life and feel your emotions boost as dopamine, oxytocin and serotonin seep into the brain and bloodstream, turning your negative state to positive with your thoughts.

Exercise: Proxy (two-minute) sleep

- Set your alarm to a gentle sound.
- The trick with this exercise is to go immediately into as close to sleep as you can.
- Find a resting place for your head, such as forehead on hands or reclining in your chair. Position your body as comfortably as you can, given the circumstances. Even better, actually lie down for two minutes if possible.
- Prepare your mind.
- Cover your eyes.
- Press start on the alarm then say to yourself: 'SLEEP'.
- Be completely still, like a rock or stone that has been in the same place for thousands of years.
- Empty your mind of thoughts.
- This may take a bit of practice, but it definitely will buy you a bit more awake time. If you are really exhausted, then two minutes will simply not be enough and your body will crave more sleep. We are only human.

Use a sleep inventory checklist:

- ☐ *Food* – Eat at least two to three hours before sleep – reduce sugar and alcohol intake.
- ☐ *Technology* – Step away from it one hour prior to sleep and keep it outside of the bedroom.
- ☐ *Temperature* – Optimal is 18°C (60–65°F).

☐ *Pre-sleep, thirty-minute wind-down* – Lights low, hot bath, stretches.

☐ *Light* – Blackout blinds or sleep mask.

☐ *Sound* – Earplugs.

You may have to sell the benefits of your preferred new sleep habits to your sleep partner. Pat's husband is still pushing back on the cooler temperature.

Having taken a thorough look at sleep and sleep hygiene, and talked briefly about how exercise helps us sleep well, next we will discover more about how diet and fitness can support the waking hours, days, weeks and years that we have ahead of us, building our stamina and vitality and increasing the likelihood of living a long, healthy and happy life.

26

NUTRITION AND FITNESS FOR ENDURANCE

How to sustain a long, healthy life with food and exercise

Take care of your body. It's the only place
you have to live.

—JIM ROHN

Our bodies need good-quality food to deliver sustained energy and create strong, long-lasting bones and muscles. We also need to push ourselves physically in our fitness regime to build stamina and energy reserves that will sustain the physical, emotional and mental effort required in tough times. It is wise to train for endurance at easier times rather than wait until we are under duress. Here are the vital aspects of food and exercise that provide us with energy when we need it most and for building and maintaining our high performance across all aspects of our lives.

Nutrition

Energy
How do we get more energy? Forget quick energy drinks and more than one dose of caffeine per day, as those will lead to

greater fatigue in the long run. Here's how to increase your energy resources:

- Drink coconut water for a quick burst of energy without the high sugar content. It replaces calcium, phosphorus, potassium, sodium and chloride, which are crucial electrolytes found in bodily fluids. Electrolytes are electrically charged molecules that facilitate all functions in the body that require the conduction of electricity, especially muscle action, including the heart and efficient nerve-signalling in our entire nervous system. While processed food diets are high in the electrolyte sodium chloride, they tend to be low in the other electrolytes. So go easy on the junk food and takeaways and cook fresh, whole foods with lots of leafy greens. Because we lose electrolytes through sweating, include coconut water in your rehydration after exercising. Other electrolyte-rich foods are celery, watermelon, cucumber, kiwi, pineapple, peppers, carrots and probiotic yoghurt. Miso soup is also great for replacing minerals, especially if you eat the seaweed too.
- Eat *slow-release carbohydrates* such as nuts, wholegrain bread, sweet potatoes, oats and avocados, which have a low glycaemic index (GI) value, instead of quick-release carbohydrates such as sweets, biscuits, cakes, potatoes, chips, crisps, white rice and bananas (high GI foods). These slow-release carbohydrates do exactly what their name says: release energy slowly in a sustained way into your system rather than in one huge sugar hit, which is what a chocolate bar, for example, does. The blood sugar spikes, giving you an energy surge, then half an hour later energy drops because it has all gone. This can lead to cravings for that energy hit. One way to overcome sugar cravings is to start to pair any high GI foods with a low GI

partner. For example, eat tropical fruit (high GI) with a handful of almonds (low GI), eat bananas (high GI) with a slice of dense wholegrain bread (low GI), eat white rice (high GI) with beans, meat and non-starchy vegetables (low GI). Some popular slow-release, low GI foods are:
- Sweet potatoes rather than white potatoes
- Non-starchy vegetables such as asparagus, spinach, cauliflower, broccoli, and celery
- Nuts and nut butter
- Dense, wholegrain bread
- Lentils and beans

I find that the best sweet snack is a piece of fruit (dried or fresh) with a handful of nuts. Pack some in your bag and reach for that instead of the chocolate bar. Low-sugar health bars also have a combination of low and high GI foods: fruit, grains and other nutrients.

Maintaining strong bones

Vitamin D facilitates calcium absorption, which is essential for healthy bones. We need our bones to be healthy and renew over a lifetime if we are to endure and have longevity. Having vitamin D in your diet boosted by getting enough sunlight keeps your bones strong and protects older adults against osteoporosis. Food sources include:

- Oily fish
- Egg yolk
- Red meat
- Fortified milk and soya products
- Fortified orange juice

A healthy diet *should* provide all the vitamin D we need, but for many people this is not the case. (NB: 15mcg (20mcg over age seventy) per day is recommended – one 85g/3oz salmon fillet contains roughly 11mcg.

Maintaining strong muscles

- Protein is important for building and sustaining muscle mass as we age, and for building up muscle when we do resistance training.
- If you are trying to build up muscle through gym training, then a drink enriched with protein such as whey, pea or hemp powder within twenty minutes of finishing training helps muscle synthesis (30g/1oz is the maximum anyone needs).
- Older adults who are trying to maintain and build muscle may benefit from protein powders such as whey powder. The usual high-protein foods we eat such as fish, meat, eggs, cheese etc. will not provide as much immediately usable protein as protein powder does. Fifteen grams (half an ounce) combined with exercise, especially resistance exercise training, has been shown to increase muscle bulk.

Fitness

If by the end of your working day you are physically exhausted, then your focus becomes 'just keep going' rather than the quality of the decisions you are making. Just as a rugby or football player is able to make better game decisions towards the end of the match if they are physically fit, a doctor or nurse doing a long shift will make better decisions towards the end of that shift if *they* are physically fit.

Fitness for endurance requires building up your capacity gradually to work that bit harder, increasing distance, numbers of repetitions and circuits and working against resistance. Long-distance cycling, running and walking are fantastic endurance sports, increasing longevity because they keep our internal organs youthful. Any type of exercise can improve your endurance if you add challenge. Push a bit harder, recover, push a bit harder, recover. However, if you are over forty, be extra-careful about how you build up your endurance. Many people I meet who used to train hard in their twenties and thirties want to get back to previous fitness levels and start training again too hard and too fast, resulting in injury. Patience is required; take small steps.

Fitness suggestions for endurance

- Gardening and household chores are good for endurance because you are often working against resistance – moving, pushing, pulling and lifting things. A good day of manual activity is a fantastic workout. The more sedentary your working life is, the more important it is to continue to require your body to be as physical as possible in your activities outside work. Putting your physical body under a bit of pressure is a good thing as long as there are no medical reasons not to do so.

- Long walks where you can pace and test yourself are a superb way to build your capacity to push through discomfort and believe in your endurance.

- Walking and running for charity can transform your view of yourself and what you are capable of achieving.

- If you want to add resistance to a walk or run, include more hills or steps on your route. Walking or running uphill strengthens muscle and bone and builds up greater endurance.

- If you decide to run a marathon, do your research and build your training up over at least a six-month period, taking advice from people who have done it before.
- In Chapter 24 – 'The Endurance Tunnel' – I gave you some endurance movements for core strength (pp. 347–50) which will enable you to build your capacity to move forwards through difficulty. Build those into your day to increase stamina for life.
- To go further with your physical training and create a long-term strategy, it is helpful to devise a plan with a personal trainer to gradually increase the intensity of your exercise regime: reps, weights and numbers of circuits in a programme you can stick to.
- Early rise – get up thirty minutes earlier for a week and use this time to do resistance training, meditation or practise the endurance movements from Chapter 24 (pp. 347–356).
- Muscle-firming (pp. 333–4) is important for determination. If you feel confident in your knowledge of your body and you travel a lot, then you may like to experiment using resistance bands that are light and easy to pack. Pat has resistance bands in her travel bag at all times. There are countless effective workouts online, but I do stress that it is best to consult with a personal trainer.
- As you exercise, if you do decide to push yourself a bit harder to improve your endurance, build up gradually. Make sure you execute the exercises correctly, too, prioritising quality not quantity.
- Using music tends to encourage many people to work a bit harder as they exercise, provided they choose warm-up tracks that support a gentle pace at the beginning, before building up to a faster pace for the more challenging part of the workout. If you go too hard too fast, you will create a negative dopamine reaction, which will make it harder

to exercise next time. Give your body time to get into gear. Music distracts your mind from the hard work and any discomfort and also gives you a sense of rhythm and emotional drive. Anyone who has attended a spinning or Zumba class will know how crucial the choice of the music is to keeping you going. Warm-down tracks are important too.

- Emotional and mental endurance can be further supported by longer times sitting still and practising mindfulness or any of the breathing techniques we have shown you in this book. Meditation retreats are also brilliant tests of endurance. If you do ten minutes a day of breathing work right now, perhaps on the train, then consider sitting still for thirty minutes each day at the weekends. You can integrate the mental focus practice from the beginning of Chapter 19 (pp. 328–9) in this longer practice while sitting still. Allocate two minutes for each area of the brain or body – giving you a total of twenty-six minutes. In the final four minutes, let your mind do whatever it wants.

It is time to put endurance into practice. In the next chapter, you will discover and decide how to rehearse and perform endurance techniques, habit stacking them into your daily life until they become effortlessly embedded.

Rehearse and Perform: Endurance

Which endurance techniques are you most excited to tackle first? Which will you choose to experiment with to give you that boost in vitality, stamina and motivation for the future? In your rehearsal week you can try them out and then go on to perform those endurance techniques every day for the rest of the month. Enjoy creating more capacity for yourself and think about an ambitious goal that you'd like to work towards in the process.

In this section, there are some day-to-day techniques, as well as techniques that are useful in the moment when the going gets tough, and a few to explore over a weekend and over the long term, depending on your purpose and plan for the future.

1. Retain the strength, flexibility and resilience techniques that are becoming habitual.
2. In addition, choose five of the endurance techniques that you would like to try first.
3. Rehearse them for one week to explore what the best way is to integrate them into your daily life and what the right triggers are. (Take a look at our habit-stacking ideas and suggestions for triggers below.)
4. Perform them daily for the rest of the month until they become second nature.

5. Give more time on weekends to the in-depth, multi-step processes such as 'Seeing the Long Game' (pp. 329–31), 'Energy Gain' (pp. 384–7) and the motivation and appreciation techniques in Chapter 23 (pp. 370–3).

(When you feel ready, come back and choose some more endurance techniques to rehearse, then perform those, too.)

Here is a reminder of all the techniques we learned in the endurance section. Read down the list and mark the ones you feel will be most beneficial to you and start with those. Then you'll put them into a programme.

☐ FOCUS PRACTICE – It is vital to rejuvenate the mind and bring it to rest when times are tough. Practise moving your focus to different parts of the brain and up and down the body, then rest it in the centre of the brain.

☐ SEEING THE LONG GAME – Visualise clearly what you are working to achieve and create a timeline.

☐ MUSCLE-FIRMING – Find an action and some words that spur you on when things are difficult for you.

☐ CREATING MILESTONES – Create and visualise milestones and imagine celebrating the achievement. Use milestones to plan projects. Walk through the timeline of a project.

☐ FEEL THE FORCE – Breathe, creating resistance to fire up energy in the brain and the body.

☐ ENDURANCE MOVEMENTS – Develop endurance, ambition, equilibrium and drive using core-strengthening exercises, 'Reach and Harness', 'Place and Balance' and 'Push and Thrust'.

☐ BREAKING THE PAIN BARRIER – Visualise the pituitary gland releasing natural painkillers (endorphins) into your system to alleviate whatever type of pain you are feeling. Remember the cautious central governor in the brain. When you feel fatigued, say to yourself, 'I have energy reserves – I can go on.'

☐ MOTIVATION

    ☐ NAMING YOUR PURPOSE – In one word, what is your underlying purpose?

    ☐ NAMING YOUR VALUES – What principles do you live your life by?

    ☐ NAMING YOUR MISSION – In a couple of sentences, what is your overriding mission in life?

    ☐ WHO BENEFITS? – Who benefits – and how – from you working on this mission? What is the social context in which you are motivated to achieve?

☐ APPRECIATION OF OTHERS – Talk/text/email people whom you would like to appreciate for what or how they did something.

☐ APPRECIATION OF SELF – Consciously make a mental list of all the good things you have and are.

☐ COLD SHOWERS – Turn the water to cold for the last thirty seconds to improve energy levels.

☐ 'WARM-UP' BREATHING – Breathe in, then breathe out, pushing the air out in short, sharp bursts until all the air is expelled; repeat.

☐ 'WAKE-UP' BREATHING – Breathe in and out, diaphragmatically, through the nose as quickly as you can for one minute.

☐ ENERGY SAVING – Commit to spending the first two hours of your day focusing without distraction on the most difficult tasks. Throughout the day, identify and adjust energy-draining activities and thought patterns.

☐ THE ART OF POWER NAPPING – A nap for twenty to thirty minutes renews focus when sleepy during the day.

☐ SLEEP HYGIENE – Adjust bedroom temperature to 18°C (60–65°F). Clear bedroom of as much technology as possible; have a notepad and pen to jot down daytime reminders.

☐ STRETCHES BEFORE SLEEP – Bend forwards, get in 'Prayer Position', put your legs up against the wall.

☐ 'WIND-DOWN' BREATHING – Slow down your breathing pattern to imitate sleep.

☐ SLEEP TECHNIQUES – 'Mind Retreat and Sweep', 'Replay Your Day', 'Count Backwards From 500', 'Count Your Blessings'.

☐ PROXY (TWO-MINUTE) SLEEP – Spending two minutes in complete stillness and relaxation, as if asleep, is very refreshing.

☐ NUTRITION – Drink coconut water, eat slow-release carbohydrates, combine low and high GI value foods, add supergreens, vitamin D foods, protein powders.

☐ FITNESS – Engage in household and garden activities, walking and running. Commit to the endurance movements and, when possible, hire a personal trainer to help you plan how to build up repetitions and resistance. Get a resistance band. Use music to motivate you and push you harder.

☐ LONGER SITTING STILL/BREATHING – On weekends, find thirty minutes each day to sit still, using any of the breathing techniques and the Focus Practice exercise.

Now, let's habit stack:

ON WEEKEND PRIOR TO YOUR REHEARSAL WEEK

- Include superfoods and top-quality protein in your diet this week; experiment with super-nutritious food. Shop at a health food supermarket instead of your normal one

and make different food choices as discussed – or book a phone call with a nutritionist.
Trigger: Creating a shopping list for the week.

- Include thirty minutes of sitting still, using the Focus Practice exercise (pp. 328–9). See if you can do it.
Trigger: Finishing coffee and completing chores.

- Practise the 'Seeing the Long Game' visualisation (pp. 329–31), focusing on one thing you are trying to achieve. Sit down with someone or by yourself. Visualise a future point.
Trigger: Finishing mental focus exercise.

- Create milestones (pp. 338–40) as a result of the visualisation above, giving you a workable plan – diarise these milestones.
Trigger: Finishing the 'Seeing the Long Game' visualisation.

- Identify your core purpose, values and mission (pp. 371–373) and explore who benefits from you achieving this (pp. 373–4) with a friend.
Trigger: Friend arrives.

ON WAKING

- Spend two minutes appreciating all the things you have – start a gratitude diary.
Trigger: The alarm goes off.

BEFORE WORK

- Get up thirty minutes earlier than usual; use the time for a short burst of resistance training, meditation, or practise

'Feel the Force' breathing technique (pp. 346–7).
Trigger: The alarm goes off.

- Run cold water for the last thirty seconds of your shower. (You'll enjoy a great boost for your nervous system and an energy release for the day – although 'enjoy' may not be the right word!)
  Trigger: Finishing rinsing.

ON THE JOURNEY TO WORK

- Set your priorities and milestones daily (pp. 338–40) and use muscle-firming (pp. 333–4) to get your energy levels raised for the difficult ones. Celebrate achievement at each milestone.
  Trigger: The train doors closing/putting on your seatbelt.

AT WORK OR IF WORKING FROM HOME

- For the first two hours, focus on the 'tough stuff'. Check for emergencies, then, after addressing any that have arisen, close your inbox or put your 'Out of Office' on. Now you are free to tackle the difficult, strategic, challenging, high-profile tasks.
  Trigger: Arriving at work or at your desk.

- Use 'Feel the Force' breathing technique (pp. 346–7) for five breath cycles. Re-fire your brain and energy.
  Trigger: Finishing the task at hand after two hours of work.

- Check thought patterns and planned activities for energy drains (pp. 385–7) and make adjustments.
  Trigger: Practising or completing the 'Feel the Force' breathing technique.

- Eat a snack that contains a mix of high and low GI value foods, e.g. fruit and nuts.
  Trigger: Going to the kitchen/opening the cupboard.

- Heighten concentration by working in 45-minute blocks – look away, take a short break, have a conversation. Begin again.
  Trigger: The pre-set reminder on your phone goes off.

AT LUNCHTIME

- STOP, check for overdrive, breathe, and take fifteen to thirty minutes to eat a nutritious lunch.
  Trigger: The pre-set reminder on your phone goes off.

- Take a two-minute sleep (p. 407) after lunch before returning to work.
  Trigger: You finish eating.

- Remember your major long-term goal by connecting momentarily with your 'Seeing the Long Game' visualisation (pp. 329–31) and your purpose, values and mission (pp. 371–373) – feel the dopamine boost.
  Trigger: Returning to your desk/logging on to start the afternoon's work.

IN THE AFTERNOON

- Concentrate on your next milestone. Stay focused on your priorities, manage emergencies and immediate expectations. See yourself achieving the next milestone of the day; muscle-firm and do it.
  Trigger: Opening up your inbox.

- Sleepy? Losing energy? Take a twenty-minute nap to boost energy (if your workplace has the facility or you can find a private space). This isn't realistic for many people; so, if you need to push through, use a two-minute sleep (p. 407) and 'Wake-Up' breathing (p. 385). You will come back with renewed brain power.
  Trigger: Losing focus, eyelids feeling heavy.

- Eat slow-release carbohydrate snacks: nuts, grains, whole foods, *low-sugar* nutrition bars.
  Trigger: The pre-set timer on your phone goes off to eat one hour before the gym.

- At the end of your workday, register achievements and set priorities for the next day.
  Trigger: Closing down your workspace, clearing away any clutter.

IN THE EVENING

- Commit to longer exercise sessions. Get to the gym/exercise space three days per week. Make it doable: increase the challenge gradually by slowly adding more repetitions or circuits of key exercises. Use music to build motivation and use 'Breaking the Pain Barrier' (pp. 361–3) to handle the pain during and after muscular effort. Remember, the central governor heralds pain and fatigue long before there is any danger.
  Trigger: Walking out of the office/station.

- On the journey home, notice the energy gains you have achieved during the day: effective conversations, decisions made about how to apply your energy positively,

fitness etc. Check energy drains, e.g. thoughts whirring about the end goal, rather than focusing on the next milestone, or accepting something when you know it is the wrong approach.
Trigger: Finding your seat on the train/sitting at a red traffic light.

- Appreciate others – send three texts or emails with thanks or appreciation.
  Trigger: Stopping at the first station on the way home/just before going into the house if driving.

- Appreciate yourself and others by enriching your conversations. Too often, when asked how our day was, we say 'fine' – minimising it. Instead, when asked, list a couple of achievements – things that you appreciated about your day, as well as a couple of challenges or energy drains. Then reciprocate, appreciating the achievements and challenges in their day. (If you don't have time to speak straight away, decide when you will connect to appreciate – e.g. 'Let me change first, then we'll chat.' Or if you don't want to talk about it now, say so and why.)
  Trigger: A partner/flatmate/family member asking, 'How was your day?'

- Use your 'Out of Office'/'Do Not Disturb'. When you have social time with family and friends, avoid all emails or work calls. This is your time as well as theirs.
  Trigger: Gathering together as family/friendship group.

- Add thirty to sixty minutes of reward/total relaxation each day – something you really enjoy doing by yourself or with others where no effort is needed, such as catching

up with a TV drama, spending an hour reading a book, or taking a hot bath. This should be something you do for no other reason than because *you* enjoy doing it. Schedule it into your diary and communicate/negotiate with others to create that time and have clear boundaries around it.
Trigger: Finishing the evening meal.

- Prepare clothes and files for the next day so that you don't have to use valuable brain power in the morning.
Trigger: Finishing brushing your teeth/logging off from your computer.

- Prepare bedroom temperature to 18°C (60–65°F) for best-quality sleep. Clear out any technology, remove your laptop and phone from the room if possible, and cover light from any screens. Remove any clutter so that you sleep in a clear space.
Trigger: The pre-set alarm on your phone goes off one hour before bedtime.

- Choose one or two stretches before sleep, e.g. 'Forward Bend' (p. 403), 'Prayer Position' (p. 403), 'Legs Up the Wall' (p. 404).
Trigger: Dimming the lights to prepare for sleep.

- Go to bed one hour earlier than normal.
Trigger: The pre-set alarm on your phone goes off at the appropriate time.

- Use 'Wind-Down' breathing (pp. 405–6), sequential relaxation (pp. 256–7) or any of the sleep hygiene techniques in Chapter 25 to get you into good-quality sleep.
Trigger: Head touching the pillow.

Extras:

- Sharing these techniques with children and family is a great way to embed them and create more endurance all around you.
- 'Breaking the Pain Barrier' (pp. 361–3) is an important technique that helps to build resistance to pain throughout your life. Next time you catch yourself thinking, *I am so tired, this is too difficult* etc., try turning that thought around to: *I have enough energy in the tanks,* or, *Maybe I am not so tired. Maybe that is a state of mind.*

(NB: If you intend to intensify your fitness programme, check changes with your doctor first if you have high blood pressure, or any other medical conditions.)

It is best to practise these endurance techniques for the first time on a week that is not too gruelling, so that you can push yourself physically and pay full attention to what works emotionally and mentally. Stay focused on *developing* endurance to prepare for tough times, even if those times haven't come yet.

Make a note of your endurance programme and triggers here:

Technique	Trigger

Rehearse: Seven days

Use the next seven days to explore the techniques and gain a good working knowledge of them. Adapt them to really suit you. Some of the endurance techniques that are about the future and planning for the long term are particularly good to practise at the weekends when you may have more time to allocate to in-depth exploration, by yourself or with family and friends.

Perform: Endurance

During the rest of the month, work through your endurance plan. Use the triggers to perform endurance without questioning your decisions or changing your schedule. As you begin to practise endurance techniques, you will start to have *more*, rather than less, energy. Alongside the key techniques that you have retained from the strength, flexibility and resilience sections, your new endurance techniques will enable you to work towards the future you want to create.

Congratulations! You have completed the endurance element of your Physical Intelligence training, supporting your stamina for the long run. It's now time to bring it all together and explore how you can continue to develop your Physical Intelligence into a lifetime of practice.

27

BRINGING IT ALL TOGETHER

How to continue developing your physical intelligence

> Great things are done by a series of small
> things brought together.
>
> —VINCENT VAN GOGH

By now, we hope you realise that Physical Intelligence techniques will empower you to achieve your potential, take on challenging assignments and realise your dreams. As a result of working through the programme, you will have rehearsed and performed twenty techniques (five from each element), through which you will have experienced the life-enhancing effect that a physically intelligent approach brings you, or you may have focused on one or two elements, habit stacking a range of techniques of your choice. Either way, well done!

So, where do you go from here? Here is some guidance around how to work with Physical Intelligence techniques in the long term, for which you will need flexibility and consistent planning and re-planning.

- Check in again with why you want to become more physically intelligent. Ask yourself, 'What is it about the way I am living my life that I want to change or enhance?'

- Observe how at different times you need to focus on some Physical Intelligence elements more than others. You may already have prioritised one or two.
- With that in mind, decide which element(s) need some focus next.
- Dip back into the book regularly. We suggest reviewing your habits every month.
- If you wish, you can repeat the whole four-month cycle over and over again; a month per element, beginning with five more strength techniques, then the following month adding five more flexibility techniques and so on. After a while you will be able to develop and customise techniques yourself, being creative with your programme as you become more physically intelligent.
- Practise techniques over time and embed them for good. For example, if you practise paced breathing technique every day for a month, it will soon become automatic and you will begin to pace your breathing without having to focus on it. Successfully attaching practices to your usual, everyday activities forms habits, and though you may not always appreciate how they are becoming embedded, they will be.
- Remember that every time you practise a single habit it is a nudge on the road to your ultimate goal.
- Don't beat yourself up. When habits become disrupted, which sometimes happens, don't worry – you can always come back to them later, when appropriate.
- Feel free to drop and pick up techniques to practise and habit stack as you see fit, based on what you need. However, don't drop techniques that you know are critical for you. Try attaching them to a different habit if they are routinely being forgotten or overlooked.

- When you face a new challenge, make a physical intelligence plan for what you need, consulting the book again and practising the habits that will help you most.
- Share this book with others, then practise together, comparing notes and supporting each other. Doing some of the exercises in pairs is fun.

Physical Intelligence is not a quick fix, but an enlightening and pleasurable journey over the course of your life. When I was in my twenties, I had very few strategies to work with to give me strength, flexibility, resilience and endurance and it was hard to make sense of how to sustain being happy, confident and productive because there were always questions and vulnerabilities. Developing the Physical Intelligence techniques, sharing them with you and others, and applying them myself has been an essential part of my journey, giving me a response to any challenge thrown my way, and bringing a great deal of fun and joy to my life.

While Pat has consistently drawn on techniques learned through dance, voice and theatre to manage challenges in life and at work, she did so subconsciously. It wasn't until joining Companies in Motion that Pat was fully aware of how she was using those techniques or the chemical shifts they were creating. She now has more techniques at her disposal and uses them consciously and strategically, experiencing benefits in all areas of her life.

Over a period of years, Physical Intelligence embeds itself, supporting your ongoing high performance. Life is rarely perfect; having techniques to apply to any situation is a huge support and puts *you* in charge of your own experience, development and achievements.

Working patterns are changing and we are living longer. Many of us will have two or three careers in our lives, generating a portfolio of things we do, rather than just the one. We may retire much later or not at all. Physical Intelligence will enable us to be ready for change and challenges at all stages of our lives and will help us to live resourcefully, healthily and happily.

We hope this book will become well-thumbed and dog-eared over the next years. Keep it near you and you will always have resources to hand when you most need them.

Before we say goodbye, we would like to leave you with some final inspiration ...

Physical Intelligence in action

The following two stories are great examples of people who have put in the work and integrated all four elements of Physical Intelligence into their lives to create the change they desired.

FRANÇOIS GAINS SELF-BELIEF AND TRANSFORMS HIS LIFE ...

François, a young banker in one of the world's leading global banks, was extremely clever but often overwhelmed by a lack of social confidence, underestimating his abilities and status in the world. He was particularly conscious of how uncomfortable he felt working predominantly with colleagues who had MBAs from the top business schools. While he had perfectly good credentials, his education was different. He had been promoted internally and fast-tracked through the global bank without the traditional MBA. He noticed how the colleagues with MBAs seemed to 'own the room' and conducted calls with ease and confidence. In addition, François' father, a brilliant scientist, had thought he was doing his son a service by constantly objecting to and critiquing his ideas about life but, instead, had unwittingly contributed to his underlying vulnerability and sense of inferiority as a result.

During the first two months of coaching, François adopted the following morning routine, practised at home: centering his body (p. 69), centering his voice using the 1–10 counting exercise (p. 90), and conducting articulation exercises (pp. 88–91). Then, on his commute, he practised paced breathing (pp. 60–4), an MOT (pp. 145–9) and focus practice (p. 328–9), moving his attention to his brain and body to prepare for the demands of the day. He artfully integrated strength and flexibility techniques, taking charge of his confidence and adaptability. He began to *feel* different. He noticed that he was laughing and joking more with team members and was becoming bolder in talking with bosses and gaining their support. If negative thoughts or worry started to take over, François became a regular user of the 'Bounce Positive' technique (pp. 268–71). He learned to handle negative events using the 'Letting Go' technique (pp. 281–284), leaving him free to perform at his best.

Having felt isolated from time to time and being highly analytical and hard-working, networking and socialising had been last on his list of priorities. So, François also worked hard on socialising more and diarising time with colleagues and mentors to became better connected all round. He practised visualising the future ('Seeing the Long Game', pp. 329–31) to help him create a strategy he could put into action. François knew he wanted to have a partner and a family, but with the long hours and commitment that the banking industry demands, he had to plan and dedicate time to socialising in order to make this a reality.

One year later, he still works to ensure his home and social life is not swallowed up by long hours, but has a partner now, has been promoted twice and has executed two of the most successful deals in his department.

TANIA TAKES CHARGE AT WORK AND HOME...

I coached Tania, a senior executive, over the period of a year. When we first met, she was working very long hours, using her weekends to catch up, and had no boundaries whatsoever between work and home. An energetic member of the senior team, she was fully involved in corporate projects, board activities and other processes critical to the business. Her and her partner's elderly parents would visit every year and stay with them for months. While these family visits were important to Tania and her partner, for Tania, this put enormous pressure on family life. They were living in a small house, there was no place for her to just be alone, and her relationship with her partner was also suffering.

Taking her unique situation into account, we identified separate priorities and techniques for work and for home. For work, these were:

1. Better resourcing – she used 'Seeing the Long Game' (pp. 329–31) and Muscle-Firming and Milestones (pp. 333–4/338–40) to envision and map out how she would do this. She integrated Posture (p. 31), paced breathing (pp. 60–4), Centering (p. 65) and Vocal Strength (p. 79) into her working life and used them to take charge of her situation. It took eight months to influence the CEO and recruit new team members to create a committed and thriving department.
2. Placing boundaries around her time, working smarter not harder, and pushing back on impossible deadlines – Tania used the energy-saving techniques from Chapter 24 (pp. 385–6) and stopped thinking *me, everything, always* and started to get clarity. She worked hard to obtain interim help and to *delegate* more; she *prioritised* the actions she needed to take

to realise her strategic goals and the goals of her department and organisation as a whole; and she *selected* the key tasks that would move the big work forwards and got on with those.

At home, Tania asked her siblings to share the responsibility for looking after her parents. 'Relationshift' (pp. 175–6), and Chemistry of Optimism (p. 263) techniques especially 'Bounce Positive' (pp. 268–71) were applied daily as she tackled entrenched relationships. She invested time and money in moving to a house with an office, her own space where she could close the door and work peacefully from home one day a week. She and her partner also committed to carving out more family time. Realising that their values and purpose as parents were being compromised, they reviewed their Chemistry of Motivation and Appreciation (p. 364), and committed to being home with their daughters for a family meal at 7pm every day. This created a fantastic new boundary that made everyone in the family happier, and helped them to feel that they were behaving with more integrity as parents.

Two years later, Tania took promotion and moved to a board position in a larger organisation with a bigger team, fully prepared to sustain her high performance, influence for resources, put boundaries around her time and get those around her performing at their highest and living at their happiest too.

Good luck and enjoy being physically intelligent!

ACKNOWLEDGEMENTS

Firstly, we would like to thank everyone at Simon & Schuster UK, especially Claudia Connal, who picked this book up and believed that the time was right for Physical Intelligence, as well as Andrew Gordon and all at David Higham Associates, who have shared their unwavering support and expertise.

Thank you to Jane Trotman and Jonathan Trotman, our partners in Companies in Motion: Jane, for staunch belief in the project, reading endless versions, providing inspiration and encouragement at key moments when we needed it most and always seeing the bigger picture; Jonathan, for creating strong foundations, going along with us, being a rock and always thinking long term.

Our panel of high performers generously gave us their time and energy and shared profound experiences from their lives that helped bring the Physical Intelligence concepts to life – Jarrod Barnes, Joan Beal, Alessandra Ferri, George Kruis, Wayne McGregor CBE, Megan Mitchell, Camilla Ross, Dawn Marie Flynn Sirrenberg, (Samantha) Claire Taylor MBE and Karl Van Haute, we thank you from the bottom of our hearts. Also, to Robert Devenport and Justine Evans, thank you for your specialist advice on fitness and nutrition, as well as time, energy and encouraging words, and to George Richmond-Scott, voice specialist. Many thanks also to our clients who agreed to have their stories shared throughout the book.

We would like to thank Andrew Wille, without whom we would not have been able to find our way to publishing this book. A chance meeting while dog-walking led to practical help on the first proposal and enabled us to meet Andrew Gordon, who in turn changed everything for us.

Thanks also to all of the pioneers who have inspired us: Guy Claxton, Antonio Damasio, Howard Gardner, Daniel Goleman, Rudolf Laban, Peter Lovatt, Candace Pert, David Rock, Alan Watkins, Jean Williams and Paul Zak, and many more researchers and writers who are thinking deeply about the place of the body in culture.

Personally, I would like to thank my husband, Adam, for supporting long periods during which my focus was on the book and for cooking and praising and loving me throughout it. Huge thanks also to my son, Angus, who contributed ideas and an epithet and was always articulate and caring, and to my parents, Tudor and Frances Williams, for supporting my career and being fantastic grandparents. My siblings, Gillian, Gareth, Rachel and Zeb, my mum, Frank and friends were always there for me when I came up for air. Jacqui Taimitarha was there at the beginning and Roz Carroll has shared a love for Physical Intelligence with me all the way. Dominic Colenso and Kath Burlinson have generously given their support and insights into Physical Intelligence and the team at RADA Business continue to inspire me. Finally, I would like to thank Pat for extraordinary clarity of thought, piercing insight, dedication and always going the extra mile with me.

Claire Dale

A very special thanks to my husband, John, for his good humour, endless patience and willingness to sacrifice even more of our precious little time together without complaint, freeing me to work on this book without (or at least with less) guilt, for ensuring that I (and, for a time, even Claire) was well fed throughout the process, and for his love, support and blind faith in me, regardless of the venture. Thank you to my stepson, Adam, and stepdaughter, Gabrielle, for sharing stories and input on early drafts, and to my brothers, Jack and Kevin, sisters-in-law, Beth and Annie, dearest friends, Saila and Jerry, and all of their families for weighing in when asked and being the respite I needed. I am eternally grateful to my first dance teacher, Joan Wilkes, and my grandmother, Alice Casey, for being my early Physical Intelligence coaches and my mother – the original Pat Peyton, my first and best teacher – for encouraging my love of dance, coaching me on posture and diction from the time I could walk and speak, and loving me beyond measure. Finally, many thanks to Claire for introducing me cognitively to the world of Physical Intelligence and inviting me along on this wonderful journey.

Patricia Peyton

RESEARCH AND RESOURCES

Below are some research sources, studies, articles and books that we have drawn on over the years. Many of them, although not all, are referred to in the book. Most articles are available online, free of charge; however some require purchasing. We have also recommended relevant apps and equipment that we use ourselves. All these resources will further support your shift towards Physical Intelligence. It is a pleasure to share these with you.

Introducing Physical Intelligence

Howard Gardner, *Frames of Mind: The Theory of Multiple Intelligences* (London: Fontana Press 1993)

Daniel Goleman, *Emotional Intelligence: Why It Can Matter More Than IQ* (London: Bloomsbury, 1996)

Marily Oppezzo and Daniel L. Schwartz, 'Give Your Ideas Some Legs: The Positive Effect of Walking on Creative Thinking', *Journal of Experimental Psychology: Learning, Memory, and Cognition American Psychological Association*, Vol. 40, No. 4 (2014): 1142–52

Pablo Brinol, Richard E. Petty and Benjamin Wagner, 'Body Posture Effects on Self-Evaluation: A Self-Validation Approach', *European Journal of Social Psychology*, Vol. 39, No. 6 (2009): 1053–64

Dr Justin Kennedy, 'Neurocardiac and Neuro-biofeedback Measurement of Financial Executive Performance as Associated with HRV Metrics', *Neuroleadership Journal*, Vol. 4 (2012): 81–7

Kirsten Hötting and Brigitte Röder, 'Beneficial Effects of Physical Exercise on Neuroplasticity and Cognition', *Neuroscience and Biobehavioural Reviews*, Vol. 37, No. 9 (2013): 2243–57

Vinoth K. Ranganathan, Vlodek Siemionow, Jing Z. Liu, Vinod Sahgal and Guang H. Yue, 'From Mental Power to Muscle Power, Gaining Strength by Using the Mind', *Neuropsychologia*, Vol. 42, No. 7 (2004): 944–56

Guy Claxton, *Intelligence in the Flesh: Why Your Mind Needs Your Body Much More Than It Thinks* (London and New Haven: Yale University Press, 2015)

The Winning Cocktail

David Rock, *Your Brain at Work: Strategies for Overcoming Distraction, Regaining Focus, and Working Smarter All Day Long* (New York: Harper Collins, 2009)

Sally S. Dickerson, Peggy J. Mycek and Frank Zaldivar, 'Negative Social Evaluation, But Not Mere Social Presence, Elicits Cortisol Responses to a Laboratory Stressor Task', *Health Psychology*, Vol. 27, No. 1 (2008): 116–21

Katrin Starcke and Matthias Brand, 'Decision Making Under Stress: A Selective Review', *Neuroscience & Biobehavioral Reviews*, Vol. 26, No. 4 (2011): 1228–48

Grant S. Shields, Jovian C. W. Lam, Brian C. Trainor and Andrew P. Yonelinas, 'Exposure to Acute Stress Enhances Decision-Making Competence: Evidence for the Role of DHEA', *Psychoneuroendocrinology*, Vol. 67 (2016): 51–60

Ethan S. Bromberg-Martin, Masayuki Matsumoto and Okihide Hikosaka, 'Dopamine in Motivational Control: Rewarding, Aversive, and Alerting', *Neuron*, Vol. 68, No. 5 (2010): 815–34

Anne Campbell, 'Oxytocin and Human Social Behavior', *Personality and Social Psychology Review*, Vol. 14, No. 3 (2010): 281–95

Derrik E. Asher, Alexis B. Craig, Andrew Zaldivar,
Alyssa A. Brewer and Jeffrey L. Krichmar, 'A Dynamic,
Embodied Paradigm to Investigate the Role of Serotonin
in Decision-Making', *Frontiers in Integrative Neuroscience*,
Vol. 7 (2013)

Strength

Pranjal H. Mehta and Robert A. Josephs, 'Testosterone and
Cortisol Jointly Regulate Dominance: Evidence for a Dual-
hormone Hypothesis', *Hormones and Behavior*, Vol. 58, No. 5
(2010): 898–906

David Rock et al., 'SCARF: A Brain-Based Model for
Collaborating With and Influencing Others', *NeuroLeadership
Journal*, Vol. 1 (2008): 44–52

Antonio Damasio, *Descartes' Error: Emotion, Reason and the
Human Brain* (London: Vintage Books, 2006)

Antonio Damasio, *Self Comes to Mind: Constructing the Conscious
Brain*, (London: William Heinemann, 2010)

Antonio Damasio, *The Feeling of What Happens: Body and
Emotion in the Making of Consciousness* (London: Vintage
Books, 2000)

Barnaby D. Dunn, Tim Dalgleish and Andrew D. Lawrence,
'The Somatic Marker Hypothesis: A Critical Evaluation',
Neuroscience and Biobehavioral Reviews, Vol. 30, No. 2
(2006): 239–71

Michelle M. Duguid and Jack A. Goncalo, 'Living Large: The
Powerful Overestimate Their Own Height', *Psychological
Science*, Vol. 23, No. 1 (2012): 36–40

Li Huang, Adam D. Galinsky, Deborah H. Gruenfeld and Lucia
E. Guillory, 'Powerful Postures Versus Powerful Roles:
Which Is the Proximate Correlate of Thought and Behavior?',
Psychological Science, Vol. 22, No. 1 (2011): 95–102

Pablo Briñol, Richard E. Petty and Benjamin Wagner, 'Body
Posture Effects on Self-Evaluation: A Self-Validation
Approach', *European Journal of Social Psychology*, Vol. 39, No. 6
(2009): 1053–64

Amy J. C. Cuddy, Caroline A. Wilmuth and Dana R. Carney, 'The Benefit of Power Posing Before a High-Stakes Social Evaluation', *Harvard Business School Scholarly Articles*, No. 13-027 (2012)

Amy J. C. Cuddy, S. Jack Schultz, Nathan E. Fosse, 'P-Curving a More Comprehensive Body of Research on Postural Feedback Reveals Clear Evidential Value for Power-Posing Effects: Reply to Simmons and Simonson' (2017)

Johannes Michalak, Judith Mischnat and Tobias Teismann, 'Sitting Posture Makes a Difference—Embodiment Effects on Depressive Memory Bias', *Clinical Psychology and Psychotherapy*, Vol. 21, No. 6 (2014): 519–24

Luciano Bernardi, Cesare Porta, Alessandra Gabutti, Lucia Spicuzza and Peter Sleight, 'Modulatory effects of respiration', *Autonomic Neuroscience: Basic and Clinical*, Vol. 90, No. 1–2 (2001): 47–56

Bradley M. Appelhans and Linda J. Luecken, 'Heart Rate Variability as an Index of Regulated Emotional Responding', *Review of General Psychology*, Vol. 10, No. 3 (2006): 229–40

Leah Lagos, Evgeny Vaschillo, Bronya Vaschillo, Paul Lehrer, Marsha Bates and Robert Pandina, 'Heart Rate Variability Biofeedback as a Strategy for Dealing with Competitive Anxiety: A Case Study', *Association for Applied Psychophysiology & Biofeedback*, Vol. 26, No. 3 (2008): 109–15

Dr Alan Watkins, *Coherence: The Secret Science of Brilliant Leadership* (London: Kogan Page, 2014)

Robin S. Vealey and Christy A. Greenleaf, 'Seeing is Believing: Understanding and Using Imagery in Sport', in Jean M. Williams (ed.), *Applied Sport Psychology: Personal Growth to Peak Performance* (International: McGraw-Hill, 2010)

Ian Robertson, *The Winner Effect: The Science of Success and How to Use It* (London: Bloomsbury, 2012)

John Coates, *The Hour Between Dog and Wolf: Risk-Taking, Gut Feelings and the Biology of Boom and Bust* (London: Harper Collins, 2012)

J. M. Coates and J. Herbert, 'Endogenous Steroids and Financial Risk Taking on a London Trading Floor', *Proceedings of the National Academy of Science*, Vol. 105, No. 16 (2008): 6167–72

Nicholas Wade, 'Your Body Is Younger Than You Think', *New York Times*, 2 August 2005: http://www.nytimes. com/2005/08/02/science/your-body-is-younger-than-you-think.html

Flexibility

Dr Jason Devereux, Dr Leif Rydstedt, Dr Vincent Kelly, Dr Paul Weston and Prof Peter Buckle, 'The Role of Work Stress and Psychological Factors in the Development of Musculoskeletal Disorders', Health and Safety Executive Research Report No. 273 (Guildford: HSE Books, 2004)

John P. Buckley, Alan Hedge, Thomas Yates, Robert J. Copeland, Michael Loosemore, Mark Hamer, Gavin Bradley and David W. Dunstan, 'The Sedentary Office: A Growing Case for Change Towards Better Health and Productivity', *British Journal of Sports Medicine*, Vol. 49, No. 21 (2015): 1357–62

C. B. Pert, M. R. Ruff, R. J. Weber and M. Herkenham, 'Neuropeptides and Their Receptors: A Psychosomatic Network', *Journal of Immunology*, Vol. 135 (2 Suppl.) (1985): 820s–26s

Joshua Ian Davis, James J. Gross and Kevin N. Ochsner, 'Psychological Distance and Emotional Experience: What You See Is What You Get', *American Psychological Association*, Vol. 11, No. 2 (2011): 438–44

T. A. Baskerville, A. J. Douglas, 'Dopamine and Oxytocin Interactions Underlying Behaviours: Potential Contributions to Behavioural Disorders', *CNS Neuroscience & Therapeutics*, Vol. 16, No. 3 (2010): e92–e123

Paul J. Zak, 'Why Inspiring Stories Make Us React: The Neuroscience of Narrative', *Cerebrum*, Vol. 2 (2015)

Lea Winerman, 'The Mind's Mirror', *American Psychological Association*, Vol. 36, No. 9 (2005): 48–57

G. Rizzolatti, L. Fadiga, G. Pavesi and L. Fogassi, 'Motor Facilitation During Action Observation: A Magnetic Stimulation Study', *Journal of Neurophysiology*, Vol. 73, No. 6 (1995): 2608–11

M. Kosfeld, M. Heinrichs, P. J. Zak, U. Fischbacher and E. Fehr, 'Oxytocin Increases Trust in Humans,' *Nature*, Vol. 435, No. 2 (2005): 673–6

Paul Zak, *Trust Factor: The Science of Creating High-Performance Companies* (New York: AMACOM, 2017)

Jim Collins, *Good to Great: Why Some Companies Make the Leap . . . and Others Don't* (New York: Collins Business, 2001)

Stephen M. R. Covey (with Rebecca R. Merrill), *The Speed of Trust: The One Thing That Changes Everything* (New York: Simon & Schuster, 2008)

David W. Merrill and Roger H. Reid, *Personal Styles & Effective Performance: Make Your Style Work For You* (Boca Raton, FL: CRC Press LLC, 1999)

Ken Robinson, 'Do Schools Kill Creativity?', TED Talk, 2006: https://www.ted.com/talks/ken_robinson_says_schools_kill_creativity

Kenneth M. Heilman, Stephen E. Nadeau and David O. Beversdorf, 'Creative Innovation: Possible Brain Mechanisms', *Neurocase*, Vol. 9, No. 5 (2003): 369–79

Ullrich Wagner, Steffen Gais, Hilde Haider, Rolf Verleger and Jan Born, 'Sleep Inspires Insight', *Nature*, Vol. 427, No. 6972 (2004): 352–5

Marily Oppezzo and Daniel L. Schwartz, 'Give Your Ideas Some Legs: The Positive Effect of Walking on Creative Thinking', *Journal of Experimental Psychology: Learning, Memory, and Cognition*, Vol. 40, No. 4 (2014): 1142–52

Carine Lewis and Peter J. Lovatt, 'Breaking Away from Set Patterns of Thinking: Improvisation and Divergent Thinking', *Thinking Skills and Creativity*, Vol. 9 (2013): 46–58

Open Space: https://www.openspace.dk

Mary B. Engler, PhD, et al., 'Flavonoid-Rich Dark Chocolate Improves Endothelial Function and Increases Plasma Epicatechin Concentrations in Healthy Adults', *Journal of the American College of Nutrition*, Vol. 23, No. 3 (2004): 197–204

Lorenza S. Colzato, Annelies M. de Haan and Bernhard Hommel, 'Food for Creativity: Tyrosine Promotes Deep Thinking', *Psychological Research*, Vol. 79, No. 5

(2015): 709–14

Des de Moor, *Walking Works* (London: The Ramblers Association and Macmillan Cancer Support, 2013) https://www.walkingforhealth.org.uk/sites/default/files/Walking%20works_LONG_AW_Web.pdf

Tom Kerridge, *Tom Kerridge's Dopamine Diet: My Low-Carb, Stay-Happy Way to Lose Weight* (Bath: Absolute Press, 2017)

Resilience

Pamela K. Smith, Nils B. Jostmann, Adam D. Galinsky and Wilco W. van Dijk, 'Lacking Power Impairs Executive Functions', *Psychological Science*, Vol. 19, No. 5 (2008): 441–7

Health and Safety Executive, 'Stress and Psychological Disorders in Great Britain 2017': http://www.hse.gov.uk/statistics/causdis/stress/stress.pdf

American Psychological Association, 'The Impact of Stress', 2012: http://www.apa.org/news/press/releases/stress/2012/impact-report.pdf

Eleanor Quested and Joan L. Duda, 'Antecedents of Burnout Among Elite Dancers: A Longitudinal Test of Basic Needs Theory', *Psychology of Sport and Exercise*, Vol. 12, No. 2 (2011): 159–67

David Dobbs, 'The Science of Success', *The Atlantic*, December 2009: http://www.theatlantic.com/magazine/archive/2009/12/the-science-of-success/7761/

Bruce J. Ellis and W. Thomas Boyce, 'Biological Sensitivity to Context', *Current Directions in Psychological Science*, Vol. 17, No. 3 (2008): 183–7

Katty Kay and Claire Shipman, *The Confidence Code: The Science and Art of Self-Assurance – What Women Should Know* (New York: Harper Collins, 2014)

H. Benson, J. F. Beary and M. P. Carol, 'The Relaxation Response', *Psychiatry*, Vol. 37, No. 1 (1974): 37–46

Toshiyo Taniguchi, Kumi Hirokawa, Masao Tsuchiya and Norito Kawakami, 'The Immediate Effects of 10-Minute Relaxation Training on Salivary Immunoglobulin A (s-IgA)

and Mood State for Japanese Female Medical Co-workers',
Acta Medica Okayama, Vol. 61, No. 3 (2007): 139–45

Stephanie A. Shanti, *Prisoners of Our Own Mind: How Different
Types of Meditation Contribute to Psychological and Physical
Health* (Createspace Independent Publishing Platform, 2010)

Edmund Jacobson, *You Must Relax* (London: Souvenir Press,
1977) (Also found here: https://joaomfjorge.files.wordpress.
com/2016/05/edmund-jacobson-you-must-relax-health-
psychology.pdf)

Carol S. Dweck, 'The Mindset of a Champion', *Stanford Medicine*,
5 February 2014: http://gostanford.com/sports/2014/5/2/
209487946.aspx

Carol S. Dweck, *Mindset: How You Can Fulfil Your Potential* (New
York: Balantine Books, 2008)

Charles S. Carver, Michael F. Scheier and Suzanne C.
Segerstrom, 'Optimism', *Clinical Psychology Review*, Vol. 30,
No. 7 (2010): 879–89

Sara L. Bengtsson, Raymond J. Dolan and Richard E.
Passingham, 'Priming for Self-Esteem Influences the
Monitoring of One's Own Performance', *Social Cognitive and
Affective Neuroscience*, Vol. 6, No. 4 (2011): 417–25

Mark Wheeler, 'Be Happy: Your Genes May Thank You for It',
UCLA Newsroom, 29 July 2013: http://newsroom.ucla.edu/
portal/ucla/don-t-worry-be-happy-247644.aspx

Richard A. Bryant and Lilian Chan, 'Thinking of
Attachments Reduces Noradrenergic Stress Response',
Psychoneuroendocrinology, Vol. 60 (2015): 39–45

Matthew D. Lieberman, *Social: Why Our Brains Are Wired to
Connect* (Oxford: Oxford University Press, 2013)

Paul Zak, 'The Neuroscience of Trust', *Harvard Business Review*
(Jan–Feb 2017): 85–90 (Also found here: https://hbr.
org/2017/01/the-neuroscience-of-trust)

Lara B. Aknin et al., 'Prosocial Spending and Well-Being: Cross
Cultural Evidence for a Psychological Universal', *Journal of
Personality and Social Psychology*, Vol. 104, No. 4 (2013): 635–52

Bethany E. Kok et al., 'How Positive Emotions Build Physical
Health: Perceived Positive Social Connections Account

for the Upward Spiral Between Positive Emotions and Vagal Tone', *Journal of Psychological Science*, Vol. 24, No. 7 (2013): 1123–32

Adam Grant, *Give and Take: The Surprising Power of the Good Guy in a Tough World* (London: Weidenfeld & Nicolson, 2014)

Kyeongho Byun et al., 'Positive Effect of Acute Mild Exercise on Executive Function Via Arousal-Related Prefrontal Activations: An fNIRS Study', *NeuroImage*, Vol. 98 (2014): 336–45

Andrea M. Weinstein et al., 'The Association Between Aerobic Fitness and Executive Function Is Mediated By Pre-Frontal Cortex Volume', *Brain, Behavior, and Immunity*, Vol. 26, No. 5 (2012): 811–19

Endurance

Gerd Kempermann et al., 'Why and How Physical Activity Promotes Experience-Induced Brain Plasticity', *Frontiers in Neuroscience*, Vol. 4, No. 189 (2010): 1–9

Susan R. Barry, PhD, 'How to Grow New Neurons in your Brain', *Psychology Today*, 16 January 2011: https://www.psychologytoday.com/blog/eyes-the-brain/201101/how-grow-new-neurons-in-your-brain

Shana Cole, Matthew Riccio and Emily Balcetis, 'Focused and Fired Up: Narrowed Attention Produces Perceived Proximity and Increases Goal-Relevant Action', *Motivation and Emotion*, Vol 38, No. 6 (2014): 815–22

Iris W. Hung and Aparna A. Labroo, 'Firm Muscles to Firm Willpower: Understanding the Role of Embodied Cognition in Self-Regulation', *Journal of Consumer Research*, Vol. 37, No. 6 (2010): 1046–64

Robert S. Weinberg and Jean M. Williams, 'Integrating and Implementing a Psychological Skills Training Programme', in Jean M. Williams (ed.), *Applied Sport Psychology: Personal Growth to Peak Performance* (International: McGraw-Hill, 2010)

Jo Marchant, *Cure: A Journey into the Science of Mind Over Body* (Edinburgh: Canongate Books, 2017)

A. St Clair Gibson et al., 'The Conscious Perception of the Sensation of Fatigue', *Sports Medicine*, Vol. 33, No. 3 (2003): 167–76

Christopher J. Beedie, 'Can a Placebo Make You Cycle Faster?', a clip from *Horizon: The Power of the Placebo*, 13 February 2014: http://www.bbc.co.uk/programmes/p01s6f3f (More information found here: https://www.aber.ac.uk/en/news/archive/2014/02/title-146509-en.html)

Christopher J. Beedie, 'Placebo Effects in Competitive Sport: Qualitative Data', *Journal of Sports Science Medicine*, Vol. 6, No. 1 (2007): 21–8

Candace B. Pert, *Molecules of Emotion: Why You Feel the Way You Feel* (New York: Scribner, 1997)

Edward L. Deci, Anja H. Olafsen and Richard M. Ryan, 'Self-Determination Theory in Work Organizations: The State of a Science', *Annual Review of Organizational Psychology and Organizational Behaviour*, Vol. 4 (2017): 19–43

L. Wang, H. Mascher, N. Psilander, E. Blomstrand and K. Sahlin, 'Resistance Exercise Enhances the Molecular Signaling of Mitochondrial Biogenesis Induced by Endurance Exercise in Human Skeletal Muscle', *Journal of Applied Physiology*, Vol. 111, No. 5 (1985): 1335–44

Kelly A. Bennion, Jessica E. Payne and Elizabeth A. Kensinger, 'The Impact of Napping on Memory for Future-Relevant Stimuli: Prioritization Among Multiple Salience Cues', *Behavioural Neuroscience*, Vol. 130, No. 3 (2016): 281–9

Alexis M. Chambers and Jessica D. Payne, 'Neural Plasticity and Learning: The Consequences of Sleep', *AIMS Neuroscience*, Vol. 1, No. 2 (2014): 163–8

Jessica Payne, 'Talking Sleep', *Movius Consulting Blog*: http://www.moviusconsulting.com/talking-sleep-jessica-payne/

Marco Hafner, Martin Stepanek, Jirka Taylor, Wendy M. Troxel and Christian van Stolk, *Why Sleep Matters: The Economic Costs of Insufficient Sleep – A Cross-Country Comparative Analysis*', (Cambridge, UK, Santa Monica, USA: The RAND Corporation, 2016)

Carol Connolly, Marian Ruderman and Jean Brittain Leslie,
*Sleep Well, Lead Well: How Better Sleep Can Improve Leadership,
Boost Productivity, and Spark Innovation*, Center for Creative
Leadership White Paper, 2015: https://www.ccl.org/wp-
content/uploads/2015/04/SleepWell.pdf

Matthew Walker, *Why We Sleep: The New Science of Sleep and
Dreams* (New York: Scribner, 2017)

Russell G. Foster, 'Body Clocks, Light, Sleep and Health',
D/A Magazine, No. 15, January 2018:
http://thedaylightsite.com/body-clocks-light-sleep-
and-health/

Anne-Marie Chang, Daniel Aeschbach, Jeanne F. Duffy
and Charles A. Czeisler, 'Evening Use of Light-Emitting
eReaders Negatively Affects Sleep, Circadian Timing, and
Next-Morning Alertness', *Proceedings of the National Academy
of Sciences*, Vol. 112, No. 4 (2015): 1232–7

Dr Guy Meadows, *The Sleep Book: How to Sleep Well Every Night*
(London: Orion 2014)

Arianna Huffington, *The Sleep Revolution: Transforming Your Life,
One Night at a Time* (London: W. H. Allen, 2016)

Dr Mike Dilkes and Alexander Adams, *Stop Snoring the Easy Way:
And the Real Reasons You Need To* (London: Seven Dials, 2017)

Equipment

Lumo Lift (Posturite) or Upright Go (Apple) – posture trainers
that buzz when you slouch, used alone or in combination
with your iPhone/smart phone or tablet.

Posturite.co.uk – sells standing desks and other ergonomic
furniture.

HeartMath emWave Pro – a computer programme and sensor
giving you biofeedback to improve heart rate variability and
coherence through breath co-ordination, improving DHEA
levels. Best if you use iPhone.

Completecoherence.com – coherence trainer. This has the same
function as emWave but is in app form. Best if you use
PC/Android.

MUSE – the brain sensing headband and app that enables you to meditate with biofeedback regarding how calm or agitated your brain is.

Headspace.com – a meditation app.

Equisync – soundtracks that provide another way of meditating: https://eocinstitute.org/meditation/

Oblique Strategies – an app by Edrease Peshtaz to stimulate creativity; it gives you a word or phrase to provoke different thinking each day.

Valkee – bright light headset. Boosts serotonin, guards against SAD and helps with jet lag.

Ultrabreathe Respiratory Trainer – a simple device to boost breath performance.

Nutrition and Fitness Specialists

Justine Evans ND, B.SC N Med, Naturopathic Doctor and Nutritionist, http://www.justineevans.co.uk/

Robert Devenport, Personal Trainer and Performance Specialist, rdfitbydesign (Facebook and Instagram)

LIST OF EXERCISES

INDEX

WELCOME TO PHYSICAL INTELLIGENCE

Think back to a situation where you needed to perform well but your nerves got the better of you, your confidence faltered and things didn't turn out as well as you hoped … or a situation where you struggled to come up with a creative solution or didn't communicate effectively with people who have different styles … or a time when you had difficulty bouncing back from a disappointment or remaining focused on achieving an important long-term goal? Most of us have faced similar challenges at some point in our personal or professional lives.

Scientific research tells us that, in the majority of those situations, we experience challenges because we are at the mercy of our physical reactions, emotions and thoughts – experiencing them without realising that we can actively manage them. There's a better way – at Companies in Motion, we call it 'Physical Intelligence' – the active management of our physiology, the ability to detect and strategically influence the balance of chemicals in our bodies and brains so that we can consistently rise to the occasion with confidence, are able to reliably generate creative ideas and flex to communicate with various people, recover from disappointment, remain focused to achieve key goals and more, enabling us to achieve peak performance.

While we are already very familiar with the concepts of cognitive intelligence (IQ) and emotional intelligence (EQ), the concept of Physical Intelligence has been generally restricted to the worlds of elite sport and art. Our Physical Intelligence techniques, all supported by neuroscience, are drawn from those worlds – breathing exercises, physical movements, mental exercises and conversations – that enable us to get in the driver's seat of our physical reactions, emotions and thoughts in order to improve our Strength, Flexibility, Resilience and Endurance.

We believe that Physical Intelligence not only sits alongside, but *underpins* our cognitive and emotional intelligence. Becoming more physically intelligent helps us create lives, businesses and societies where people take responsibility for themselves, are more informed and thoughtful about how to use their capacity, and are equipped with techniques that foster harmony and help them achieve and sustain peak performance.

Read about the impact Physical Intelligence has had on individuals and leading organisations globally:

'All of these techniques have enabled me to manage pressure in the work environment and have improved my sleep and my personal and family life – all with techniques that don't require much time or effort.' **Chief Legal Officer, Leading Financial Institution**

'Physical Intelligence should be part of everyone's education in business – the earlier the better. It's a gift and the quicker the business gives you this gift, the healthier you will be – physically, mentally and emotionally – inside and out of work. It is not just about work; it's about life and it is the most amazing gift for people in all walks of life and at all levels.' **Head of Business Development, Global Pharmaceutical Company**

'I work for a company that attracts the top 1 per cent of the world's graduates – so it is an intellectually challenging environment. We do a lot of training on wellness but it is too generic and broad. No one except Companies in Motion is tying these concepts to business. I liked that Physical Intelligence is tied to science and connects movement to the ability to quickly manipulate brain chemistry. Physical Intelligence had a much faster impact than anything else I've experienced … I saw a woman who was quite meek completely transformed … Physical Intelligence gives you really quick tools that transform your presence or performance – techniques you can quickly apply and that you can apply time and again. Physical Intelligence is empowering and informative and you can make it about yourself – your work and life. I'm a very visual person. I do a lot of visualisation and meditation. I'm obsessed with innovation and like to work in a challenging environment. Physical Intelligence supports me in all of those areas.' **Head of Content Partnerships, Multinational Technology Company**

FOR MORE INFORMATION ABOUT Companies in Motion, please visit us at www.companiesinmotion.com or call us at + 1 44 (0)20 8588 0631. *Keep an eye out for our Physical Intelligence app – coming soon!*